To Pat Slade,

Keep Em Laughing!!

James S. Robertson

2-92

HOW THE PLATFORM PROFESSIONALS KEEP 'EM LAUGHIN'

James "Doc" Blakely
Joe Griffith
Robert Henry
Jeanne Robertson

Rich Publishing Co.

Houston, Texas 77070

First Edition 1987
Second Printing 1989
Library of Congress Catalog Card No. 85–63110
ISBN 0–9607256–4–4
Printed in the United States of America

NEWT "DAD" HIELSCHER

Acknowledgement

The idea of forming a group of Platform Professionals was conceived in the mind of Newt "Dad" Hielscher, Shreveport, Louisiana. A seasoned professional humorist with a sterling reputation long before "Doc" Blakely, Joe Griffith, Robert Henry, or Jeanne Robertson arrived on the professional scene, Newt often presented a meeting planner with a challenge. After a great performer like Newt Hielscher, what does a meeting planner do for next year? Invariably the planner would ask Newt for his recommendation. Not only did the program organizer want quality humor and fast-paced entertainment, but also a clean, wholesome talk that would appeal to family and business audiences of all types.

Realizing that his own reputation was on the line when he made a recommendation, Newt assembled the current group of Platform Professionals.

It was a bold move for a seasoned professional to recruit four other speakers, all of whom were 20 years or more younger, and promote them, in a sense, as competitors. But Newt believed that meeting planners would appreciate this service for continued excellence in their program planning and he was exactly right. Many associations and conventions to this day alternate Platform Professionals until they have completed the roster and then repeat the schedule.

In personal letters to his colleagues, Newt always starts out with "Dear Children," so it was only natural that the others reciprocate, out of respect, with the affectionate term "Dad."

"Dad" has been not only a mentor, friend, supporter, and founder of the Platform Professionals, but also a great student of humor techniques and delivery. He was always going to write a book "one of these days." Somehow, with a busy schedule of speaking engagements, he managed to avoid getting it all down on paper. Although he is still actively involved in the speaking business, working out of his office in Shreveport, Louisiana, Newt is spending a little more time fishing when not on the circuit.

"Well, "Dad," we have not forgotten the valuable lessons of life and living you have taught us, the inspiration you have given us in touching people's lives through humor, and the sterling example you have set before us as a professional's professional both on and off the platform. Your "children" gratefully acknowledge your guiding hand and dedicate this book to you and in memory of your dear wife Polly.

"Doc" Blakely, Joe Griffith,
Robert Henry, and Jeanne Robertson

Contents

ABOUT DELIVERING A HUMOROUS SPEECH   52

PART IV

Over 2000 Jokes, Stories, One- and Two-Liners Perfected
Before Live Audiences 73

INDEX

PART I

WHO ARE THE PLATFORM PROFESSIONALS?

Four seasoned professional humorists comprise "The Platform Professionals." Their purpose is to serve professional meeting planners, training directors, and program organizers with very high quality educational/entertaining presentations for individual and company growth, inspiration, and enjoyment.

Doc Blakely, CPAE   Robert Henry, CPAE

     Jeanne Robertson, CPAE   Joe Griffith, CPAE

A brief description of the specialty of each speaker follows:

DOC BLAKELY, CPAE
3404 Fairway Drive
Wharton, Texas 77488
(409) 532–4502

Doc Blakely speaks internationally about 100 times annually receiving invitations nationwide and from as far away as Malaysia. His creativity with humor and the spoken word have led to authorship of 7 books and Pokin' Fun, a weekly syndicated humor column.

Speeches

ACCENT ON LAUGHTER, THE GIFT OF LAUGHTER, WORDS IN STONE, TO SOAR WITH EAGLES, and SUCCESS CAN BE FUN.

Seminars

HOW TO KEEP YOURSELF INDISPENSABLE—3 to 6 hour seminar tailored to meet the client's needs. Revolves around communication, human relations.

THE 10 SECOND EXECUTIVE HUMORIST—2–3 hour seminar to teach business people how to use humor in their own presentations like a professional.

ROBERT HENRY, CPAE
P. O. Box 1350
Auburn, Alabama 36830
(205) 821–2415

Robert Henry, (1983–84 President of the National Speakers Association), pharmacist, mixes clean humor with wit and wisdom to penetrate contemporary issues. He's an exciting speaker appropriate for sales and management meetings, after dinner talks, as a keynoter and as a seminar leader. He speaks internationally, having just returned from trips abroad on the speaking circuit that included Canada, Mexico, London, and Copenhagen. He's a humorist, motivator, comedian, and raconteur, averaging 3 appearances weekly.

Speeches

YOU'RE A PROFESSIONAL WHAT?—Hilarious look at every day actions—85% humor, 15% inspiration.

WIN WITH ACES—Guaranteed to make your audience feel great, high cards of humor dealt face up.

Seminar

BUILD A BETTER YOU—starting now! Three hour seminar emphasizing guaranteed steps to success.

JEANNE ROBERTSON, CPAE
2905 Forestdale
Burlington, North Carolina 27215
(919) 584–9641

Jeanne Robertson, (1985–86 President of the National Speakers Association), a former Miss America contestant, regales her audiences with tales of a 6'2" beauty contestant. She is adept at turning personal experiences into stand-up comedy routines while covering some pretty serious situations.

Speeches

THERE HE IS—Clean Fun. A little audience participation, a little music, a lot of laughter, and an underlying clear message.

HUMOR: AN EFFECTIVE STRATEGY FOR SUCCESS—Jeanne uses humor to illustrate how to use humor to be more successful.

For The Spouses

HOW TO ENJOY YOUR CONVENTION . . . AND SURVIVE!—Jeanne pokes fun at the annual meeting. Humorous and informative. Guaranteed to make the meeting planner look great.

JOE GRIFFITH, CPAE
13608 Midway Road, Suite 124
Dallas, Texas 75244
(214) 233–7130

Joe Griffith has given over 2,000 speeches. His face may be familiar because he has been in movies, in over 200 TV Commercials (Holiday Inn, McDonald's), and in segments of CBS's Series "Dallas".

His background also includes aviation, advertising, and investment analysis. He regularly consults with Fortune 500 Companies and Senior Executives on effective public speaking.

Speeches

THE FUNNY SIDE OF THE STREET (90% humor, 10% message).

SUCCESS WITH EVERYTHING ON IT (60% humor, 40% message).

Seminar

CHECKPOINTS TO SUCCESS (Covers attitude, change, goals, and how to better manage yourself and others.) One-half or full day seminar tailored to meet client's needs.

Here's How It All Began

Newt Hielsher, Platform Professional Emeritus, Shreveport, Louisiana, initiated the idea of organizing a team of professional humorists to meet the needs of satisfied clients who wanted more of his brand of speaking talent. Newt, already busier than a fellow wearing bifocals at a burlesque show, found such a speaker in "Doc" Blakely, Wharton, Texas. Blakely, who claimed his earned Ph. D. stood for "Post Hole Digger" and that his hometown of Wharton, Texas, was between Houston and Buenos Aires, reciprocated by recommending Hielscher for the same reason. That worked fine until it was discovered that they were following each other back to back in succeeding years. Often times meeting planners felt it was too early for repeat performances and asked for referrals for future programs. This was the signal to expand. Newt and "Doc" began searching for other top professional humorists who subscribed to the same prerequisites of philosophy and standards to join this loose cooperative association.

That's when Joe Griffith, Dallas, Texas, entered the picture. Joe loved the business as much as the others. "It's the only job I know of," he says, "where they applaud you just for showing up for work." The demand for these humorists continued to grow while at the same time they were branching into seminars in areas of human relations, humor workshops, communications, and speech training programs. This created more demand than the three speakers could fulfill. It was decided that another one or two members should be added, provided the same standards could be continued.

Robert Henry, Auburn, Alabama, was added for obvious reasons. He was an established speaker, thoroughly professional, humorous, and also experienced in the seminar field. Robert admitted having a slight weight problem until he went on a special diet. It consisted of two shots of scotch and one shot of Metrecal. "Then," he claims, "I lost 80 pounds and my driver's license."

After the "boys" personally saw humorist Jeanne Robertson, Burlington, North Carolina, in action, the decision was unanimous to add her as the final member of the group. A 6'2" former Miss America contestant, she claims two titles. "I was the tallest contestant ever to compete in the Miss America Pageant. I was also the tallest contestant ever to lose in the Miss America Pageant."

The founder of the group, Newt Hielscher, decided to cut back on his speaking engagements to catch up on his fishing. He took emeritus status, and left his four proteges to conduct the business. "Sure he's rich," says his four partners, "but he won't loan us a dime; says all his money is tied up in cash."

Together, these four speakers address over 500 audiences and travel over a million miles annually. They produce enough theraputic laughter to mend anything from a broken heart to the crack of dawn. They speak for conventions, associations, business meetings, and virtually all the Fortune 500 companies. They have appeared before English-speaking audiences throughout the U.S., Canada, Central and South America, Europe, and on cruise ships, wherever their services are needed.

PART II

WHAT THIS BOOK WILL DO FOR YOU

How often have you wished for a bit of guidance on how to add a little humor in a speech, a joke or line to support a point, yet make the audience laugh? How often have you searched for reference material to spice up your speech, a story or anecdote that adds zest and interest to spark audience enjoyment? You may be scheduled to present a speech about business activities or speak at a service award banquet. You may have to address a community function, respond at a political gathering, speak to an association or similar group meeting. Maybe you want to take a bold step and enter the world of professional speaking. Whatever your speaking role may be the appropriate use of humor, the right joke or line will generate audience understanding and acceptance of your message beyond belief.

Wish no more. Search no more. You hold a TREASURY of material in your hands. The material has been assembled by four of the nation's top humorists, The Platform Professionals, whose biographies and careers are described in Part 1. Their combined speaking experience totals in excess of 60 years.

This book reveals their personal approach to the business of using humor in speech. Part III provides a vivid insight into their methods through a series of "20 most frequently asked questions" collected from over 200 seminars and humor workshops conducted by the Platform Professionals. Each tell how they DEVELOP—STRUCTURE—DELIVER a humorous speech.

Part IV offers you a vast collection of over 2000 jokes and lines personally selected, tried, and perfected before live audiences by the Platform Professionals.

A closer study will reveal hours of treasured material for your reference and use. It is no secret that leadership gravitates to the person that can present an effective speech. People love those leaders who can make them laugh. Some, such as Lucille Ball, are known more for their wit. Others, like John F. Kennedy, are known primarily for statesmanship. But whether their leadership role was in the arena of superstars, politics, or business, these gifted communicators have one common denominator . . . good humorous material.

This book will become an integral part of your own communication skills development. It will not replace a group of good writers, but it is the next best thing because the jokes and lines contained in this volume have passed the toughest test. They have been personally edited by the Platform Professionals who must rely on editing instinct for their living. Furthermore, the material had to pass not one editor but FOUR . . . unanimously, before acceptance.

What does this mean to you? It means that for the meager investment of a few dollars, you have hired four of America's premier professional business speakers to screen over 20,000 lines, try them before live audiences and then select one-tenth of that number as worthy of being included in this book.

Over 2 years were spent in diligently categorizing these witticisms by subject and indexing them for rapid and easy reference. So, the next time you need a few lines to liven up a presentation or want to develop a whole routine, the material is here at your fingertips.

Let's take an example. Suppose you are to make a speech on the dangers of pollution of the local river by a variety of sources. Not very humorous, right? Wrong.

Humor is still the most effective carrier for a lasting message. Perhaps just a few lines appropriately placed in your talk will do more good than all the hues and cries of impending doom. Let's expand the pollution example. Make a list of the subjects related to pollution in this case and then check the alphabetized categories, and index, for applicable lines.

Subjects might be:

| America | Congress | Electricity | Police |
| Biologists | Doctors | Fishing | Scientists |

Since all of these subjects are easily associated with pollution, a logical connection can be made between the line or joke selected and the moral or message carried.

Then look in the index for those subjects not found elsewhere. As your mind researches the idea, other subjects will appear. Jot them down and follow up until you have at least 30 lines from which to choose. At this point, YOU become the editor. You may use half a dozen of the lines or all of them. The main thing to remember is to use only those lines that make a specific point more memorable. Select those lines which you believe are not only funny but can alert your audience to the dangers you wish to address. Your opening remarks might be something like:

> "Many of us have been complacent about the potential pollution of our water supply. I too was unconcerned until a guy told me he went fishing the other day and saw our river catch fire.
>
> I'm told the fire department put it out but then our lake died.
>
> Yes, we can joke about it now but let's look at some facts that are not too far from fantasy . . . ."

By sprinkling a few lines like these throughout your presentation, you will do more for your own art of communication and grab the imagination of listeners in a way that even the movies would be hard pressed to visually duplicate. Never forget that you are dealing with the most powerful image-producing mechanism on earth . . . the human mind. It thrives on images and humor is a trigger to release a most explosive, powerfully positive form of communication energy.

The raw materials are here waiting for your selection and arrangement into everything from sparklers to blockbusters.

If you are an experienced speaker, you may grasp the principles more quickly. But whether you are a veteran orator or new at making speeches, you will gain insight into how four Platform Professionals reach the same level of excellence through the variety of methods outlined in Part III. By studying answers to the series of questions posed to the Platform Professionals about "How To Develop and Present a Humorous Speech," you will find a wealth of information on: How to research a speech; how to structure it with humor techniques and philosophy; how to use various forms of humor, manage the environment for successful communication, handle adversities, motivate listeners to action, and much more.

Add to that a selection of the "right stuff" contained in Part IV and you too will share in the secrets of how the Platform Professionals . . .

KEEP 'EM LAUGHIN'.

PART III

**20 QUESTIONS POSED TO FOUR
PLATFORM PROFESSIONALS ABOUT
"HOW TO DEVELOP AND PRESENT
A HUMOROUS SPEECH."**

- About The Speech Foundation

- About The Speech Structure

- About Delivering A Humorous Speech

About the Speech Foundation

1. **What Are Your Thoughts on the Value of Humor as a Speech Tool or the Power of Laughter as a Form of Therapy?**

Robert Henry — To stand before an audience, tell a joke, and have the laughter explode around me is the most exciting thrill I know. It is just as if the audience has reached out, wrapped their arms around me, and said, "Robert Henry, I like you. You have formed a friendship with me today, stamped and sealed with humor. I want to be your pal. I want to accept your point of view. I want to buy whatever you are selling. I want to vote your way. Might even more readily agree to be your sweetheart." Now, if I just let the audience know how much I like them, we are going to be successful together.

I believe that humor is a wonderful gift from God both in the ability to create it and enjoy it. Humor is a precious natural resource. It comes to us absolutely free and our responsibility is to add value to it and pass it on for others to enjoy.

Humor made jesters the favorites of kings. It has made some people wealthy and driven others from high office. Berthold Brecht said, "One should not fight dictators; one should ridicule them." A dictator does not fear force and thrives on hatred. But humor, this powerful emotion expressed with laughter, can topple a dictator that no mighty army could budge.

Humor is a powerful weapon; it can make unbearable suffering bearable. It can relieve unrelievable pain. It can even heal a broken heart.

As a pharmacist, I'm very interested in healing illness and especially eliminating pain. It has been proven that humor is a valid, quantifiable therapeutic agent.

When we laugh, a substance called endorphins is released in our brain. This is a chemical similar to morphine. It promotes a sense of wellness and confidence.

This is the Henry family about which Robert talks so much. Merrilyn, Patrick, Brent, and Robert.

Studies have been done with cancer patients in which they were repeatedly shown movies of Laurel and Hardy, Abbott and Costello, and others. The incidence of improvement and even cure was startling.

The evidence is in. Humor is good for us. Properly used, it has no bad side effects. You have much to gain and virtually nothing to lose. You can have a lot of fun, possibly make some money, spread a little happiness, and even heal someone, though you may never know it.

Years ago, I spoke in Buffalo, New York. I did not feel the program went well. Six months later, a fellow approached me in the lobby of a Washington hotel. He introduced himself and told me he had been at the Buffalo speech and thought it was terrific. I laughed and said, "Boy, I really died in Buffalo." He said he could not imagine what I was talking about and told me a story.

His sister had a small child dying of Wilm's tumor, a malignancy of the kidneys. For four months, she had been terribly depressed and refused to step outside her home. He had managed to get her to come hear me speak in Buffalo.

He said his sister laughed for the first time in four months. He believed she laughed harder than she had in her whole life. He left me saying, "Thank you for the gift you gave my sister."

When using the material and techniques available in this book, you never know when you might reach out with humor and touch someone in a dramatic and personal way.

Jeanne Robertson — I believe very strongly that humor is a powerful tool in helping us live through what could be unpleasantries in life. As a young child, I would have certainly never chosen to be 6 ft., 2 in. tall and therefore I would have never had one of my greatest advantages. But at age 13 . . . when I reached my "peak" . . . I had the choice of letting this unusual height become a liability or an asset. I decided to make it an asset and was able to do so by seeing the humor in the situation.

For example, all children hear the words "My, how you've grown." With me, I would usually hear, "Myyyyyy." On a trip to Auburn, Alabama, to visit relatives who had not seen me since my latest growth spurt, my father knew I would encounter this very typical response. Rather than watch me go through the pain of being a little embarrassed, he suggested that when the relatives came running out to greet us, I should jump out of the car and before anyone could say anything, shout, "Myyyyy, how I've grown." Sure enough, it stopped them in their tracks. They didn't have anything to say and we all laughed. This is a small, but significant, example of how humor can be used to ease the pain of what could be life's unpleasantries. It will work in most situations and is an excellent form of therapy.

Joe Griffith — The power of using humor with even the most trying subjects can bring unexpected rewards. As a lay speaker, you are being judged on how your speaking ability fairs with the audience's expectations of you and what you do professionally. Not long ago, a friend of mine said he heard a speaker at a meeting. He recounted how the man was very entertaining. He told lots of good jokes. I asked him if he was a professional speaker and he said, "No. He was a college president." He went on to say that had he been a professional speaker, he wouldn't have thought he was that good. So the man was perceived as good because the audience was comparing him to other college presidents.

The lay speaker does not have to live up to the high expectations of a professional speaker. I've heard economists tell some of the oldest jokes and get laughs and I think most of the laughs come from the audience's excitement that an economist can tell a joke, and that if he can tell a joke, maybe he will not be boring after all.

Remember, humor is a simple tool that in the right hands can produce tremendous results.

Doc Blakely — One technique used by professional joke tellers is to follow the standard of telling at least one joke per minute. Some of the old time professionals use this as a guideline for their speeches. If they were asked to speak for 30 minutes, they simply told 30 jokes. If they had an hour, they told 60 jokes. Perhaps that led to the description of good humorous speakers as "a laugh a minute." It is not a bad philosophy for the professional humorist. However, for the lay-speaker, this may be unnecessary or an unattainable standard.

Yet, any speaker can utilize humor in some form to reward the audience for listening to his/her remarks. I believe that a good executive speaker getting a laugh every 5 minutes will exit the platform as one of the highlights of any meeting. That laugh does not have to come from a long, drawn out joke. By using a witty line every 5 minutes, you risk almost nothing. Yet, the rewards can be extremely satisfying in many ways, perhaps even leading to the advancement of a career.

Suppose you have a one-hour, serious presentation to make. By following the philosophy of one laugh at least every 5 minutes, it would take only 12 well-chosen lines which through trial and error could be arranged in a logical presentation to help illustrate your points and re-enforce your thoughts. In all probability, those 12 lines would take no more than 10 seconds each to deliver. That means 120 seconds, or a total of two minutes out of the entire hour to reward your audience for listening. You may find that shared laughter becomes the highest form of communication, enhancing everything else you have to say.

Let me give one final example to illustrate the power of humor.

Early one morning as I was leaving a hotel in Topeka, Kansas, after having made a speech the night before, I was paged to the telephone in the hotel lobby. A lady identified herself and remarked that she had attended my talk entitled "Livin' on Love and Laughter" the night before and had met me at a reception. I remarked that I remembered her, to which she replied, "Oh, you silver-tongued devil, you don't remember me!" But when I described the dress she was wearing, she sounded genuinely surprised, continued to joke around and then said, "I had not planned to go to the meeting last night, but something about your subject 'Livin' on Love and Laughter' kept nagging at me until, at the last moment, I decided to go. I had been sitting around the house feeling so sorry for myself that I didn't want to get out and break my black mood. I just had to catch you before you left the hotel to let you know how much I appreciate you and your philosophy. I face today with a brighter outlook and can even accept what an uncertain future holds in store for me with a smile. Now, don't you tell anyone, because not even my closest friends know, but I'm dying of a terminal illness. I only found out a couple of months ago and that's the reason I was in such a deep, dark mood. I want you to know that the hour I spent listening and laughing with you and the others last night was the greatest therapy imaginable because for an hour I was able to forget and once again truly enjoy myself."

There was not a hint of self-pity in her voice. She was filled with a joy that stunned me as tears welled up in my eyes and a lump came to my throat. With great composure, I expressed my personal concern for her condition, asked for her address, and suggested that we should keep in touch. She suggested, "That won't be necessary. Just keep on making people laugh whether they think they need it or not. Believe me, it is the greatest therapy in the world. God bless you for coming our way."

I never heard from her again . . . except in the giggles of a child, the chuckles of private conversations, and the uproar of a crowd.

2. One-Liners and Jokes are Forms of Humor. What are Other Forms of Humor and Their Use?

Joe Griffith — There are three major forms of humor:

1) Surprise—this is where the audience cannot see the punchline coming. I tell a joke where I build myself up to be the nicest, most

wonderful person in the world. I really have the audience thinking I'm wonderful. Then suddenly, on the punchline, they discover that I'm totally opposite. This is where the surprise comes in. The audience laughs because they did not see the punchline coming; it was a surprise.

2) Exaggeration—this is where something is blown so out of proportion it makes it funny. Watch Johnny Carson's monologue and observe the use of exaggeration. For example: "It was so cold . . . ," "How cold was it?;" or "He was so old . . . ," "How old was he?"

I recently heard one joke where the speaker said, "The lady was fat. She was so fat, she could kick start a 747." Now there's an exaggeration joke.

3) Understatement—Mark Twain was the master of understatement, the exact opposite of exaggeration. He could take a subject so important to everybody and point out the most insignificant part of the subject and have it become the most important thing in the world. For example, "You could take his brains, put them in a gnat's navel and still have room left over for two mustard seeds and a banker's heart."

Doc Blakely — Three other forms of humor are the pun, irony, and satire.

The pun is a very risky form of humor for the average lay speaker and should generally be avoided. Basically, a pun is a joke which includes a punchline or word that has a double meaning. For some reason, amateurs often misuse the pun form of humor. Unless the pun is handled in a highly professional manner, it receives more groans than laughs. An example of a low-quality pun is, "The bald headed man's motto is 'Hair today and gone tomorrow.'" A pun with a moderate chance of success is, "Old superintendents never die, they just lose their principles." However, if used sparingly and with great selection, the pun can be effective.

An example of a high-quality pun is, "Mr. Smith may not have much personality, but his wife is a pure delight. She is friendly, smiling, and always laughing. I asked her, 'Don't you ever wake up grouchy in the morning?' She replied, 'No, I usually just let him sleep.'"

Irony is a different form of humor which not only has a surprise ending, but also a totally different twist. An example is given by an attorney who explains his defense techniques in this way; "Suppose my client is accused of having a dog that attacks a neighbor. My first line of defense is that the neighbor was trespassing and the dog was merely guarding his owner's property. My second line of defense is that the neighbor not only was trespassing but also provoked the dog into attacking him. If those lines of defense fail, then I must prove beyond a shadow of a doubt that my client doesn't even own a dog." Note the irony of this subject.

Satire is also a very effective form of humor in the hands of some individuals. It is usually more difficult to handle by lay speakers simply because they have not had enough experience to determine when satire might be inappropriate. This form of humor is actually a way of degrading an individual, object, or organization in such a way that the line is both funny and true. However, it is not the kind of subject that would be talked about seriously in public. For example, suppose at the halfway mark in the season, the local football team had lost every game. At a city-wide banquet, a speaker on the program might remark, "There's a rumor going around that the Houston Oiler organization has just hired a new Chinese coach . . . fellow by the name of Win Won Soon." Interestingly this line is both satire and pun. Obviously, satire can be great if it is accepted in the spirit of fun. There is the possibility that a line will not be accepted as very funny, so extreme caution should be used.

The key to the use of puns, irony, and satire is to trust your instincts on the use of each. If you don't feel totally comfortable with the acceptance of any of your material in the spirit of "laughing with one another" instead of "laughing at someone," then it may be advisable to use other tactics.

Jeanne Robertson — We all use the forms of humor Joe and Doc mentioned, but I have had more success with a different type of humor—describing everyday situations. The nonprofessional may be comfortable doing the same. Specifically, I use words to paint humorous pictures of everyday situations. If the pictures are painted clearly and lead the audience to see the humorous side of an event, not only do they respond with laughter, but they want to shout, "I've been there!"

Two well-known humorists who excel at describing everyday situations are Bill Cosby and Bob Newhart. When Bill Cosby describes visiting a dentist's office, I want to shout, "It happened to me, too, Bill!" The same occurs when Bob Newhart gives driving lessons. They successfully use words to paint humorous pictures of those everyday situations; I see their pictures and respond.

And where does the nonprofessional find those humorous ideas? Observing local people and events is an excellent way to obtain ideas for material.

Most professional speakers are glad to do "freebies" in their hometowns when convenient. One such occasion for me was when I was asked to "do a little program" during the October meeting of a twenty-five member book club in my hometown. It was convenient for me because I was keynoting a convention in a nearby city the morning of their meeting, but I did ask them to change their meeting time from 1:30 to 2:00 P.M. just to make sure I would be back when they convened. The program chair mused "we've always met at 1:30," but agreed to check. She later said the change would be fine.

October rolled around and I found myself seated in their midst waiting to speak and listening to the secretary read the minutes of the previous meeting. I could not help but smile when she said, "It was proposed that we change the time of the October meeting from 1:30 to 2 o'clock to accommodate our speaker. The motion passed . . . twenty-one to four."

I had forgotten this incident until something in a joke book triggered my memory. Therefore, I suggest the speaker looking for this type of humor should 1) read the joke books and joke services to trigger their own memories of humorous events, 2) watch and listen to local people to pick up on their wit, and 3) be aware that local events are a never-ending source of everyday situations that can be painted humorously through words. Other forms of humor are superb and I use all of them from time to time. But I suggest we do not forget that describing everyday situations is a valuable way to entertain people.

Robert Henry — Another form of humor often heard is insult comedy. This means aggressively attacking a member of the audience and using him as a foil for humor. Don Rickles is the king of insult comedy. About half of us love Don Rickles while the other half is disgusted by his style. I happen to enjoy Rickles because I have never perceived that he really means those seemingly unkind things he says to people. I feel that he is having fun and genuinely loves the people he insults. Many would quickly disagree with this opinion.

My suggestion is that you stay away from insult comedy. The risk is too great. Turn the insult on yourself or refer to a Slobovian fellow from outer Slobovia. Since no such person or country exists, you are generally safe.

What about dialects and ethnic humor? Dialects are great fun and need not be considered a put-down of anyone. The first rule of dialect humor is that you had better be able to do it letter-perfect. A hokey dialect is embarrassing. I know some great Jewish stories but I don't use them. Can you imagine a fellow from Alabama with a pronounced southern drawl trying to do a Yiddish dialect? A dialect story is not meant to be demeaning and it's far from insult comedy. Dialect stories can actually lift up the nationality being recognized for greater respect. Doc Blakely has a program called "Accent On Laughter" in which he uses many different dialects. I think this is one of the most delightful programs I've ever heard and when it's over, everyone in the audience feels good about himself.

Ethnic humor is quite another matter. Years ago, ethnic humor was popular. Times have changed and people have become more sensitive. Possibly, we've become too sensitive and have lost a great source of humor. Nevertheless, it is a real risk to single out an ethnic group and appear to demean their values.

Incongruities are an effective form of humor. They do not fit. They are abnormal. They present a surprise. Here is an example: A college counselor asked a freshman, "What do you want to do with your life?"

The young person says, "I want to be a great physician. I want to stamp out disease, eliminate pain, and heal the sick and suffering."

"What if you can't get into medical school?" queried the counselor.

"In that case, I think I'd like to drive a cab."

What makes this joke funny? Obviously, the ideas do not fit; they are incongruous. On one hand, the goal is enormous, the ambition unrestrained. On the other, a job which requires very little training will satisfy.

Finally, we should mention the use of dirty jokes or blue humor from the platform. Platform Professionals say do not do it. Period. It is not worth the risk.

Research tells us that 80% of a typical American audience will laugh quickest and loudest at a sexually-oriented, alcoholic-based joke. I could start a joke by saying, "There was a drunk hooker in a bar." I know beforehand that 80% of a general audience will laugh quick, loud, and hard at that story. But, twenty percent won't laugh. Twenty percent will be offended and not appreciate your disrespect.

Let us say that you do not use dirty jokes. How about cute, risqué humor? Again, research tells us that over 90% of a general, American audience will laugh at a well-told cute, risqué story. But something less than 10% of the audience will not laugh. Sooner or later, someone will come to you after a talk and tell you how much they resent the offensive material you used.

There are some people who go to programs looking for something at which to be offended. They usually find it. Some folks are offended at a generic invocation. Starting with "Ladies and Gentlemen . . ." could offend some weirdo because they figure that's an unfounded assumption.

There is certainly a gray area in humor. A joke or remark that may be totally acceptable to most of your audience may offend someone. My suggestion is to go through your material carefully, before the talk, with a critical eye. Eliminate anything you think could be considered dirty or risqué. Then, if someone takes offense, just figure they came there looking for it and would have found it if you had read nursery rhymes.

Profanity fits into the category of dirty or blue material. Should you use it? No! It's not worth it. Even though most people will use some degree of profanity in conversation once in awhile, those same people will resent you using it from the platform. It's a very real double standard and you do not need the grief. Some comedians get away with it in Las Vegas, but they would not last a week at the civic clubs, chambers of commerce, corporate annual meetings, or association banquets worked by Platform Professionals.

3. In Addition to the Humor Found in Various Books and Tapes, What are Some Continuing Sources of Humor?

Robert Henry — If you are going to be a successful humorous speaker, be willing to invest a few hundred dollars in a humor library, then add to it on a regular basis.

I haunt book stores. I especially love old book stores and purchase any book on humor that I do not have in my library. I skim through it very quickly. Ninety percent of the jokes are inappropriate for me to use for one reason or another. Now, I go back through the remaining ten percent of the book and study the jokes closely. I am only interested in the premise or the punchline of the joke. If I use the story, I will build the storyline up front, using my imaginary characters and style to make it my story. Importantly, I decide under which category I will file the joke and what point I will make with it.

If I find two jokes in a $20 book that I can use in the next two dozen speeches, I figure I have found a great bargain. I will pay $10 for a good joke all day long.

There are so many books available to fit every speaking style. For instance, *"Doc" Blakely's Push Button Wit,* 3404 Fairway Drive, Wharton, Texas 77488 ($20.00).

Do not forget your local library. I live in a university town and have access to Auburn University's library. There are literally scores of books on humor available for the asking.

Joe Griffith — Humor sources are everywhere, but good humor is hard to find. One suggestion is to buy cassette tapes of the top professional speakers whom you enjoy. This gives you an opportunity to hear them tell their jokes. Sometimes a joke in print does not look as funny as it will sound if it is heard live. Also, you will benefit from hearing an expert tell the joke properly.

There are numerous publications on humor: *Quote Magazine* 405 Sussex Place, 148 International Boulevard, Atlanta, Georgia 30303; *Comedy and Comment,* Mack McGinnis, 448 North Mitchner Avenue, Indianapolis, Indiana, 46219; *Current Comedy,* 700 Orange Street, Wilmington, Delaware, 19801; *Round Table,* P. O. Box 13, King of Prussia, PA 19406.

Joe Griffith is climbing aboard a T-38 at Columbus Air Force Base. The T-38 flight was arranged by Jess Moore with the Columbus, Mississippi Chamber when Joe was their annual banquet speaker.

Jeanne Robertson — The sources mentioned are certainly good and I subscribe to all of them. Although I seldom find a piece of material in them that I use verbatim in a presentation, they are valuable tools for me when used in another manner. I use these services and joke books to trigger ideas when I am creating material. I would suggest a nonprofessional speaker do the same. Let the printed joke remind you of something from your experiences and then tell that story. Your material will be fresh and you avoid the risk of repeating material the audience has heard. Naturally, the professional humorist devotes much more time to creating and finding humor. For the lay speaker, joke services and joke books can serve as a quick way to find material that is ready to use in the event there is not enough time to create your own.

My greatest source of material, as mentioned during my response on forms of humor, that is often overlooked—is local people. Many local people have great wit. They do not want to go on stage and stand behind a microphone, but they do perform. You will find them at neighborhood parties, little league games, garden clubs, and even church. Folks in Burlington, North Carolina, generally agree that one of the funniest people in our town lives on my street . . . next door to me. And people wonder where I get my original material. The humorist is not always the funniest individual at a gathering but is probably more aware of humor than others present and has developed a knack of looking for humor. The nonprofessional speaker should do the same thing.

A second source is local events. Several years ago, the Burlington Hospital Auxiliary sponsored a "Celebrity Night" in conjunction with a Little Theater production. In the initial planning stages, it was to be a grand event, spotlighting a number of North Carolina celebrities. The invitations went out and, one by one, folks such as Andy Griffith and Catfish Hunter "regretfully declined." When the big night rolled around, the celebrities consisted of me, a couple of ex-football players, and a local tennis pro who had won the State Seniors Tournament title the year before. We dined with the Hospital Auxiliary dignitaries at the local country club and then gathered in the parking lot for the limos to take us to the theater where we would each be spotlighted as we entered. Of course, the limos came from the local funeral home, and because of the number of people, we also used the long, black hearse for the spouses. The "spotlight" turned out to be two kids with jumbo flashlights on the roof of the building. I could go on and on, but the point is—it would be difficult to make up something like this. It happened, and is an example of an excellent source of material . . . local events.

Doc Blakely — I agree with Jeanne. One of the best sources often overlooked by lay speakers is the casual conversation of people. Always keep your antennas out and your ears open for good humor. For some reason, most people do not mentally record good lines that are adlibbed. People say witty things all day long, but most simply laugh and let the line slip by without recording it. Start a humor diary. Record those lines that you hear people laugh at and you will find a use for them. For example, I heard two high school superintendents from different school systems talking recently. One asked the other how their football season turned out. The superintendent replied, "We had a 5 and 5 season. We lost 5 at home and 5 on the road."

Also, some great ideas can be picked up from humorous tapes of other speakers. Nightingale—Conant Corporation, 7300 Leigh Avenue, Chicago, Illinois 60648, recently published a series of tapes on humor titled the EXECUTIVE TREASURY OF HUMOR—Volumes I and II. These albums contain the works of the top 12 humorists in the United States. All four of the Platform Professionals are included in albums I and II. The albums may be ordered from Nightingale—Conant or any of the Platform Professionals. (See addresses page 3)

4. Do You Ever Change Material or Use of Key Words to Fit the Background, Age or Other Characteristics of Your Audience?

Doc Blakely — Definitely. Just as an exercise, talk to a group of first graders. You will find yourself choosing both your words and stories to fit their level of understanding. In the same manner, but less dramatic, you have to change your approach slightly by using technical jargon for engineers, agricultural talk for farmers, and colloquial expressions for some areas of the country. For example, I recently presented a talk in New Orleans. In a casual conversation prior to my speech I discovered that a sidewalk is called a banquette (bankit), a front porch is a gallery, and the middle of Canal Street is referred to as neutral ground. Apparently, this terminology is familiar only to citizens of New Orleans, and they are well aware of these colloquial expressions. In the "setup" for a joke, I told a story about this guy who "got off his gallery and walked down the bankit to neutral ground . . . ." This got an immediate laugh and even drew applause, yet I hardly knew what I had said. It just proves the power of tailoring your material to fit your audience.

Joe Griffith — Yes, I change material to fit every audience. Years ago, I told a story with the word fireplug in it. The joke worked well until one time I was doing a series of talks in Iowa. During the first talk, the joke fell flat. Driving to the second talk, I commented to the program chairman that I couldn't understand why the joke fell flat. He told me that people in Iowa did not know what the word fireplug meant. Then it dawned on me that fireplug was a Texas phrase. So, the next day I changed "fireplug" to "fire hydrant" and the joke got a laugh again.

There are times when you do not change your material, but you will have to change the pace of your delivery to fit the audience. City audiences think faster because their lifestyles are faster. When talking to rural audiences, slow down to fit their slower lifestyles.

There is a story that I heard years ago about Bob Hope when he was playing in Dallas. He did not do too well and the man who ran the theater where he was playing told him to slow down. He did and soon became a big star.

So adjust your delivery to each audience and you too may become a big "executive" star.

Jeanne Robertson — The more professional speakers travel the more they know about various areas of the country and what will or will not "go over" in those areas. The same thing applies to the types of groups a speaker addresses. Material told to an agricultural group in Luverne, Alabama, may have to be changed slightly if told to corporate executives in New York City.

For example, I have a routine poking fun at the "dress for success" people. It goes over well in agriculturally related groups where folks like to poke fun at the three-piece suit set. I am not as quick to use that same material, however, in a corporate speech where everyone in the audience is sitting there literally "dressed for success." Material about "our friends in the North" goes over well down South. Forget it in Maine.

When in doubt, the professional and nonprofessional should mentally associate themselves with members of the audience and adjust terminology accordingly.

For instance, I have a humorous program for spouses titled "How To Enjoy Your Spouse's Convention . . . AND SURVIVE!" When

I give this speech, I do not give it as Jeanne Robertson, professional speaker, but as Jeanne Robertson—a spouse who for years has attended her husband's conventions. The pronouns switch to "we" and "our" because I'm speaking as a spouse. I can identify with them and vice versa. For example: "We cannot remember our room numbers . . . but we can remember who has won door prizes for the last 15 years."

Do not misinterpret changing material as being two-faced. The speaker is not changing values but rather knows the audience and relates to the particular surroundings. It boils down to knowing your audience, the background of the group, particular problems, likes, and dislikes. It is important to check in advance with the person who asked you to speak to obtain this information.

Robert Henry — Jeanne is right. That is one of the most important rules for speakers to follow.

Since my humor springs from the "Heart of Dixie," I have had to learn a very important lesson. There is English. There is Queen's English. And, then there is Southern English. A fellow from Bombay, India, who is fluent in Queen's English, will not have the foggiest idea what I am talking about. If I am speaking before a group that may have trouble with my accent, I make a conscious effort to speak distinctly.

Colloquialisms and faulty grammar will be accepted by an audience if they come from a platform character. However, when speaking "straight" or putting over the message, bad grammar and poor syntax will brand one as intellectually inferior.

All audiences have similarities, but a number of variables makes each audience different. Different word choices are used for audience variables such as young-old, men-women, management-labor, native-foreign born, married-single, city-country.

It is the ill-prepared speaker who would go before the AFL-CIO and praise the "right to work" labor policy. A man speaking before the National Secretary's Association better clean the sexist language from his speech. Do not come off as a city slicker to farm groups or a hayseed to bankers. The key to platform success is to get on the level of the audience or as close as possible and never give the appearance of "talking down" to a group.

Imagine that you have been offered a 5-minute spot on Hee Haw. What kind of material would you choose? You certainly would not use the same material if you were to exchange wit with Johnny Carson on the Tonight Show.

5. How Does One Handle Humor with Dignity so the Speaker Does Not Come Off as a Clown or Buffoon?

Doc Blakely — That's a good question and the answer is quite simple. Do not let anyone talk you into doing something you don't feel comfortable about. If you feel okay about a routine, the audience will sense it and allow you to slip "into character" while still retaining an air of respectability. For instance, I have a gift for doing dialects well enough that an audience can "see" the character I am portraying. I can be a Swede, a Scot, or a St. Bernard and still demand the

The Blakely Clan. From left to right, grandson Eric, son Mike, also a professional writer-speaker, daughter-in-law Becky, granddaughter Torie, daughter-in-law Kim, wife Pat, and Doc Blakely. Inset is photo of son Perry (1956–1979).

respect of the audience because they realize I have slipped into this character for a specific purpose. The key is to start out with dignified remarks, even though those remarks may be quite humorous. Gradually build with the less dignified material so that the senses are not shocked immediately with a change of direction that is too severe. Then end with a disclaimer to rapidly bring respectability back to your part of the program. Here is an example of such a disclaimer: "The humorist is not always understood because they say we hear the sound of a different drummer; we march to a different beat. In case you have misinterpreted what I have said tonight, let me explain it, especially for the more intellectually inclined, in the following way. . . ." Then your remarks can be easily concluded with a dignified, profound philosophy of your choosing making the audience realize why you used the material. Most audiences will laugh with you while granting you both dignity and respect.

Jeanne Robertson — At the end of a series of humorous stories, during which I may act a little like a clown, I find it effective to completely change my tone and posture, utilize a pause, and then contribute three to four more serious lines to tie together the points of the material. This signals my audience that I am not just a clown and they later let me return to humor if I choose.

By using a casual conversational tone, rather than shouting or being sarcastic, a speaker signals "we are here to have fun together." People in an audience sense very quickly the real purpose of the speaker's humor. More important than what is said is how it is said. Everything from facial expressions to posture portrays the speaker's ulterior motives. If the people in the audience trust these motives, they may think the speaker is a clown, but they will think so in loving terms.

Perhaps the best way to avoid being thought of as a clown or buffoon is to refrain from acting like one. Many speakers who use a great deal of humor believe they must be "on" from the time they come through the door. This often wears thin quickly. People believe they are seeing a show, not meeting an individual. When others on the program are making remarks, the buffoon doesn't act interested, and when he does get "on," he stops at nothing to get a laugh. In these instances, it would not be WHAT was said that labeled a speaker a buffoon, but rather HOW he acted and treated others.

Robert Henry — I believe it is important for speakers to stay within their platform character or personality. Does your humor feel right for you? For a laid-back, dry-witted performer to suddenly start braying like a jackass would be unsettling. However, I would not accuse Red Skelton of being undignified and he is the world's greatest clown.

The Robert Henry that audiences see is in character. I speak a little louder and talk a little faster when on platform. I exaggerate my conversational tone a bit in telling my stories with poetic license and enthusiasm. I might shout, whisper, wail, and whine, but it is all in character and contributes to the point being made by the story.

Importantly, I agree that dignity is never lost on a good laughline. If anything, it is enhanced because good humor is often perceived as a sign of intellect.

Platform humor should never be derisive, sarcastic, or demeaning. Deliver your humor with love. If you strip away the dignity of your audience by demeaning them and diminishing their value, you will inevitably lose face.

Joe Griffith — Some of the most memorable humorists delivered their lines in a dignified way. People like Mark Twain, Will Rogers, and Bob Hope depended on timing and good material for laughs, not buffoonery. Presidents like Kennedy and Reagan are well-known for their use of humor, but yet, they do not come off as a buffoon or clown. Watch Bob Hope on television and see how he sets his jokes up. If he is going to tell a joke about the President, he always starts off by saying something positive about the Commander in Chief and then, bang, the punchline. So, it is the contrast between the setup and the actual joke that keeps a speaker from having to come off as a clown.

Also remember that when you select jokes for speeches, choose the kind you can tell without having to be a clown or buffoon.

6. What Chance Does the Average Lay Speaker Have in Thinking Funny? Are Not Most Good Speakers Just "Born" That Way?

Doc Blakely — Will Rogers once said, "The guys who say they can think funny on any subject at any moment ain't funny to anybody but themselves." His point was quite simple; even the most respected humorists in the world have to expend a great deal of effort to create the kind of humorous communication for which the best are so famous. Just as in any other field, there are some individuals blessed with extraordinary talent. It is true that many speakers are simply born with the gift and this is especially true in the case of the humorous speaker. However, history is full of examples of men and women who excelled in speechmaking because they had a burning desire to communicate a great message. The key for the less gifted speaker is to be on fire with enthusiasm for a certain subject or cause. The audience senses the sincerity, urgency, or entertainment value of the speaker. That "feedback" has made great speakers out of many people who were not "born" to be great speakers. Will Rogers himself, for instance, was one of the most beloved speakers ever produced by this country. Yet Will was shy, had a nasal twang in his voice, and butchered the English language. When he spoke, no matter what he said, everyone laughed. He capitalized on his peculiarities and became one of the most famous humorists of all time. Although he had the innate ability to "think funny," he was not a "born" speaker. The thing that made him successful as a speaker was the fact that he worked extremely hard at his profession, spending 10 or 12 hours per day reading, writing, and thinking to come up with his famous "ad-libs." The lesson is apparent. Anyone who wants to speak humorously can do it with proper dedication of time and effort. The "born" speakers simply do it more quickly.

Robert Henry — All people are born with an identical disadvantage—the inability to speak a single understandable word. However, it is not long before differences in the ability to communicate begin to appear. Personality type plays a major role in one's ability to stand before an audience and speak, especially to speak humorously.

I believe there is such a thing as a "natural born" funny person. Some people have a knack for seeing things funny. Their perception is a bit skewed and it is the funny aspect of a situation that first comes to mind.

I also believe there are some truly unfunny people in the world. I know people who could not get a laugh with the best material ever written. Those folks should never let anyone try to turn them into a humorist.

Someone once asked a speaker, "Do you have to be funny when you speak?"

His answer was, "Only if you want to get paid."

I have often heard this answer repeated at speaker's conventions and it is absolutely false. I know some great speakers who are not funny at all.

If you are laying them in the aisles at the pool hall or if you have got them belly laughing at the barber shop, you are going to be a hit. If you are an average lay speaker with the slightest bit of talent for being humorous, exposure to the experience of platform professionals, their books, tapes, material, and techniques will help you present a polished platform performance.

Jeanne Robertson — The average lay speaker has just as much chance to "think funny" as the seasoned humorist. The difference is that the seasoned humorist has learned to take funny thoughts and turn them into material for speeches.

The wit of my friends in North Carolina never ceases to amaze me. Yet most have no desire to be speakers. There are more one-liners and humorous stories told at most small town parties than during any major speech presentation. Unfortunately, the lay speaker will attend one of those parties, enjoy the humor, even contribute to it, and not recognize it is a source of "funnies" for speeches. The professional speaker could attend the same party, pick up valuable humor and turn it into speech material. At that point, people say the pro has the ability to think funny.

We are all born with the ability to think funny. The professional has learned to be aware of thoughts that are potential speech material and to construct humorous material from funny thoughts.

Joe Griffith — A speaker does not have to think funny to be funny. I always recommend a simple guideline for using or not using humor in speeches. If you have trouble remembering jokes, you probably should not use them. If you enjoy jokes and can easily recall them, then you probably should use jokes. For added protection, always make sure that the joke makes a point. If the audience does not laugh, you can remind them that the joke made a serious point with a reference to the humorous illustration.

About the Speech Structure

7. What Is the Very First Step for You in Developing a Humorous Speech?

Robert Henry — I am a motivational entertainer. Generally, my talks are approximately 70% humor/entertainment and 30% motivational message. I have three 45–60 minute talks and two three hour seminars. Two of the 45–60 minute programs contain lots of motivation and inspiration which can be varied according to the objectives of the meeting planner. The third talk is 98% humor for those audiences who simply want to have fun.

When developing a speech, I begin with the message. It might be goal setting, how to be a winner, principles of leadership, or there is no such thing as a free lunch. I then select the humor that will set it up, tie it together, and drive the points home.

I am basically a joke teller. I use lots of jokes to get across the message. When I collect jokes/stories, I have several thoughts in mind: where can I use this, how will it fit, and what point will it make?

Joe Griffith — I collect jokes and put them in a file. When the file begins to bulge, I begin writing a speech. First, I determine which five jokes will get the biggest laughs of all. Then I decide which of the other remaining jokes best fits in the category with the five big ones. Now I have five vignettes, each one ending with a belly laugh which is one of the original five jokes. So each vignette starts with a chuckle, a chuckle, a laugh, a laugh, and ends with a belly laugh.

Jeanne Robertson — I have been told by many professional speakers that I develop a speech backwards. They may be correct, but it works for me.

I do not plan my points and then search for humorous material to illustrate those points, nor do I write a clever title and build a speech around it. I usually do not even have an underlying message that is waiting to get out for the world to hear. I am a humorist, which means I am asked to speak to make people laugh a lot and think . . . a little.

Therefore, my first step in developing a new humorous presentation is to list the pieces of material that I would like to try out, or that I previously used but not for this particular audience. After I have obtained the stories, it is a simple matter of determining what points they illustrate and if the points are worthy of my audience's time. If they are, I'm set. A little reworking usually lets several stories go together to illustrate a main point. Remember, the overriding objective for the humorist is to entertain and slip a message in under the door.

Collecting and working on humor is an everyday occurrence for

Jeanne Robertson fights to keep the basketball away from her son, Beaver, left, and husband, Jerry. What else would a tall family do during spare time?

humorists and it should become a priority for anyone interested in speaking. Keeping accurate lists of humor that you are positive will work and humor you would like to try is a must. If a speaker has these lists, the first step in developing a humorous presentation becomes natural. Simply review the lists and see what you have at your disposal.

Platform Professionals usually average 15 speeches per month. With such a schedule, I find it best to devote my time to perfecting speech #1, speech #2, and so forth. I prefer that a meeting planner ask what my topics are rather than assign a topic to me. The lay speaker should be wary of being trapped into a topic that will demand an extraordinary amount of time.

Doc Blakely — I select a topic first; actually the topic usually chooses me. At some point, a title jumps out at me, screaming for my attention.

For example, I had been speaking since 1964. It was my practice to constantly try out new routines, lines, and bits of humor. Every time I told a story that involved some ethnic group, such as the Irish, English, German, someone in the audience would comment on my ability to handle the accent representing that particular ethnic group. It was not something I consciously did. I thought of myself as more of an actor playing the role of a character with a certain dialect. I became so immersed in the character that even the accent was convincing to the audience.

One night after a speech filled with humorous anecdotes, many of which utilized an English dialect, a native of England approached me, shook my hand, and said, "You know, ol' chap, you sound more like we do than we do. Your accent was smashing." Numerous people of other nationalities complimented me in similar fashion and since all of them had derived a great deal of laughter from my stories, the topic "Accent on Laughter" gradually evolved and now it is my most requested talk. Other people began to comment on what a "gift" I had been given and the topic "The Gift of Laughter" has evolved. All my other talks had similar beginnings.

8. After Your Initial Inspiration, How Do You Develop an Outline of What You Will Say?

Jeanne Robertson — Remember now, I am working "backwards," first listing the humorous material I could use in a specific presentation. If the list includes a good story that I really want to tell on a particular occasion, but requires some modification, I will twist and mold it to fit the audience. In this way, I find developing an outline becomes a natural. After listing my pieces of material, I arrange them by similarities and natural flow. For example, all stories about losing the Miss America pageant go together . . . tallest to ever lose in the Miss America Pageant . . . finished 49th out of 50 girls . . . was better than the girl who played the comb; as do stories about my size . . . six feet, two inches tall . . . 11B shoes . . . 160 pounds. Those clumps of stories illustrate major points of my outline.

Joe Griffith — Always study the great speakers. Get cassette tapes of the speakers you most admire and enjoy. Listen to how their speeches build and flow. Since a speech is spoken, so much can be learned from listening to speeches instead of reading them. This is why listening to cassettes can be very beneficial.

We all develop a style that follows those we admire most as speakers. When I was a child watching Red Skelton on television in the 1950's, I had little idea of the influence he was having on me. Today, I think I reflect so much of what I saw and heard him do. Had I read his monologues, I would not have learned much because his delivery and pacing is what makes the humor work.

After listening to the tapes of your favorite speakers, try to outline them, and you will see how they developed their talks. Outlining is not easy, but it will be very helpful.

Doc Blakely — In my case, after I have the initial inspiration of a title, I research books, newspaper articles, and anything else that comes to my attention. The speech development begins when a specific number of points gel in my mind to get across the major message.

The key to communicating with humor is to keep the message to a minimum. Illustrate with jokes, lines, and anecdotes in such a way that people will remember the major point or points which you are obligated to get across. Let me explain with an example that magnifies the point. I have a friend who is a stand-up nightclub comedian. He decided he wanted to become a professional humorist and speak at convention meetings. He explained to me that he had developed a tremendous speech and had 17 major points that he was going to present to his audience. He asked if he could sit in on one of my presentations to gain a few pointers and some insight into the professional humorist's method of communicating.

Later, when I had finished my presentation, he said, "I was absolutely amazed. You spoke for an hour, but you only made one point." The reason for that in my case was quite simple. My client had asked me to make only one point—productivity. Although my presentation was 90% humor, you can bet that when that audience left the ballroom, they remembered my message. That was an extreme case, but a good rule of thumb I follow is to never have more than six points to make. That generally constitutes my outline. All the rest is humor, fact, or inspiration to support those points.

Robert Henry — The best speakers are those who have something significant to say and a burning passion to say it. When I fall in love with a subject, whether it is goal setting, being a better you, or making the most of what you have, I read everything I can get on the subject. The ideas I feel are most important begin to float around in my mind. My next step is to dream up a theme that will tie the points together.

I have a speech called "Win With ACES." It is a foot-stomping, exciting, humorous, and motivational talk about goal setting and how to reach your personal mountaintop. I explain that once you know where you are going (goals), you will get there by playing the hand you have dealt yourself. If you are holding a handful of aces, you will be a winner. I then talk about the "ACES" of success: "A"—Ambition and Attitude; "C"—Commitment; "E"—Enthusiasm; "S"—Service.

The ACES acronym keeps me on target and aids the audience in recalling what I have said.

9. How Do You Organize Your Thoughts and Decide on the Best Arrangements for Your Remarks?

Jeanne Robertson — Earlier, I mentioned natural flow in organizing groups of material. This is a good thing to remember when organizing thoughts and arranging remarks.

Compare a speech to a flowing river, going in a natural direction, and visualize the audience on a raft with a speaker on that river, going with the flow. As long as the speaker's thoughts are organized in logical order the trip will be smooth. Failing to put thoughts in a logical arrangement can be compared to trying to take the raft upstream. More often than not, the speaker will find the audience will not go along on that trip.

Time sequence is one logical arrangement that seems to work well. For example, it is natural in one of my presentations to first tell stories about being a large baby . . . "23 inches long at birth," then stories about being tall at age 13 . . . "6 ft., 2 inches in the seventh grade," and finally material revolving around being the mother of a tall son . . . "my 6 ft., 8 in. 'little boy.'" The audience is comfortable with this logical movement through time.

Arrangement to illustrate is another surefire method of organizing thoughts. Quite simply, material is put together that illustrates a certain point. For example, being persistent. The audience will permit the speaker to use stories that seemingly have nothing in common, if, in the end, they all serve to accomplish the same purpose.

There are many ways of organizing thoughts. Arranging them by time and for illustration are two that have proven successful for many professional speakers and would serve the nonprofessional equally well.

Joe Griffith — Professional speakers are often asked to cut down their speaking time to get a program back on schedule. Because of this, we become adept at organizing speeches. We develop shortcuts to achieve the same positive results in a shorter time frame. There are three formulas that can help you in organizing a speech.

One is problem-solution-benefit. First discuss the problem; next, discuss the solution or possible solutions; and then discuss the benefits of the solutions chosen to solve the problem.

The second organizing technique is past-present-future. How was it, how is it, how is it going to be? Think of what you would like to relate from the past, what you presently know about it, and how you see the future.

The third organizing principle is pros-cons-conclusions. In other words, if I asked you to determine if flex time should be implemented at our company, you would go out and get all the pros and all the cons of flex time, and then come to a conclusion. So, if you put all of this into a speech, you would organize it with all the pros, cons, and conclusions.

These three organizing principles are good in that they provide a definite place for your information and keep the audience on a progressive journey. The audience feels like they are going somewhere and ending up with a memorable trip.

Over 3000 attendees at the annual Texas School Boards Association convention enjoy the humor of Joe Griffith.

Doc Blakely — As previously mentioned, I select a title first, then develop the body of the speech using from one to six major points that I re-enforce with illustrations. A major key to my style is to keep my thought processes developing in a logical progression just as you would lay a firm foundation for a home, add the walls next, and the roof last. The logical progression that you may want to develop in the minds of the audience is that the firm foundation refers to a large dues-paying membership. The walls could refer to the strong support received from those willing to hold up the association through voluntary service on committees. The roof could refer to those at the top who owe their positions to all those below them.

A tip to the executive who might be planning a program of this sort is to use a professional technique of getting at least one laugh for each minute of presentation. If you plan to speak for 30 minutes, then use 30 lines that illustrate your more serious thoughts. Keep in mind that the humor must also be in a logical progression. Each line must make sense by supporting the more serious thoughts you plan to impart. If you use 30 ten second lines in a 30 minute presentation, you have consumed a total of 5 minutes of the audience's time, leaving 25 minutes for your message. However, because of the re-enforcement with humor, your presentation very likely will be the hit of the convention and the most memorable speech made among other executives.

Robert Henry — Let us imagine you have five points or ideas that you want to present in your speech and they will each stand individually. You could imagine a pie with five equal slices. Since each point stands alone, you can start with any slice and tie the points together with segue lines (transitions). You can progress through the speech until the imaginary pie plate is empty.

If you have some points that will arouse controversy, it is better to put them last. Early on, discuss the ideas on which most people agree. This will build a sense of shared purpose in your audience. Finally, slip in the least controversial issue and progress to the most serious issue to be discussed. As the points get heavier, the judicious use of humor is more appropriate.

Once, in a board meeting of the National Speakers Association, a point of contention had been debated ad nauseum. In the heat of discussion, a board member suddenly pounded the table and with an overexaggerated sense of authority demanded, "I just want to know, what is the penultimancy here?"

The board collapsed into helpless laughter. In this case, the humor was unintended, which made it even funnier, because the questioner was well known for using $10 words where they would not fit. The tension was broken with humor.

Your title might be "Climbing the Mountain of Success." The speech could begin on the valley floor where everything is lush, green, and easy. That is where you will find most of the people. As you progress toward your peak performance, your comments will correspond to the difficulty of the climb. Finally, the toughest of all, you reach the peak where the fewest people and the greatest rewards are to be found.

I like acronyms where the first letter of each point makes up. a word. If your speech is about achieving real success, the title could be "You gotta have STYLE." Style would stand for Sacrifice, Tact, Yearning, Love, and Energy. Plug in appropriate humor to drive these points home.

10. Is There a Formula for Determining the Number of Lines or Jokes to Use on a Particular Subject?

Joe Griffith — If you watch the Johnny Carson TV show, you have heard him say more than once that he violated the Rule of Three. This means he told one too many jokes on a particular subject. This is a rule of comedy and it has to do with rhythm. There is a rhythm of three's in comedy. So I always try to have only three jokes about one particular subject.

What if I have six jokes that are good on a particular subject? Well, the secret is to use the other three later on and the rhythm will start all over again.

Remember to use your best joke as the last joke in each of the batches of three.

Jeanne Robertson — I agree with Joe concerning the Rule of Three when referring to one-liners or little asides, as speakers call them. Here is an example: "I was worried when I went to the Miss North Carolina pageant. Basically, I'm a small town girl and I knew most of the contestants would be from BIG cities, like Charlotte, Raleigh . . . Haw River."

The Rule of Three is also good when involving the audience by asking questions. For example, "How many of you have sons? . . . How many of you have daughters? . . . How many of you have children . . . who are not sons or daughters?" See, again, a set of three.

Please do not confuse the Rule of Three with needing three stories to illustrate a point. If one good, long story that contains a number of humorous asides will illustrate a point, tell it and move on.

Robert Henry — The Rule of Three that is so effective in humor establishes a rhythm or pattern, either consciously or subconsciously, in the minds of an audience. This rhythm heightens the impact of the humor. You can even organize your thoughts, material, or speech titles around the magic of three.

As examples, Christians believe in the Trinity of Father, Son, and Holy Spirit. The world can be divided into earth, sea, and air. Time has three aspects: past, present, and future. After establishing this pattern in the minds of the audience, add jokes by three to each point or subject.

After organizing your ideas by three's, you can further employ the rule to grab attention with the title of your speech. For example, "Politicians, Polecats, and Potlickers" will immediately draw a smile to the lips and stir curiosity. It's not only the Rule of Three, but the alliteration that's interesting.

Let me emphasize that I use more jokes than one-liners. My stories might last from one to three minutes. Therefore, I do not always use the Rule of Three. If it is a substantial involved story with a plot, it will stand alone. I will tell a story, segue to the message or point, and move on.

Doc Blakely — The only apparent exception to the Rule of Three is in the monologue, such as a string of 25 to 30 one-liners on the same subject. However, even then it may hold true by switching thoughts within the monologue. For example, the monologue may be about a fictitious airline. It may go something like this—"I'm not going to say the planes were old, but did you ever see a plane take off from the kneeling position? They did, however, have all the latest equipment. . . radio, radar . . . curb feelers. Their definition of first class was inside the airplane. And you should have seen the crew that got on board. . . ." Note in this example that the monologue followed the rule of three by joking first about the airplane, then switching to the crew. By the same token, the monologue will continue following the Rule of Three by switching again to the navigator, stewardess, passengers, air controllers, weather, and so forth. Always keep the Rule of Three in mind and you will not run the risk of tiring an audience by staying too long on one subject or aspect of humor.

11. After the Body of a Speech is Prepared, What is the Next Step?

Doc Blakely — There are three parts to speech. Years ago, Plato referred to them as the head, body, and feet. I previously used an example of foundations, walls, and roof. The more common terminology referred to in speech courses is opening, body, and conclusion. At this point, we are still working on the body and we should fine tune that body before going further. Take a second look, warm it up. It is very much like a hamburger. You cook the meat first and get it thoroughly prepared, even though the condiments are what give it appeal. The buns can be thought of as the opening and conclusion which can be added later. For the moment, let's concentrate on the meat, which is the message. Humor is represented by lettuce, tomatoes, mayonnaise. The addition of this combination of condiments in a creative arrangement is what makes people say "Whataburger" instead of "Where's the beef?" when they hear a speech that has a thoroughly prepared message.

Doc Blakely joins in the fun at an outdoor function in Phoenix. A western party after his talk was the perfect place to coerce a partygoer into mugging it up in imitation of "Deadeye," a character he popularized at the Arizona meeting.

Jeanne Robertson — After preparing the body of the speech and before going to the opening and closing, I search through my files for material that ties in with the stories I have selected or supports the points those stories illustrate. I am simply gathering finishing touches. Be reminded, a speaker sifts through much more material than she actually winds up using.

By this point of the preparation process, the speaker has decided against using certain material; so, it is a good time to study the remaining material for weaknesses and shore up those areas. A story that originally seemed right may need just a little twist to make it perfect and fit with the other material selected for use.

Three great stories about my teenager may lose impact when used in succession. For example, when I spoke at my son's high school graduation—"finally, a speech that counted" according to him—I needed to put together a completely new presentation and followed the steps I have been suggesting. First, I went through my material and listed what I had not told these students during past speeches and what I thought would be appropriate for this situation. Then I proceeded to put the material in smaller clumps to see what worked together and what good points were illustrated, putting aside material or points that simply did not fit. It was at this stage I realized that while some of the remaining stories were good ones, and very appropriate, too many of them mentioned my son. I considered this a weakness to the overall effectiveness of the speech just as telling all basketball or all beauty pageant stories would be considered a weakness. But rather than discard good material, I strengthened the material by involving other members of the class. Everything went well except for a son who grumbled a little bit about "giving away some of my best lines."

Therefore, critical review and evaluation of the speech body is a vital step before proceeding to the opening or conclusion. You should carefully recheck the flow of your material and insure that the humorous lines will work well together. Remember, a speech may flow naturally, but lose impact if too many stories of one type are used.

Robert Henry — The body of the speech contains the message, the main ideas I want to plant in the minds of the audience. The serious part of my talk, which may well be presented humorously, zeroes in on being a success. I select stories about people who have overcome great obstacles on the way to the top. I will use these stories to illustrate the importance of having ambition, or being committed to one's goals, or consciously choosing the right attitude. Or, the stories are often hilarious but with a very serious intent, to embellish a key point the audience should remember.

To say a person should have a good attitude is rather unremarkable. We have heard that dozens of times. To say success is determined by attitude and give a startling true story of how the right attitude propelled a loser to a mountaintop will move an audience to consider changing its own circumstances.

Joe Griffith — The first thing I do after finalizing the body is go to the opening. After the body is written, you know where you are going and can better determine how to get there. The body is your destination and the opening is the road map that gets you to your destination. Always remember that the purpose of the opening is to get the audience's attention and to create interest in the body that is to follow.

12. What are the Principle Ingredients of Effective Openings?

Robert Henry — Remember, I am a motivational entertainer and my ideas are born on the wings of humor. In order for the audience to accept my humor they have to be "in fun" or "in the mood."

My opening actually begins with the proper introduction. This is so important I prepare a written introduction that, if read properly, will hand the audience over to me in the right frame of mind. After the introduction, I have about two minutes to create an atmosphere and form an impression that will last for the next hour. If I fail here, I may never get the audience with me. Conversely, if I open well, I can make some mistakes and will not lose them.

I want to start like gangbusters with several big belly laughs right up front. Also, since I am an animated, physical speaker, I quickly give the audience lots of nonverbal and facial expressions to convey the idea that this program will be fun.

I would never start a talk by calmly thanking the chairman, the president, the august members, honored guests, reverend sisters, and the bread boy in the rear of the room. My philosophy is grab their attention, make them laugh, and bind them to me. The rest will follow as appropriate.

Doc Blakely — Take the hamburger example that I previously used. There are different kinds of buns that can be used to enhance the appearance of hamburgers and appeal to the tastes of the consumer. You can use sesame seed buns, whole wheat, rye, or some other creative arrangement. In my own case, I want to use an exotic opening that really delights the taste buds of the audience. My rule of thumb is to get a laugh within the first 15 seconds after I am introduced. That constitutes my opening. If at all possible, I want to use an original line that lets the audience know that I am aware of what has been going on at this convention. If you can allude to some "inside story" that everyone is chuckling about, the line does not even have to be real funny, it will usually get a big laugh.

For instance, at one large convention, everybody was grumbling because the hotel had been overbooked and at least half the conventioneers had to stay in hotels outside the major hotel where the meeting was being held. My opening line was, "I was standing outside this beautiful hotel just a few moments ago . . . that is where I am staying . . . outside the hotel." That turned out to be a great opener and the fact that it did not have anything to do with the body of my presentation did not matter to the audience. In other instances, you can have a set opener that will work regardless of the situation. A professional speaker friend of mine always mentions how happy he is to see the ladies in the audience and then opens with a funny line about ladies. If there are no ladies present, he simply mentions this fact, wonders out loud what they might be doing, and then uses the line anyway.

Jeanne Robertson — In planning the opening material, I go straight back to my lists of humor on which material is arranged in a logical order. Certain material, i.e., about location, travel, or the group, lends itself to be used in an opening and, therefore, is listed under opening material. Pulling out the material to use for a particular speech depends on what I think would fit on this occasion and, quite frankly, what I have used in previous speeches to this group. It is preferable to use opening remarks that are original and relevant to the speaker rather than use supposedly surefire winners you have heard other speakers use. More than likely, the audience has also heard other speakers and you are off to a weak start.

While we are discussing openings, let me hitchhike on Doc's thoughts. All speakers who go to an event with their speech prepared should always be on the lookout for things that are happening during the meeting that could be incorporated into the opening remarks. The audience then knows you have been observant and are not giving them a canned speech and they appreciate that fact. In addition, the speaker eliminates the risk of opening with something that might have been used by a previous speaker.

Opening material is generally used to warm-up or loosen the audience. Of course, we have all experienced banquet groups that do not need to be loosened any more! If this occurs it is usually best to lead the audience direct to your message.

Opening remarks should achieve an appropriate warm-up if practical; they do not have to be relevant to the purpose of your speech.

I find it successful to open with material that the audience thinks at the time is incidental to the message and then, later in the speech, refer back to those remarks to further illustrate a point. In some cases, a speaker does not even have to refer back, because it is evident as the speech progresses that the opening incidental remarks were not "incidental" at all. For example, my introducer usually tells the audience I was Miss Congeniality in the Miss America Pageant. It sets me up to include in my opening remarks that "Miss Congeniality is the contestant whom the others believe to be the least likely to win the title of Miss America." Later in the presentation, this seemingly incidental remark supports the point that we have to be able to laugh at ourselves and things that happen to us.

Joe Griffith — I always try to open by talking about the audience. This is especially effective if you have an audience with a head table. A joke on a member of the audience is much funnier if the audience can see the person's reaction. It is also good to check beforehand with the people whom you will be talking about to make sure they do not mind what you are going to say.

One time, I saw a speaker tell a joke on a minister and the minister did not crack a smile. The entire audience followed the reaction of the minister and did not crack a smile. It put a damper on his entire speech. In fact, the speaker never recovered from this early misfortune and is now a lighthouse keeper.

Also, if there are six vice-presidents at the head table and you mention two of them, the other four are going to be offended because they were omitted. So be sensitive to who it is you kid as much as who it is you are not going to kid.

13. What Are Your Recommendations for Humorous Closings?

Robert Henry — The close to a humorous talk does not necessarily have to be humorous. If I am doing a mostly humorous talk, I like to leave an audience laughing on a high note. However, most of my talks involve a substantial message which I have illustrated with humor. In this case, I want to close differently so that the message is remembered rather than the jokes. I like to leave an audience on a very emotional plane. I want them feeling deeply about the ideas I have planted in their minds.

Robert Henry will make you laugh too.

My favorite close is done with poetry which touches our most basic emotions: love, family, and God. Audiences admire a speaker who makes the effort to memorize a poem just for them. And, if the poem is an old favorite, quickly recognized, the audience appreciates it even more.

Jeanne Robertson — It is amazing how varied speakers are when it comes to conclusions. Robert just told you about closing with poetry. Having heard him on numerous occasions, I can vouch that he is successful with this technique. And yet, in over 20 years of speaking, I have never closed with poetry. It is not natural for me; each speaker must work within their comfort zone. Some humorists roll them in the aisle for 30 minutes and then hit the audience with a message "in conclusion. . . ." My preference would be to entwine the message throughout the speech, review the points at the close and leave them on a laugh. With this in mind, my standard rules for conclusion are: Always restate your points; don't try to make them again, just restate them. Refrain from inserting new thoughts; it is too late. Leave them on a laugh; it is not so quiet walking back to your chair. I usually do something that is completely unexpected to generate spontaneous laughter.

Problems in concluding a speech do occur when a speaker has not made any points to restate. The problems are magnified when the speaker realizes this fact and attempts to fit missing points in the conclusion. The impact of a special ending is lost in audience confusion.

Several years ago, I developed what I call a "ditty" and have used it in closing a speech called "Humor: An Effective Strategy for Success." I snap my fingers and repeat a group of words in rapid succession to almost a musical beat. While I repeat the words, I restate my points. It is quick, gives me that unexpected ending and gets a spontaneous reaction.

Joe Griffith — Let me give you a real live example of just how far you can go to come up with a close. I was speaking to a group of bankers in the Midwest. It was a black tie affair with over 1,000 people present. An hour before the banquet, I discovered that I did not bring the pants to my white dinner jacket. I only had a pair of blue jeans. I gave the speech behind the podium, so everything was okay. Nobody knew the difference until the end when I used this unfortunate incident as a closing example. My closing message was that things can go wrong in banking, but you do not have to let them affect your performance. And then I told them what had happened to me, stepped out from behind the lecturn to expose my blue jeans. The room exploded with laughter. I made a great point and ended with a laugh.

Doc Blakely — Basically, there are two ways to close. You can leave them laughing or laughter can be used as a set up for a radical departure from your otherwise highly humorous remarks. An example of a "leave 'em laughin'" closing would be to select a very funny line that also makes a point you will make in concluding. Suppose you have given your speech on your theory of economics and what the future holds for this country. You have used some humorous remarks throughout your presentation so that the audience is familiar with your style of humor. An example of a great closing line in this case would be something like, "There you have it, my friends. That is my best appraisal of where we are headed in the next year. However, let me caution you that economics is merely a theory. As the old saying goes, 'If you took every economist in the world and laid them end to end . . . it might be a pretty good thing.'" By making light of yourself in this situation, the audience will generally love you for it, yet realize the sincerity of your projections while respecting you for admitting the possibility that this situation could be different because no one can forecast the future for sure.

In the radical departure department, an entirely different approach should be used. Here is an example. After you have entertained the audience with as much humor as you feel has been appropriate, and especially after a hearty laugh at the conclusion to your humorous remarks, you may want to close with a more profound thought, such as "The more intellectually inclined in this audience may have thought some of my remarks to be inappropriate. In case you have misinterpreted what I have really been saying in this session today, let me explain it to you in a little different way. We come into this world without our permission and leave it against our will, but it is what we do with the time we have allotted to us that makes the living worthwhile. We can approach each day expecting the worst and find it. Or, we can put on a happy face, pull ourselves up by our attitudes, and live life to the fullest. A part of that fullness is laughter. It is one of the most wonderful therapeutic tools known to mankind. It is one of the most wonderful drugs on the market and it is totally free to all those who will embrace it.

It is completely safe and there is no possibility of harmful after-effects from an overdose. Here's hoping my remarks have given just a little insight into happier living by getting high on life. So the next time you see someone on the street who appears to have no happiness in him, not even a smile to share, give him one of yours because there is none who need humor so much as those who have none left to give."

About Delivering a Humorous Speech

14. Do You Have a Problem with Stage Fright? If So, How Do You Deal with It?

Joe Griffith — Yes, but it is the good speakers who learn how to control it, or at least make it unnoticeable to the audience. On one occasion, I was scheduled to speak in St. Louis, and the president of the association was to speak ahead of me. He was a nervous wreck—shaking papers, wiping his brow, and not eating any of his lunch. I leaned over and asked, "Are you nervous?" He said, "Am I nervous? I am about to die!" I asked him who spoke in his place last year and he pointed to a man sitting near the head table. I asked him, "Do you think he was nervous last year?" He said, "No." Then I called the man up and asked him if he was nervous last year and he said, "Was I nervous? I was about to die!" So, I said to this year's speaker, "You see, he was just as nervous as you are, but he did not let anybody know it." The point is most people are nervous when they speak, but the secret is not to let it show with too many telltale signs such as shaking papers. We can control a lot of our nervousness if we do not telegraph it.

Another thing to remember is that stage fright is at its height during the beginning of your talk. The secret is to learn your openings so well that nothing will keep you from pulling them off. Confidence in your opening will eliminate a lot of stage fright.

Jeanne Robertson — A fool is born every minute . . . and quite often, we want to become speakers.

I rarely experience what is commonly called stage fright. Most individuals see a group of people in an auditorium or at a banquet and comment, "I am glad I am not up there with the microphone." For as long as I remember, I have been the opposite. When I have found myself in those situations, I have wanted to be the one with the microphone. Interestingly enough, it is not important to me to be "on stage" when I am with friends, but put me, for example, in a banquet setting when there is a speaker, and I enjoy being that person. I cannot explain this strange phenomenon any more than I can explain why some people get sick at the thought of giving a report at a PTA meeting. I do know there are others like me because of the number of members in the National Speakers Association. I enjoy speaking so much, as well as the events surrounding the speech, that most of the time I just sit happily waiting to be introduced with no thought of being nervous.

But over the years I have noticed that there are certain occasions . . . and only on these occasions . . . when I must overprepare or I experience something similar to stage fright . . . panic! It tends to occur in three situations: When addressing my peers in the speaking profession; speaking at events in my hometown; in situations when I steer away from what I normally do. Unfortunately, for nonprofessional speakers it is in these exact situations that they usually find themselves designated the speaker. As mentioned, I try to control the panic in these circumstances by over preparing. Through the years I have learned to turn down an engagement that will require extra preparation unless I have ample time to develop appropriate material.

Doc Blakely — I still have stage fright every time I speak. The trick is to be so confident of your material and so well rehearsed in your delivery that you know your fears cannot stand between you and the success of your presentation. As a private pilot, I always have some anxieties about taking off, flying through the air and landing safely at my destination. However, because I am well trained and experienced, that has never prevented me from taking off. A little stage fright for a speaker or a little anxiety for a pilot both make good copilots.

Robert Henry — I know the expected answer is "Yes, I still get nervous, but that keeps me on my toes." The truth is, I almost never get noticeably nervous before I speak if it is a typical program. After more than a thousand professional talks I know my material well and I am confident in my delivery. Most importantly tens of thousands of people have repeatedly laughed at my humor so I have little reason to expect a problem.

However, if the audience is unusual or significantly different, I can expect my stomach to turn into a mass of knotted muscle and my mouth to dry out. Like the time I was asked to speak to 19 millionaires, the oldest being 42, and tell them how to be successful. Or the time I spoke to 12,000 people at a Positive Thinking Rally.

In those cases when you feel terribly intimidated and you are convinced you will bomb before the audience, there is a solid rule to fall back on. It goes like this: "Go with what brung you." There had to be a reason you were invited to speak in the first place. Your reputation surely preceded you. Do not ever let an audience bluff you into changing your style or delivery at the last minute. You might change the material to fit the particular situation but, to change your style, personality, or delivery will always be a mistake.

15. How Do You Tie Thoughts Together for a Smooth Transition from One Point to Another?

Joe Griffith — Transitions or segues should be so smooth that the audience is not aware of them. Segues can take many forms. One can be as simple as laughter from a joke. You simply pause after the laughter and begin your next point. Another segue is to number your points. For example, if you have five points to make in your speech, you number them. After finishing point number three, you say, "Point number four is . . ." and you are off and running to your next point. Just mentioning the numbers is your segue.

You can take the audience from one place to another by using geographic segues. A speaker I know uses this method over and over in every speech. He will say, "I was talking to a lady in Detroit last week . . ." or "They were telling me about a man in Phoenix. . . ." With geographic segues, the audience can go all over the world and never leave the palm of your hand.

A segue that I use frequently is tone of voice. By changing tone of voice, you can lead an audience from one mood to another. When I tell jokes, I speak louder and faster than when I am saying something serious. So when I go from something funny to something serious, I lower my voice and slow down my speech pattern. This subconsciously alerts the audience of a change in mood. When I go from serious to funny, I reverse the order.

Good segues can make a speech seem more important to the audience because they feel like they are being taken to a positive conclusion without having to travel a bumpy road.

Doc Blakely — One way I use segues to get from one point to another is through what I refer to as an internal summary. I present a talk called "Livin' on Love and Laughter" which breaks down love into the various ingredients, supported by stories, jokes, and one-liners. A way to segue from one point to the other is to keep going back over the material just covered in a very brief summary. For instance, the first point I cover on love is "Love is Patience." The point is supported by humorous material. Then I cover "Love is Kindness," going on to "Love is Generosity," until I have finished all the desired points. Each time I do a very rapid internal summary by saying, "Love is patience, love is kindness, love is generosity, love is . . . ," then give the next supporting facts and humor. This makes a very smooth transition from one point to the other. It also keeps the audience informed of the direction of your thought process as well as material covered.

Robert Henry — It is inappropriate to tell a joke and let it hang there. Since we are humorous speakers, it is important that our humor have a purpose. That is why segues are necessary to tie thoughts together and connect the humor with a specific point you wish to make.

Sometimes a segue may be as simple as one word. These guide words or connecting words could be "like," "therefore," or "also."

Here is an example: "You can fool all of the people some of the time and some of the people all of the time . . . and usually that is enough. Therefore, I ask you to be vigilant for the people who would deceive you." Here, we have taken a humorous quip and used the word "therefore" to tie it to a call for vigilance.

Sometimes a short sentence, a statement, or a question is an effective segue or lead-in to a point you wish to make.

"My son keeps a hamster in his room. At first the smell was terrible . . . but the hamster got used to it. Does this sound like your son? Love, with discipline, may solve your problem."

Ideas may be tied together by enumeration, specifying letters of the alphabet, the corners of a square, or the points of a pyramid.

"There are three points of power on the pyramid of success: God, family, and work!"

"There are four equally important points I wish to make, each fitting appropriately in the corners of a square deal."

Often, proverbs, maxims, or even clichés can bridge ideas or lead into a change of thought.

"If you are going to be a success, take action, any action, just do something. The Chinese say, 'A journey of a thousand miles begins with one step.' Your first step should be. . . ."

"Don't do anything today you can put off until tomorrow. 'Cause if it's any good today, you can do it twice tomorrow. This is the kind of thinking that keeps some people from getting started. They're always waiting for a better deal tomorrow."

Remember this sequence: humor, segue, point.

"A man in his 80's was marrying a 20-year-old go-go dancer. His children were alarmed and said, 'This could be fatal.' He said, 'If she dies, she dies.' Let's look deeper into the potential problem for the good things: one, two, three. . . ."

With this timeworn joke, you could get a laugh. Get a laugh, grab their attention, and make your point.

Platform Professional Jeanne Robertson is a funny woman, but her peers saluted her business sense when they elected her President of the National Speakers Association.

Jeanne Robertson — The segues already mentioned are excellent, but while we are on the subject of smooth transitions, it is appropriate to remind the nonprofessional speaker to avoid segueing the speech to death. There is nothing wrong with the audience knowing the speaker has completed thoughts on a certain point and is shifting gears. The comment "I never knew when he went from one point to another" is not necessarily a compliment.

16. How Important is Timing and Rhythm in Delivery?

Robert Henry — Timing is extremely important for the platform speaker. For the humorist, timing is the very essence of the art.

There are four kinds of "TIME" with which the speaker/humorist must be concerned.

First is the timing of the speech itself. If the program chairperson asks the speaker to speak for a specific length of time, there may be a compelling reason for the request. If the speaker needs more time, a simple request often clears the way. However, if the program coordinator insists on a specific time frame, under no circumstances should a speaker violate the guideline.

If several speakers are on a program, it is inexcusable for a speaker to use portions of another speaker's time.

There is nothing more difficult than shutting up when you are hot. When the jokes are popping and the audience is rolling on the floor, obviously in love with your effort, you are easily convinced that you could keep them euphoric for hours. You can not! I once saw a speaker work an audience to a frenzy with an unsurpassed comedic skill. At 50 minutes, the audience would have carried the speaker from the room on their shoulders. At an hour and 20 minutes, the group turned hostile and all of the speaker's good work vanished. I overheard a member of the board of directors of the association say they would never invite the speaker back.

What happened? How can a speaker go from the "penthouse" to the "outhouse" in the span of a few minutes? The answer . . . too much time. It has been my observation that a superb platform performer, using every trick that years of experience will teach, can hold an audience for 50–60 minutes without a break and under ideal circumstances. The less experience one has, the more time one should shave from this maximum.

I am not suggesting that every speech, or even that most speeches, should last this long. And, of course, seminars/workshops are handled with different techniques.

The second kind of "TIME" with which the speaker/humorist should be concerned is timing of the delivery. Pacing of the speech, more specifically, the way the "surprise" is set aside or the cat is let out of the bag is paramount to success.

Every joke may be reduced to a punchline . . . quite often a punchword. Usually, there is one word that, if set aside neatly, will double the impact of the story. It is this setting aside that heightens the surprise and separates the amateurs from the pros. Often, the variation in timing is quite subtle, almost imperceptible, unless one knows exactly what to look for. But, it is inevitably the timing that makes one humorist tower over another.

Those who do not have an innate sense of timing can be aided by actually counting or talking silently to themselves. Set up the joke, tell it well, then silently count . . . "One, two, three," or think "Pause, pause, pause" before hitting the punchline.

The third kind of "TIME" worthy of discussion is that time the humorist allows for laughter after the punchline (word) has been set up correctly and told well.

The amateur is easily spotted as one who continues to talk after the punchline (word), or who pauses momentarily then jumps in with both feet and stomps all over any laughter that might be deserved. The explanation is usually simple. One is afraid the audience will not laugh and in order to obviate this potential embarrassment, the speaker continues to speak. The result is that the audience is never allowed to thoroughly relax into laughter.

The real pro—the one with the confidence, the trooper who has polished the delivery, got the material, and knows that it works—will tell a story and then stop . . . do absolutely nothing more than stare the audience right in the eye as if to say, "I have done my job to the best of my ability—telling the story—now you do yours—laugh."

The hard part is to stand there and do nothing. This takes raw courage. But, it is important to let that laughter live as long as it has value. I often talk to myself as the audience is laughing. That is, talk to myself mentally. I will say . . . "Hold it . . . hold it . . . h-o-l-d it . . . NOW!" And, I am off to the next point.

It is a fine distinction to be made. You do not want the laughter to die, creating an awkward silence. But, you want to let it go as long as it has drive.

The fourth kind of "TIME" might be the most difficult of all. This is the time that exists between stating the punchline and the realization that the audience is not going to laugh appreciably at what you have just said. This is cold sweat time . . . the dry mouth . . . that big lump in the pit of the stomach.

If the audience is not going to laugh at a story you have just told, you have a fraction of a second to recognize your impending doom and leap in to minimize your embarrassment. I have no formula that will help you recognize this situation. I guess it comes with experience. It is something that will develop in your gut and then you operate on instinct.

I know this; if you have to stop and think . . . "They are not laughing," it's too late. Everyone knows they are not laughing.

We have discussed timing: the length of the speech, the telling of the story, and the pauses for laughter. Some people will say timing is innate and cannot be learned. I think some speakers get it much easier than others and have a better understanding. But, I believe any speaker can improve their timing if they work at it.

Jeanne Robertson — Timing and rhythm in speaking are a matter of pausing at the right time and placing words in the correct order for those pauses. Yes, some people do come by it naturally, but timing, rhythm, and delivery can be improved. The best way I have found to do so is to tape every presentation and later listen carefully to determine why something did not go over as well as anticipated. Did I rush a word? Cut off a laugh? Put the words in the wrong order? Taping presentations is also an excellent way to hear what went over well and to listen carefully to the phrasing and pausing in order to recreate the same effect.

Let me share an example of how pausing and placement of words can be changed to gain or lose an effect. As a professional speaker, I provide a short introduction that a presenter may elect to use. I suggest that if they use it they might want to use it verbatim. At one place in the prepared intro, I have set up the introducers to get a prepared laugh if they deliver the words as printed and put in the indicated pauses. The line is: "Jeanne speaks two languages fluently: English . . . and Southern." This line, if read as written, gets a laugh. The pause gives the audience an opportunity to wonder what is coming; French? German? Spanish?. The placement of the word "Southern" serves as an unexpected twist and brings laughter—applause, in God's country. There are no words after "Southern" because they would step on the laugh.

Now, let me share several of the ways the line has been given and let the reader judge how changing the placement of certain words and eliminating the pause affect the line:

"Jeanne speaks English and she has a good Southern accent." No anticipation. No laugh.

"Jeanne speaks English very slowly like the people do in the South." No pause. No laugh.

"Jeanne speaks two languages fluently: Southern and English." No unexpected twist. No laugh.

"Jeanne speaks two languages fluently: English and You All." What?

"Jeanne speaks American and English if she can when she is in the South fluently." This introducer had been drinking.

The list could go on and on. The point is that while some people inherently know to say "English . . . and Southern," others can learn to change phrases and insert pauses by taping and studying their speeches.

Joe Griffith — I had a comedian friend tell me that when he buys jokes, he buys jokes that are funny no matter who delivers the jokes; but with his timing and rhythm, he can make a good joke a great joke.

An important part of timing is not to step on your laughs. Speakers who step on their laughs either do not have confidence in themselves or they do not have confidence in the joke they are telling. I have one joke that if I do not wait at least four or five seconds, the audience will not have time to catch the joke. Once they do catch it, it gets a belly laugh.

Some words have a rhythm that makes jokes funnier. In one story I tell, I have learned that saying "Buick" gets a bigger laugh than using Ford, Oldsmobile, Cadillac, or other names of cars. The reason is that words with the X, L and I sounds are funnier to people than words without them. These sounds add to the rhythm of a joke.

Doc Blakely — Rhythm is one of the most important ways you have of selling a piece of humor. We have all seen comedians on television "blow the punchline." The audience usually thinks this is very funny because it embarrasses the performer. If the performer is a very skilled one, they can take advantage of this blown punchline and come back with a saver which often is funnier than the original line. However, no comedian or humorist ever wants to blow a punchline. The usual cause of this miscue is a breakdown in rhythm or timing. My definition of timing is to be able to speak as rapidly as practical in situations where that seems most appropriate to sell the setup or payoff. In other instances, you may want to lower your voice, slow down your pace to build up suspense just as background music in a suspense movie is used to control your emotions. Therefore, timing is basically controlled by the speed of your speech, tone of your voice, and the raising and lowering of your voice. Rhythm is a much different thing. Here is just one example from an actual setup I use in telling a story about my early days as a bullrider. Read these lines aloud and emphasize each capitalized word and I think you will understand what rhythm is all about. "Do you know what it takes to be a bullrider? You gotta WALK like a bullrider, TALK like a bullrider, THINK like a bullrider, DO like a bullrider DO . . . and before you know it, you'll be a bullrider." That setup never gets a big laugh; it was not designed to do so, but because of the rhythm, it always gets chuckles, grins, smiles, and heightens the anticipation of what is yet to come.

17. Is There a Place for Visual Aids in Humor?

Robert Henry — Yes, indeed. First of all, the speaker is a visual aid. You should look appropriate for the speech you are going to give before that particular audience. If you are doing a keynote at a banking convention, wear your best power suit. If you are scheduled for a Hawaiian luau, by all means, wear a loud shirt or muumuu. You should always ask the meeting planner what dress is appropriate. There is nothing more embarrassing than showing up at a banquet in brown loafers when everyone else is wearing tuxedos.

Use of props can be very effective in punching up the humor in a program. I have terrifically funny friends who do magic with humor, wear funny costumes, use funny hats, blow whistles, use huge cardboard cutouts, show comical slides, slice the air with fake swords, and show phony arrows piercing their heads.

Again, if you are comfortable with this humor, it can be devastatingly funny. If it is not you, do not try it.

Jeanne Robertson — "Do you sing during a speech?" is a question I am often asked. The fact is that in some presentations I do pull out a baritone ukulele and do a song. To call it singing would be a gross overstatement and, believe me, the routine is included because it illustrates a point, not because of any musical talent. Although it may be stretching it a little to call the ukulele a visual, it has served as a reminder. The more visuals or props of this type that a speaker uses, the greater the chances of something going wrong.

Over the years, about everything that could happen with the ukulele has occurred, from the string breaking in the middle of a song, to one person at the head table using the instrument to hit another—high class clientele. By this stage of my career, I have developed recoveries from these possible circumstances, and have found I can roll with the punches. This is made easier because a presentation does not depend on using the ukulele. When humorists depend upon visuals or props for the success of a program, they add to the list of things that have to be checked and double checked.

For a speech several years ago, I decided that a certain funny magic trick involving fire would further illustrate a point. No, I am not a magician, but this particular trick could be purchased at the nearby "House of Houdini"—I believe for a grand total of $7.95—so I gave it a try. I actually caught my dress on fire in front of a thousand people . . . quite a visual! Of all the things I said that night, there is no doubt about what the audience will most remember.

An elderly auditorium custodian I met at a beauty pageant years ago summed it up best. In my role as pageant emcee, I waited with everyone else during the rehearsal while the stagehands set up the props for a contestant who was to sing for her talent. The props literally consisted of a complete bedroom suite. The fellow pulling the curtain asked no one in particular, "Does all that stuff help?" The custodian slowly shook his head and replied, "Not if she can't sing." And this is a good reminder for humorists who believe visuals might carry a speech. They will not, "not if they can't make people laugh without them."

Joe Griffith — Is there a place for visual aids in humor? I think the question should be reversed. Is there a place for humor in visual aids? The answer to that question is a definite yes! Anytime the audience expects you to do the unexpected, you will have the audience in the palm of your hand.

I was on a program in San Diego with a chemist. He was giving a very technical presentation to other chemists. I will never forget that after showing six slides that were serious, the seventh one was a photo of himself sleeping in his pajamas in his laboratory back at the office. When the slide popped up, the audience began to chuckle, and he commented, "You can see this stuff bores me, too." They roared with laughter. The comic relief added greatly to his presentation and the audience was always waiting for his next attention-getter.

There is an old joke about two golfers about to tee off and one said to the other, "Let's play for a little money, but since you're so much better than I am, why don't you give me two gotcha's." Well, the better golfer agreed to give two gotcha's. As he was about to tee off, the other guy hauled off and kicked him in the rear, knocking him three feet off the tee box. The better golfer got up and said, "Why did you do that?" And the other golfer said, "That's one gotcha." The poorer golfer won the tournament because the other golfer kept waiting for the next gotcha.

As a speaker, you will win your audience because the audience does not know when the next funny slide is coming.

Doc Blakely — Visual aids can be used in humor very effectively, but it would be my recommendation to use them in moderation. Years ago when I was an inexperienced speaker, I asked an old

This is not the only book for Doc Blakely. PUSH BUTTON WIT, his 5th book to author is shown here at a bookstore autographing party, a familiar scene also at many of his talks. He quips, "This book is already in its 4th printing. The first three were kinda blurry."

mentor of mine to serve as a critic of one of my talks. At that time I was relying heavily on visual aids which I thought greatly enhanced my performance as a humorist. For instance, I would roll an old hat, red bandana, and other items inside the daily newspaper to conceal any evidence of props from the audience until I was introduced to speak. I used the silly hat and other props in various ways to add comedy to my stories, even resorting to cutting funny things out of the newspaper with scissors and a variety of other visual tricks. The most memorable criticism I received from my mentor was about the visual aids. He commented that I needed to make a decision as to whether I was going to be comedian or a humorist. "Slapstick comedians need a lot of props," he said. "A good humorist uses the mind to create the desired images." It is a lesson I have never forgotten. There is a place for visuals in humor, but they are not necessary and if used at all, should be used in moderation.

18. Some Speakers Use Notes; Others Do Not. What Do You Recommend?

Doc Blakely — It varies with the individual. One should use whatever works best. In my case, I prefer not to use notes. I have always had a natural tendency to speak without notes, so it is very easy for me. This style was further re-enforced very early in my speaking attempts when people commented that they were impressed that I was able to speak humorously, at length, without notes. To use notes would destroy eye contact for me which is very important. It would tie me to a lectern which is not my preference because I have a very animated style of speaking and use a lot of body language in my presentations.

However, this does not mean that I simply memorize all my lines. I do not. For years, I have used mental image tricks that I stumbled upon myself and later re-enforced with modern memory training techniques. For example, Plato was reported to have been able to speak for several hours without the use of apparent notes. When they asked him how he was able to cover such meticulous detail at such length, he replied, "It is quite easy. I simply take a mental stroll down a familiar street and enter the homes of all my friends along the way. As I am escorted through each room, I recall where every table, chair, lamp, and other articles are located. I attach an important point to each of these articles through a strong mental image and go from house to house until my speech is concluded." If you think speaking without notes is something you want to try, you may want to pursue memory training in more depth. One of the best books on this subject is *The Memory Book* by Jerry Lucas and Harry Lorraine, available at any bookstore.

Joe Griffith — I avoid notes whenever possible, but there are times when I use them. For example, when doing a three or six hour seminar, I use notes, but they are very skimpy, just a few key words to remind me of what is coming next. I try to make them as unobtrusive as possible and I can do this by using 3 × 5 cards or writing the notes on the sides of the overheads that I am using in the seminar. However, when working in front of a lectern, I cannot use notes while being funny. They are a distraction. So I arrange the jokes to the point where they trigger each other.

For example, I have a joke about health food stores. I follow that joke with a joke about dogs. I tied these two jokes together by asking myself a question after the health food joke and the question is, "Whom would I not feed health food to?" The answer is "My dog."

I have a joke about bartenders and it is followed by a joke about automobile mechanics. I tie these two jokes together by asking another question. "After you have been to a bartender, what is it you should not do? The answer is drive a car." Now I am into automobile mechanics.

Notes can be eliminated by using words to organize your speeches. I recently wrote a one-hour speech on enthusiasm. I organized everything using the word enthusiasm. For example, the E stood for excited, the N stood for new, and so on. Each letter reminded me of what I wanted to say in that particular point in my talk. When I ran out of things to say on E, I went to N until I finished the word enthusiasm an hour later.

Jeanne Robertson — In the late sixties, I arrived in a small town in Alabama to rehearse for a beauty pageant I was to emcee the next night. The local sponsors had spared no expense in building an elaborate set on which the contestants entered from the back of the stage, descended at least a dozen steps, and walked toward the audience. The first three girls fell down the steps. They would be falling still if I had not overheard one of the girls say, "We'd do better if we could look where we are stepping." It turned out they had been instructed that under no circumstances should they look down at the steps. Ridiculous. If they needed to look down to keep from falling, why not?

The same goes for speakers and notes. If a speaker needs to glance at notes to keep from falling, why not? I do not use notes for speeches, nor do my associates in Platform Professionals; but remember, we speak every other day. It is a different situation for the nonprofessional speaker.

While it was certainly permissible for the contestants in that pageant to glance at the steps, it would not have been acceptable to enter from the back of the stage, and stare at the floor until reaching the front, glancing up every so often to see if the audience and the judges were still there. The same goes for those who use notes. To insure that this is not the case, avoid writing more than three words to be said in a row on the notes. Speakers cannot read verbatim that which is not written down. Three words or less remind a speaker of what should be said and that is what notes should be, reminders.

Robert Henry — When I first started speaking, I wrote my speeches and read from a manuscript, word for word. That is the least desirable, but it was not as bad as it sounds.

First, I typed my speech in orator-type. Those are very large letters that can be read at a distance. Secondly, I was a very good reader and most people never realized I was reading. At appropriate spots, I would write in, "Tell joke." I would tell the joke I had selected with lots of eye contact and animation. Then it was right back to the script.

I progressed to an outline, often on index cards, and a mere glance would give me the sequence of ideas.

Ultimately, I learned to speak without notes.

We professional speakers often give the same speech over and over. People sometimes step forward amazed and say, "How do you ever speak for an hour and never look at a note?" The answer is simple. Get three hours of material. If you forget one thing, slide into something else; if that goes, jump to another idea. The audience will never know you blew it.

You can memorize a speech, word for word, and throw away the text. This is very dangerous. If all you know is what you have memorized and your memory blanks out—this is guaranteed to happen sooner or later—you are in desperate trouble with nowhere to go.

Finally, you might number the points you will use, both humorous and serious. Associate each point with the number using memory techniques. If your fourth point is "a free society," imagine that four rhymes with door and when you open the door, you're free. Your memory, with visualization, will key you: four . . . door . . . free . . . free society.

19. Some People Use Gestures When They Speak. What Are Your Thoughts on Their Use and Misuse?

Robert Henry — I believe that a speaker should give an audience something interesting to look at as well as listen to. Your interesting look might come from a low-key performance standing behind a lectern. Mine is just the opposite.

I am a physical, kinetic speaker. I like to work in the open, in front of a head table, with a hand microphone and about 40 feet of cord. If the audience is larger than 300, I want a riser with plenty of room to move.

Gestures should never be planned. They should spring from the gut. Be totally natural. Do what feels right for you. If you get excited, it is okay to throw out your arms. It is not okay to throw out your arms and pretend to get excited. Phony or faked gestures are as obvious as a sign held high saying, "Fake!"

It is okay to move about, even into the audience. Do not move halfway into the audience and stay there for a long time. That means you will be working to the backs of half your listeners. Stay in front and work side to side most of the time.

Movement will be emphatic if done for a purpose. Move to make a point. Do not wander aimlessly with mike in hand. Never shift your weight from foot to foot pointlessly.

I create a character for the audience that is ebullient, fun-loving, enthusiastic, and happy. I love what I do and want it to be obvious from the platform. When telling the stories I enjoy, I assume a role and become an integral part of the story. I act it out. Therefore, any gestures that keep me in character are appropriate.

Along with gestures, eye contact with the audience is very important. Never pick a spot on the back wall and talk to the spot. Also, do not scan the room from side to side or front to back, never stopping on a person.

Speak to one person at a time. Pick someone in the front row, stare deeply into their eyes and speak just to them for 10 seconds. Then look at someone in the middle of the room, to the left, to the rear, up front. Cover the whole room, but always talking to one person at a time.

Jeanne Robertson — Robert is correct. Faked or poorly used gestures only serve to detract from a presentation. Actually, as far as gestures are concerned, perhaps it is more important to refrain from putting yourself into a category of using one type of gesture or another. It is better to let the material dictate the type of gesture. No, I do not mean to mention a cloud and point to the sky. Let the tone of the material set the gesture.

Most of my gestures involve subtle movements of the head, hands, and eyes except when telling a story that requires exaggerated action. I have found that to get the desired audience response, a slow turn of the head is more effective than an overexaggerated fling of the arms. A hand on the hip, a wrinkled brow, or raising the eyebrows may be all the gestures a speaker needs for a particular one-liner.

While it is fun for me to use sly, subtle gestures I would not use them if the speech material required more action. For example, at a beauty pageant I was emceeing years ago, a funny thing happened to one of the contestants who was twirling a baton for her talent. That incident—stretched a little, of course—has slowly evolved into one of my best longer stories, but there is no way to mock a person twirling a baton without getting into it. So, when telling that story, I use a variety of gyrations, i.e., body crouched, hands over my head, legs swinging, and any number of exaggerated facial expressions. While the story is funny enough when heard on cassette, the gestures make it one of those classics all speakers look for. The secret: Let the material dictate the gesture.

Joe Griffith — My belief on gestures is to use them, but do not abuse them. So often, gestures are referred to as body gestures, but speakers can gesture with their voices. If you are speaking in a consistent low voice range, then to raise your voice is a gesture as it adds impact to the words that you are saying. I know one speaker that seldom gestures; then when he makes a big point, he takes off his glasses and shakes them at the audience. It is a very effective gesture only because that is the only time they see him take his glasses off.

I have trained thousands of people to speak in my speech training school, but there is one classic story about a politician who came to see me. He was running for the United States Senate. I could

Joe Griffith (r) gets two birdies in a row at beautiful Desert Highlands in Phoenix. The miracle was witnessed by Joe Larson.

not get him to gesture, so I told him to write gesture on his notes. Then, when he got to that part of his speech, he would know now is the time to gesture. Unfortunately, that did not work either. He finished a statement, looked over and saw the words "gesture here," and then made a gesture. Instead of being together with his words, he separated them. It did not work. Finally I told him, "Just do not gesture at all unless you feel like it." I think that is good advice. It is better to undergesture than to overgesture or to have bad gestures.

Doc Blakely — I discovered years ago that I was a naturally animated speaker. This came to my attention at the first speech I ever gave. The lectern was out in front of the head table at a banquet.

After my talk, quite a number of the people at the head table, who were seated behind me, were joking about the best show being my back side, watching many movements of my body which were hidden to the audience. This was not a conscious movement on my part, simply something I was naturally inclined to do because I throw myself into the acting out and telling of a humorous story. I reasoned that if people behind me were enjoying those movements, people in the audience would react equally as well in response to body language humor.

As I emerged from behind the lectern, I discovered some very interesting things about an audience's reaction. If you are doing a good job of acting or selling your story, many people in the audience will be a mirror image, especially of facial expressions. Watching the facial expressions of your audience, at least for an animated speaker, is one of the best shows in town. People often ask me, "Do you always laugh at your own jokes that way?" I usually reply, "If you were looking at what I was looking at, you'd be laughing too."

20. How Do You Rehearse Material to Perfect It?

Jeanne Robertson — At a small dinner party years ago, I told a story about a dog and a steak to our six guests. While they laughed, I noticed my husband was only grinning. He had heard the story several times. Later that evening, I commented to him that our friends seemed to like that story and he said, "Yes, you have about got that one down pat."

My husband is well aware of, and puts up with, a system I have used for years to rehearse new humorous material. It is not earth-shattering, but it works. Quite simply, I perfect my material in conversations before I try it in speeches.

Back to the list . . . you remember it . . . the list of material I am ready to try in speeches? May I suggest that a person interested in speaking also keep a list of material to be worked on or perfected, and from this list, try material in conversations. Just as my husband knew from our guests' reactions that I had that particular story down pat, so will the reactions of your friends tell you if that piece of material needs more work.

When I reach a point that I have a number of stories down pat, I call a local senior citizens group or nursing home and set up a time to do a free program in which I try out as much new material as time will allow. One could say it is similar to doing off-Broadway in a small theater. But in Burlington, North Carolina, it would be called off-Main in the basement of the Front Street Methodist Church. The results are the same though, and the reaction of the crowd and studying of the tape let me know what is ready . . . not to mention the goodwill done in my town.

Joe Griffith — I read a joke over a few times to get the feel or the rhythm of the punchline. Once I do that, then I try it out on anybody I can find—service station attendants, toll booth attendants, anybody. I seldom tell a joke before an audience without first telling it to at least three different people.

When you can tell a joke or story without having to think of the words, you are probably ready to deliver it before a live audience. If I am going to tell jokes that I have not told in some time, I listen to a previous tape just to hear my rhythm, making it come back to me faster.

Everybody has a best time to rehearse. Mine is early in the morning or after I have had my daily run. Find out what your natural bio-rhythm peak is and try to use that time to maximize your rehearsal period.

Doc Blakely — I use methods that are similar to my colleagues, but in addition, I picked up a fascinating idea from a lay speaker. This fellow was a student of humor and tried out his lines on his friends and associates on a daily basis. He did this with a very simple technique. Each day, he would come up with a line that he thought was funny, one that he could tell using his own unique personality. Then when he met a close acquaintance on the street instead of saying, "How are you?," he would ask, "Have you heard the thought for the day?" He was always very careful to keep the subject in tune with current events. For instance, if he was attending an investment seminar, his thought for that day would be something like "Never invest in anything that eats or needs repainting."

The advantage of using such a technique is obvious. You get experience delivering the line plus an idea of the feedback you might expect if the line is delivered to several people during the course of a day. Of course, you have to be careful not to repeat this line to the same person or let others overhear you using it frequently or you run the risk of becoming a bore. One other precaution. Do not let a negative response from one or two people discourage you from trying it on an audience. Sometimes, a "thought for the day" that is only mildly amusing on a one-on-one basis is hilarious to an audience. By trying it out on a few individuals to gain confidence and feedback, one has some idea of what to expect from an audience.

One last hint in this area—never simply walk up to someone and say, "What do you think about this line?" They will invariably tell you that the line is not funny and discourage you from using it on an audience. In my experience, I have found that it is best never to confide in anyone. Just use the line at the proper time and place and let your listener's reaction be the judge. Think of the "thought for the day" as a mini-rehearsal. You may be surprised at what you learn with this little used technique.

Robert Henry — Every aspiring speaker needs experience to improve. Someone once asked the great orator, Dr. Ken McFarland, how to become a good speaker. He gave a one word reply, "Speak."

In the beginning, you should speak free at every opportunity to develop poise before an audience. After you have become a confident, polished speaker, you can return to those freebies to try out new material.

I recommend going to the local Chamber of Commerce and ask for their listing of local clubs. The list will identify every service/civic club in the area and give you the president's and program chairperson's name, address, and telephone number.

Every Rotary, Lions, Civitan, Kiwanis, Ruritan and other club in town are looking for at least 45 speakers a year. You will need a 30 minute program. They allocate 30 minutes for lunch and 30 minutes for a speaker. Then the room empties as if by magic as members dash back to their business.

Call the program chairperson. Tell them you have a program. They will be thrilled at your offer. You will be put on the schedule, but all you will get paid is a free lunch. During the program, be sure to mention that this is just a sample of your work. Your best stuff is being held in reserve and they can hear that if they invite you back to speak at their annual ladies' night banquet. Of course, you charge a modest fee for those appearances.

If you become a professional speaker, these clubs will be even more excited at your offer to speak at a regular meeting. I know of no better place to try out new material before you take it on the road.

PART IV

**OVER 2000 JOKES, STORIES,
ONE- AND TWO-LINERS PERFECTED
BEFORE LIVE AUDIENCES**

Accidents

1. The neighbors were still talking about the night Fred arrived home late after a long evening of drinking. "I saw it all," said one. "Can you imagine? He roared into his driveway, clipped the tree, tore up 20 feet of hedge, knocked over the yard light, and smashed into his garage door."

"It must have been terrible," replied another neighbor. "But it could have been worse. Can you imagine the damage he could have done if he'd been driving a car?"

2. A lady bent a fender on their new car and a neighbor asked if her husband got mad. "He didn't say much," said the wife. "But his boss said the smoke alarm went off when he got to work."

3. Six-year-old Scott came into the house covered with mud after finishing a rough day at play. "Mom," he shouted at the top of his voice, "if I fell out of a tree, would you rather I broke a leg or tore my pants?"

"What a silly question," his mother answered from the next room. "I'd rather you tore your pants."

"Well, I got good news for you then," the boy replied triumphantly. "That's exactly what happened."

4. Rookie officer's report of his first traffic accident: "Miss Jones was involved in the accident which bruised her somewhat and injured her otherwise but apparently did not hurt her elsewhere."

5. Two hippies walking down the street met a Catholic priest with his arm in a sling. "What happened to you, man?" inquired one of them. "I fell in the bathtub and broke my arm," replied the priest.

The hippie turned to his friend, "Man, what's a bathtub?"

"How should I know?" replied the second one. "I'm not a Catholic."

6. Just got some news from back home. Uncle Schyder was accidentally tarred over while they were putting in the first shopping center, but he is being honored as our town's first speed bump.

7. A kindhearted farmer came upon a young boy who had just lost a load of hay along the side of the road, and suggested that the boy come home with him and have dinner before reloading the wagon.

The boy said he didn't think his father would like that, but the farmer persisted, and finally the boy agreed. After eating dinner and relaxing a bit, the farmer drove the boy back to the scene of the accident and started to help him put the hay back on the wagon.

"By the way," the farmer said, "you're awfully young to be pitching this hay yourself. Where's your father?"

"He's under this hay," the boy replied.

8. The hippie awoke in the hospital and found himself covered from head to toe with bandages, and naturally felt terrible. "What happened, man?" he said to another long hair who was sitting next to his bed.

"Like, baby," said his comrade, "you remember last night after the party in the Village, when you said you were going to fly off the roof and land in the Bronx?"

"Well, yeah, man, I sort of remember, but why on earth didn't you stop me?"

"Man," reasoned the other cool one, "I thought you could make it."

9. A city slicker went to the mountains for the first time in his life this spring. One morning, he returned to his hotel from a walk in the woods; his clothes torn, his face and arms all scratched and bruised. The hotel owner, alarmed, asked him what in the world happened. "A big black snake chased me," the New Yorker said.

"But a black snake isn't poisonous," replied the innkeeper.

"Listen," the city fellow said, "if he can make me jump off an 80-foot cliff, he doesn't have to be."

10. In filling out an application for a factory job, a man was puzzled for a long time over this question: "Person to notify in case of accident."

Finally he wrote: "Anybody in sight."

11. Dr. Perkins and Mr. Spencer, an attorney, were driving in separate autos along the mountain highway one foggy night. The cars collided, but the fault was questionable. Both men were shaken up, and the lawyer offered the doctor some whiskey from a pocket flask. Perkins took the flask with a shaking hand and took several long swallows. When Spencer started to cap the flask, the doctor said, "A stiff drink could help the nerves. Why don't you have one also?"

"Oh, I will," replied the lawyer, "right after the highway patrol gets here."

12. A running joke around town at the height of the blizzard: "Did you hear about the bad accident up near Peoria? Two hundred

geese suffered whiplash when the lead bird made an abrupt turn to the south."

13.   For 25 years, Morris had never been late for work. However, one morning instead of checking in at 9:00, he arrived at 10:00. His face was criss-crossed with adhesive tape and his right arm was in a sling. Mr. Sapman, his boss, demanded to know why he was late. Morris explained, "I leaned out a window after breakfast and fell three stories."

His boss just shrugged and said, "What, that takes an hour?"

14.   A local factory's bulletin board has this suggestion: "In Case of Accident or Injury, Notify Your Supervisor Immediately." (Underneath, someone had scribbled, "He'll kiss it and make it better.")

15.   Garageman giving estimate to owner of wrecked car: "First, the good news. Your glove compartment and sun visor are in excellent condition."

16.   It seems this fellow was really brainwashed about not having his safety belt on if he had a fender bender. So, obsessed with keeping as safe as possible, he buckled up constantly. But one day, he put his own auto in the shop for minor repairs and was given a beltless loaner by the garage. Everything was fine until he reached his destination, unbuckled, and got out. His pants fell down.

17.   A woman driver pulled into the garage with a badly dented fender and asked the mechanic, "Can you make this look like new by 5 o'clock this evening when my husband comes home?"

He said, "No, ma'am, I can't, but I can fix it so you can ask him tomorrow how he did it."

18.   A woman, after a fender bender with a male motorist, exclaimed, "You had no right to assume that I had made up my mind."

19.   A lady rammed her car into her house and it finally stopped inside the den. When her husband asked, "How did you drive the car into the den?" She replied, "I turned left at the bedroom."

20.   Yesterday, our teenager came in and said, "I don't want to upset you, but I scratched the left rear fender a little."

I asked, "Was it bad?"

He said, "Oh, no, not really, but if you want to look at it, it's in the trunk."

21.   A man's ear was bleeding. A friend asked how it happened. He replied, "I bit myself on the ear."

"How did you do that?" asked the friend.

"I stood on a chair," the man replied.

Ads

22. Another commercial . . . "Four out of five doctors recommend. . . ." Think how the fifth doctor must feel when he sees that. (In Voice) "OH, my God, I was the only one!"

23. In a local paper: "Free LITTLE puppies. Choose black or black and white spotted . . . but choose NOW. Will soon be free LARGE dogs."

24. "Puppies For Sale. Mother registered AKC St. Bernard. Father, a VERY REMARKABLE beagle."

25. "Found," said a small item in a Southern newspaper, "bird or hat, which flew or blew into Smith's Service Station. It's sort of round with green and red feathers and quills on it. If you've lost a bird or a hat, maybe we have it. Even if you haven't, drive by and see it. It's worth a trip."

26. Two businessmen were discussing the merits and drawbacks of advertising. "Is your advertising getting results?" queried the first. "Yeah, I guess it is," replied the second. "Just last week we advertised for a night watchman and the next night we were robbed."

27. Advertising really works. There are seven peaks in Colorado higher than Pike's Peak. Name one of them.

28. Running a business without advertising is like winking at a girl in the dark. You know what you're doing, but she doesn't.

29. Classified ad: "For Sale: 100-year-old brass bed. Perfect for antique lovers."

30. A young man applied for a job at an ad agency. He was told, "Your resume is full of distortions, half-truths, and bald-faced lies. Welcome aboard."

31. Some employers have a tendency to make their classified job ads sound better than the jobs really are. For example:

"Usual benefits"—free coffee in a paper cup.

"Comprehensive benefits"—cream and sugar.

"Outstanding benefits"—slice of cake when employee has a birthday. or:

"Seek soft-spoken, sympathetic person with dark suit"—casket sales.

"Challenging position for person with martial arts skills"—to deliver pizza in a high crime area.

"No experience needed, $5,000 per week to start"—smuggling cocaine.

32. In the Personal Ads column: "Lady with bad feet, poor eyesight, full of arthritis, otherwise friendly and nice personality wants to meet an old man with same qualities. . . ." Now, that's truth in advertising!

33. Classified ad: "Help wanted—saleslady for cosmetic counter in department store. Must like people part or full time."

34. Ad in a newspaper: "For sale. Complete set of encyclopedias. Never used. Teenager knows everything."

Age

35. Mr. Collins was seventy years old, but he still enjoyed chasing after young ladies.

A friend asked Mrs. Collins if she was upset that her husband chased after young girls.

"Why should I be?" Mrs. Collins replied. "Dogs chase cars, but when they catch them, they can't drive."

36. Thirty is the ideal age for a woman—especially if she's forty.

37. As I grow older, I'm just thankful for lots of things. Just think of the state we'd be in if wrinkles hurt!

38. The secret of longevity? Get to be 99 and then be REAL careful!

39. Don't think for a minute that women who subtract years from their ages waste those years. No, indeed! They add them to the ages of their female acquaintances.

40. A very wealthy 72-year-old man who married a shapely 21-year-old blonde was asked, "How did a 72-year-old codger like you manage to marry such a young, beautiful woman?"

"I told her I was 90," he replied.

41. Old is . . . when you start talking to your sister again.

42. A senior citizen approaching his 100th birthday said, "I attribute my longevity to the fact that I lived most of my life before America and the rest of the world went nuts."

43. A lady was talking to her elderly uncle and they were discussing

some of the current problems of life in these United States. The lady sighed. "Do you think, Uncle Frank," she asked, "that things will ever get back to normal?"

"I don't know," he replied. "There aren't very many of us left who remember what normal was."

44. It's not that she's too old. But she's got beautiful antique jewelry . . . and she bought it when it was new.

45. As Confucius said . . . , and she WAS THERE when he said it.

46. A man celebrating his 100th birthday was asked by a reporter what his secret for long life was. "Nothin' to it," replied the oldster, chompin' his toothless gums. "Jest keep a-breathin'."

"Well," the reporter continued, "is there any one thing to which you would attribute your longevity?"

"I can't rightly say yet," replied the oldtimer, "I'm still dickering with two breakfast food companies."

47. A fellow said, "I don't want to be 73 years old."
Another said, "Yeah, that's because you ain't 72."

48. Doctor: "You should live to be seventy."
Patient: "I am seventy."
Doctor: "See there. What'd I tell you?"

49. My wife is something. She never lies about her age. She just tells everyone she's as old as I am. Then she lies about my age.

50. A friend's delightful response to a query about his age: "I'm 53, but I prefer to think of it as 11 Celsius."

51. "Grandpa, it says here that there are 20% more women at age 75 than men."
"At age 75," sighed Grandpa, "who cares?"

52. Old age is when you wonder how Bo Derek would look with a snow shovel in her hand.

53. An old-timer says he didn't realize how much advancing age had affected him until he sat down in a rocking chair the other day and couldn't get it going.

54. He's so old his hairpiece is turning gray.

55. You are over the hill when the opposite sex looks good to you, but you don't remember why.

56. "Dear Clara," wrote the octagenarian. "Pardon me, but I'm

getting so forgetful. I proposed to you last night, but really forgot whether you said yes or no."

"Dear Will," 78-year-old Clara wrote back. "So glad to hear from you. I knew that I had said no to somebody last night but had forgotten who it was."

57.   An elderly woman was filling out an application for residency in a retirement village. With some anxiety, she answered the questions relating to the state of her health, then signed her name and put down her current address. After "Zip," she printed: "Normal for my age."

58.   One of the blessings of old age is that when your face gets so saggy and wrinkled that you don't like to look at it anymore, your eyesight starts to fail.

59.   An oldtimer is someone who remembers when human hair came in only three or four basic colors.

60.   "Why is it that a woman of 40 looks older than a man of the same age?"

"It's because a woman of 40 is probably 50."

61.   Phyllis Diller on her 62nd birthday: "I'm really only 35 because I have been taking birthday control pills."

62.   An old man—whose birth certificates and all family records had been lost years ago—had gone to a doctor and asked him to determine his age. "Well, Doc," asked the ancient one, "how old am I?"

"According to all mortality tables I've ever seen," said the doctor, "I'm all alone in this room."

63.   An elderly gentleman was overheard complaining to a friend: "You know the worst thing about getting old? I'll tell you—it's having to listen to advice from your children."

Airplanes

64.   The commuter I fly provides goggles and a scarf upon boarding.

65.   My commuter is different. I asked the captain, "Will we need a parachute?"

He said, "Naw, we won't be goin' that high."

66.   Fred and Archie were sitting on a park bench. "I'm afraid to fly. Those airplanes ain't too safe," announced Fred.

"Don't be a baby," said Archie. "Didn't you read last week there was a big train crash where 300 people were killed?"

"Three hundred people killed on a train—what happened?"
"An airplane fell on it!"

67. You know you're in trouble when you go to the airline desk to complain about losing your luggage and the guy behind the counter is wearing your clothes.

68. How about those airlines that still cut frills in order to offer better passenger rates? I know one that doesn't show movies. It just buzzes the drive-ins.

69. Muhammad Ali was confronted by a flight attendant on a recent flight.
Attendant: "You have to buckle your seat belt."
Ali: "Superman don't need no seat belt."
Attendant: "Superman don't need no airplane."

70. If God had really intended for people to fly, he would have made it easier to get to the airport.

71. Our favorite preacher saw a member of the flock off at the airport yesterday: "May God and your luggage go with you."

72. A flight attendant says she was on duty on a recent flight when she was summoned by a little old lady who was taking her first nighttime trip and had been looking out the window at the blinking wingtip marker light. "I'm sorry to bother you," the little old lady said to the attendant, "but maybe you should tell the pilot that he has left his turn signal on."

73. Don't knock airline meals. For at least 20 minutes, they keep you from worrying whether the wings are going to fall off.

74. Pilot to passengers on a commuter flight: "I've got some good news and bad news. The bad news is that we're lost. But, the good news is that we've got a strong tailwind."

75. A man walked up to the airline counter and set three pieces of luggage before the clerk. "I want the brown bag to go to Dallas, the black one goes to Milwaukee, and I want you to send the other to Orlando."
The clerk said, "I'm sorry, but we're not a parcel post, sir! We can't do that."
In a slightly raised voice, the man said, "Why not? That's what you did with my bags the last time!"

76. First woman: "Last year we went to Majorca on vacation."
Second woman: "Where's that?"
First woman: "I don't know, we flew."

77.   Two women were preparing to board the airliner. One of them turned to the pilot and said, "Now, please don't travel faster than sound. We want to talk."

78.   A man who had just bought a plane was giving his wife her first ride in it. "What I like about traveling this way," he said, "is that there are no road signs to watch and no pedestrians. So I don't think I'll be bothered by backseat drivers up here."

Peering through the windshield, his wife snapped at him, "Watch out for those birds!"

79.   Airlines subscribe to the same philosophy as my mother. If you don't eat what is on your plate at lunch, you get the same thing again for dinner.

80.   The host asked a contestant on "I've Got A Secret" what made him decide to be a parachute jumper, and the fellow replied, "A plane with three dead engines."

81.   Everybody's cutting back. Instead of movies, one airline asks passengers to just pass around pictures of their children.

82.   When his engine conked out, the pilot of a light plane glided to a landing on the N.Y. State Freeway. The pilot jumped out and walked back to the only car in sight, which had pulled off the road out of the way, to ask for a lift to the closest interchange. As he neared the car, the woman sitting beside the driver stuck her head out the window and said excitedly, "We'll get out of the way, Mister, if you'll just show us where to go. This clown here is the only driver in the country who could start out on a freeway and wind up in the middle of an airport!"

83.   It's a mild shock when you realize that if you want to board an airplane early, you stand a better chance with "needing special assistance" than "with small children."

84.   We thought those cut-rate flights had a catch to them. Flying from New York to Dallas, we got over Tennessee and had to fork up another five dollars.

85.   In South America, scientists have found strange, ancient lost airstrips. They've also found strange, ancient lost luggage.

86.   An airline was conducting a training flight for new personnel and, during the take-off, the trainee flight engineer noticed that one of the engines was on fire. With the wrench that he had in his hand, he touched the pilot's shoulder and said, "We're on fire."

The pilot soon had the plane safely back on the ground. The green engineer was explaining to the ground crew how calmly and coolheadedly he had spotted the trouble, how quietly he had called the pilot's attention to it without panic or excitement. As he was talking, he saw the pilot being carried from the plane on a stretcher.

"What's the matter with him?" the trainee engineer asked.

"Broken shoulder," came the reply.

America

87.   Overheard: "If Christopher Columbus was so smart, why didn't he discover Saudi Arabia?"

88.   You know what's wrong with America today? Guns have silencers when it's electric guitars that need them!

89.   They talk about American efficiency, yet the secretary always answers the phone, and most of the time it's for her boss.

90.   What this country really needs is a car that gets 100 miles to the gallon and runs on junk mail.

91.   I went to the movies last night. Incredible! Cars crashing . . . buildings burning . . . people fighting with guns and knives. And that was just on my way home.

92.   Autumn is a wonderful time of the year even in Pittsburgh. You can sit for hours in the smog and watch the birds change colors and fall out of the trees.

93.   America is still the land of opportunity. An immigrant came here 10 years ago with absolutely nothing. Today he owes $261,000.

94.   What this country needs is a tailpipe and muffler that will last as long as a beer can.

95.   America is the only country in the world where you can go on TV and kid politicians, and the politicians go on TV to kid the people.

96.   The great disadvantage of American democracy is that so often you find yourself in agreement with people you can't stand.

97.   Americans love healthy, outdoor sports . . . especially if they are played indoors.

98.   America is the land where half our salary goes to buy food and the other half to lose weight.

Animals

99. You never realize that a dog is man's best friend until you start betting on horses.

100. Strolling through the card room of a businessmen's club, a member was surprised to see three men and a dog playing poker. Pausing to watch, he commented on the extraordinary performance of the dog. "He's not so smart," the dog's owner said in disgust. "Every time he gets a good hand, he wags his tail."

101. A man brought a parrot at an auction after some very spirited bidding. "Now you're sure this bird talks?" he asked the auctioneer.

"Talk?" replied the auctioneer. "He's been bidding against you for the past 10 minutes."

102. The trouble with Florida? One person describes it this way: There was this cat, this real cat, that had a mouse trapped in a hole in a Key Biscayne house. He tried to reach in the hole with his paw, but the mouse had room to slip away from him. So the cat said to himself, "Well, I got nothing to do . . . I'll just outwait him. He's got to come out sometime." But the mouse was very patient and he wouldn't risk his neck. A day went by and then two, and the cat was starving. He knew he would have to get some food or he would pass out. So he said to himself, "I used to do imitations. I'll imitate a dog."

So the cat took a deep breath and barked, like a big, big dog. The mouse heard it and said to himself, "There's a big dog out there and cats don't hang around when there's a big dog, so the cat must have left. Dogs don't eat mice, so it must be safe to come out." The mouse came out and the cat grabbed him and ate him. And the moral of the story is that you have to be able to speak two languages to get anything to eat in Miami.

103. First Duck: "That was a new twin-engined jet that just went by. Don't you wish you could fly that fast?"

Second Duck: "Listen, I'd be moving that fast too if I had two tails that were both on fire."

104. Well, our cat died. My daughter ran in shouting, "Daddy! Daddy! Fluffy is dead! Fluffy is dead!"

I said, "Honey, don't cry. Fluffy is gone to heaven to be with God."

She said, "What would God want with a dead cat?"

105. Do you know how to make an elephant fly? Well, you start with about six feet of zipper. . . .

The group's reaction tells it all as Jeanne Robertson uses audience participation to illustrate a point.

106. The door-to-door salesman stared doubtfully at the rather formidable looking animal lying on the doorstep. "What kind of dog is that?" he called to the old lady.

"Don't reckon I know," she said. "My son sent that to me from Africa."

"Well," the salesman hesitated, "that's the strangest looking dog I ever saw in my life."

She nodded her head and said, "You shoulda' seen it before I cut its mane off."

107. My farmer neighbor says he has one rooster so lazy that when the other roosters crow, he just nods his head.

108. It is rumored that a zebra is a horse whose mother was scared by a Venetian blind.

109.   You can lead a horse to water . . . but if you can get him to float on his back . . . well, then you've got something.

110.   The boss complains his dog isn't very smart.
"I bought one of those dog whistles," he said, "and he won't use it."

111.   An old woodsman gave this method as the best way to catch a porcupine: "Watch for the slapping tail as you dash in and drop a large washtub over the animal. This will give you something to sit on as you plan your next move."

112.   Did you hear about the mother hen who was having trouble controlling her chicks? One day they had a fight with a robin over a worm and came home all messed up and bedraggled. Mother hen was very upset and scolded her offspring. "If your father could see you now," she said, "he'd turn over in his gravy."

113.   There once was a cat who lived aboard one of the ships of the British Royal Navy. One day, during a storm, the cat slipped on the wet deck and fell into some machinery. One of its fore-legs was mangled. The pharmacist's mate had to amputate the leg. But, the pharmacist's mate was a kindly fellow and, while the cat was under sedation, he whittled out a little wooden leg for the Tom. The cat got along nicely with the artificial leg. As a matter of fact, the artificial limb didn't seem to hamper the cat's activities at all.
One day, the crew heard an unusual hammering noise. They investigated and there was Tom, holding a mouse down with his front paw and beating it to death with that wooden leg.

114.   A nursery school put on a dog show and our 6-year-old daughter entered the family Irish setter, Scarlet. When she returned from school, her mother asked her how Scarlet came out. "Well," she explained, "Scarlet almost won best of the breed, but then at the last minute, another Irish setter showed up."

115.   The youngster was crying in the street after an encounter with a big, stray dog. A man came up and asked, "Did he bite you?"
"No," sobbed the child, "but he tasted me."

116.   There was a story about a man who insisted there was a cat in his stomach. Shortly after, the man was rushed to the hospital for an emergency appendectomy, and his doctor thought it was a good time to cure the man of his cat obsession. So when the man

came out of the ether, the doctor held up a black cat and said, "Well, we got him out of you. All right?"

"You've got the wrong one," screamed the man. "It was a white cat!"

117. A man took his cocker spaniel to a vet and ordered him to cut off the dog's tail. "I want it all off," he said, "So that not even a hair of the tail remains."

The vet asked, "Why in the world would you want to cut the tail from an innocent little dog?"

"My mother-in-law is visiting us next month," the man replied, "and I want to eliminate any possible indication of welcome."

Around the World

118. The sun never sets on the British Empire. God wouldn't trust an Englishman in the dark.

119. Here's to the Frenchman who loves his wine,
And the German who loves his beer.
The Englishman loves his 'alf and 'alf,
Because it brings good cheer.
The Scotchman loves his whiskey straight,
Because it gives him dizziness.
But the Irishman has no choice at all . . .
So he drinks the whole darn business.

120. Fidel Castro has his share of problems. His country is in the Caribbean, his government in Russia, and his people in Miami.

121. Napoleon never knew the meaning of the word "quit." He was Corsican and could not speak a word of English.

122. Those Canadian-French hockey players can give some odd twists to the English language:

After an opponent had scored four goals: "We've got to stop him. He's going like a horse afire."

Praising an outstanding performance: "He's a one-man guy out there."

Poor performance: "That was the worst game I never saw."

The potential of a new player: "I don't know whether or not he'll extinguish himself."

123. The best way to make an Englishman laugh in his old age is to tell him a joke when he's young. ASHLEY MONTAGU

124. Tad McAdoo got sotted at the Brannan wake. After an hour, he tiptoed up to the hostess and said, "Do lemons have legs?"

"Lemons with legs?" exclaimed Mrs. Brannan. "You must be losin' your mind!"

"In that case," said McAdoo, "I'm afraid I've just squeezed your canary into me whiskey!"

125.   How about just a token grain embargo against the Russians? In other words, we keep the corn and send them the cobs.

126.   After fighting only 24 hours, the British RAF released the following communique: "TODAY WE DOWNED 90 PLANES: 60 DEFINITE, 30 PLEDGED."

127.   What's dumber than a dumb Irishman? A smart Scot.

128.   After visiting Ireland and Scotland last year, a couple got into a debate with another pair as to which whiskey was stronger, Scotch or Irish. One explained why he was so sure Irish was stronger: "My wife and I drank a quart of it one night and got up the next morning and went to six o'clock mass."

A challenger demanded just what that proved.

"We're both Methodist," the man explained.

129.   Know what's Irish and comes out in the spring? Patti O'Furniture.

130.   Rudolph Groutenski, the Russian general, was taking a stroll with his wife in Moscow. As they walked along, a bit of moisture fell on them.

Mrs. Groutenski turned to her husband and said, "Tovarich, I believe it's snowing."

And the General said, "No, my dear, it is raining."

"No," said the wife, "it is snowing."

"Don't argue with me," said the general. "Remember, Rudolph the Red, knows rain, dear."

131.   A Frenchman, a Japanese, and an American faced a firing squad. Offered a last wish, the Frenchman asks to hear the Marseillaise. The Japanese asks to give one more lecture on Japanese management. The American asks to be shot first. "I can't stand one more lecture on Japanese management," he exclaims.

132.   Five Scotsmen decided to go horseback riding. So they sent Sandy to bargain with the stable owner. Sandy inquired the price of a horse. The stable owner, before answering, asked, "How long?"

"The longest ye've got," replied Sandy. "There will be five of us goin'."

133.   I like the Chinese recipe for a happy marriage: "The wife

should love her husband less and understand him more . . . and the husband must love his wife and not try to understand her at all."

134.   In a Moscow park, an elderly Jewish man was studying Hebrew. A Russian soldier, passing by, remarked, "What are you studying Hebrew for? When you die, you won't go to Israel."
   The man replied, "So, I can use it in heaven."
   The Russian soldier asked, "What if you end up in hell?"
   The old man said, "Big deal. I already speak Russian."

135.   There is a new Mexican-Japanese restaurant called "Taco-Yaki." After eating there you have an urge to build a small car and hide in the trunk.

136.   After the first hole at a golf course in Scotland, the host turned to his American guest and said, "Ha' many strokes d'ye have?"
   "Eight."
   "I took seven. Ma' hole."
   After the second hole, the Scot repeated the question. "No sir!" said the American, "MY turn to ask!"

137.   Do Chinese people go out for American food?

138.   Know what you get when you cross two Italians? Killed!

139.   The Russians may be ahead of us in missles, but we're 5 years ahead of them in Japanese cars.

Bachelors

140.   Bachelor: "A chap who believes it's much better to have loved and lost than to have to get up for the 2 A.M. feeding."

141.   A rather fickle bachelor was telling a married friend about the talents and accomplishments of a girl he had just met. The married man listened quietly. He had heard him rave like this before. "And you know," the bachelor enthused, "this girl has brains enough for two." His companion's terse comment was: "Then you ought to marry her right away."

142.   Being a bachelor is really a grind. You wash the dishes, make the bed, and then a month later you have to do it all over again.

143.   And it's hard to explain, but when you're 35 and a bachelor, you feel guilty even talking to a young girl. You have the feeling that any minute a cop is going to come over and arrest you for Statutory Conversation.

144. You can tell he's a bachelor. He has a scotch-and-waterbed.

145. My bachelor friend says, "I'm ashamed of my telltale gray and the rings around my collars, but that's what comes from doing the laundry in the backyard with a garden hose."

146. A playboy type reportedly told some friends, "Once I gave up drinking, smoking, and chasing women all at once. It was the worst 20 minutes of my entire life."

147. Bachelor: "I keep waiting for the perfect woman to come along. Meanwhile, I'm having a lot of fun with the imperfect ones."

148. A bachelor described a blind date this way: "She's okay to take out on a credit card, but I wouldn't want to spend cash on her."

149. Bachelor explaining why he always eats out: "During the last meal a date cooked for me, I broke a tooth on her jello!"

150. A bachelorette about town says that what she is really looking for is an older man with a strong will—"You know, one his relatives can't contest."

151. Friend: "Surely you must have met one man you would have married."

Playgirl: "I have and I have met one man who would marry me, but unfortunately, it wasn't the same man."

152. My girlfriend likes me just the way I am—single.

Banks

153. A bank is an institution with so many vice presidents that, when there's a director's meeting, it looks like a run on the bank.

154. A woman told a bank teller: "I want to make this withdrawal from my husband's half of our joint account."

155. My bank . . . I don't know if you've heard of it. It's called Security Run On. Their idea of a vault is a money clip and a can of mace. Its banking hours are November.

156. One of life's big disappointments is discovering that the person who writes the advertising for a bank is not the same one who makes the loans.

157. A college student found her checkbook in such a mess that she had to telephone her bank for help. "What balance do you show?" asked the bank clerk.

Replied the caller: "I asked you first!"

158.   Banker: "A pawn broker with a manicure."

159.   I told my wife we were overdrawn at the bank. She said, "No problem. I'll write a check to cover it."

160.   Sign at the local bank: "We serve the farmer who has everything, but hasn't paid for it."

161.   A longtime customer recently made a loan application at the bank where he conducts his financial business.

Since the applicant's credit rating was A-1, the loan was quickly approved. But as the paper work was being completed, the bank officer said jokingly, "Since you're 75 years old, don't you think you need a co-signer?"

The applicant finished signing his name on various dotted lines, put down the pen, and looked the banker squarely in the eye. "No," he replied firmly. "I assure you that the bank has no worry on that account. If I die and go to heaven, I'll see that payment is sent to you. And, if I go to hell, I'll hand it to you."

162.   The nicest thing about bank machines is that they don't smile and wish you a nice day after you've withdrawn your last cent to pay a utility bill.

163.   Bank president: "Where's the cashier?"
Assistant: "Gone to the races."
President: "During working hours?"
Assistant: "Yes, sir. It was his last chance to make the books balance."

164.   A volunteer worker for the United Givers Drive called on the town's leading banker. Thinking she would flatter him into making a sizeable contribution, she said, "I'm honored that your name was on my list because you are rumored to be the most generous man in town."

The banker quietly wrote out a check, handed it to the woman and said, "Here's a check for $10. Now you can start denying that rumor."

165.   "I hear the bank is looking for a cashier."
"Thought they just hired one a week ago."
"They did. He's the one they're looking for."

Baseball

166.   One foggy night at the ballpark the umpire had called two strikes on Yogi Berra who hardly saw the ball zip by him.

On the next pitch, the umpire yelled, "Strike three!"

Yogi looked at him and said, "That one sounded kinda high."

167. A diamond is the hardest natural substance known, ranking just above a baseball umpire's head.

168. Responding to charges that he "doctors" baseballs with a "foreign substance," a Los Angeles Dodgers pitcher said: "Not true at all. Vaseline is manufactured right here in the U.S."

169. "Atlanta signed me for a $3,000 bonus. The Braves officials took me to one of the finest restaurants in the city. I rolled down the window of the car after we were there 10 minutes, and the hamburgers fell off the tray."

170. Someone remembered the time Bobo Newsom was picked up by the Philadelphia Athletics in a last-ditch drive for the pennant.

Bobo was notorious for staying out late. He made Babe Ruth look like a divinity student.

With a big ball game coming up, Bobo's manager said, "Get a good night's sleep tonight. You're my pitcher tomorrow."

Next day, the game was rained out. Bobo's manager came up and said the same thing: "Get a good night's sleep. You're my pitcher tomorrow."

Once again, the game was rained out. Bobo's manager was determined to keep his pitcher alert for the game. "Get a good night's sleep tonight," he said one more time. "You're still my pitcher tomorrow."

Bobo shook his head. "Sorry," he said, "I don't pitch three games in a row for nobody."

171. A rookie who thought he was hot stuff pitched his first game, but he walked the first seven batters; so the manager took him out of the game. The rookie stormed into the dugout mumbling, "How do you like that dumb manager? He takes me out of the game just when I had a no-hitter going."

172. One day, manager Tom Lasorda of the L.A. Dodgers went to mass on Sunday morning in Cincinnati and who should come in and sit in the same pew but the manager of the Reds.

They eyed each other but neither spoke. When the service was over, they walked out in silence and Lasorda got nervous when he saw the Reds manager pause to light a candle.

"Right away, I figure that gave him an edge," said Lasorda. "So I walked back to the front of the church and came down the aisle again . . . and when I see he's gone, I go over and blow out the candle."

173.   One thing you have to hand professional baseball players— they can always find an old place to spit and a new place to scratch.

174.   At today's baseball ballpark prices, you can't hit a homer into the cheap seats anymore.

175.   The coach called the Little Leaguer in from center field for a conference. "See here, Eddie," said the coach, "you know the princi- ples of good sportsmanship that the Little League practices. You know we don't tolerate temper tantrums, shouting at the umpire, or abusive language. Do I make myself clear?"

"Yes, sir," replied Eddie.

"Well, then, Eddie," sighed the coach, "would you please try to explain it to your mother?"

176.   Houston bumper snicker: "Support Little League Baseball— Cheer For The Astros."

177.   Boy in Little League uniform runs into the house, gets a drink, and then says to his mother: "The score is 20–0 in their favor, but don't worry, Mom, we haven't come to bat yet!"

178.   You can always tell when Spring is near . . . by the first screech of a Little League mother.

179.   St. Peter and Satan were having an argument one day about baseball. With a beguiling leer, Satan proposed a game (to be played on neutral grounds) between a select team from the heavenly host and his own hand-picked Hades boys.

"Very well," the gatekeeper of the Celestrial City agreed. "But you realize, I hope, that we have all the good players and the best coaches too."

"I know," said Satan calmly, "but we have all the umpires!"

180.   It wasn't really a Little League disaster, but the home team's star outfielder was pretty upset when she snagged her pantyhose sliding into third.

181.   The baseball manager, when asked what terms his Mexican- born pitching sensation might settle for in his upcoming contract negotiations: "He wants Texas back."

182.   "The best part of being retired," says retired baseball catcher Tim McCarver, "is showering alone."

Basketball

183. Old basketball players never die. They sit in front of you at the movies.

184. A basketball coach reportedly told some friends about a dream he had. "I was walking down the street," he said, "when this Rolls Royce pulled up beside me. Inside, there was a beautiful young girl—blonde, maybe about 18 or 19 years old. She asked me to get in. She took me to a fantastic restaurant where we ate and drank and she paid the bill. Then she asked me if I wanted to go home with her. And I said yes. And we did."

"Then what happened?" a listener urged.

"The best part of all," the coach drooled. "She introduced me to her two brothers and both of them were over 7 feet tall!"

185. The coach of the State basketball team said, in reference to their losing record: "We have a great bunch of outside shooters. Unfortunately, all of our games are played indoors."

186. A teacher had asked her pupils who the five greatest Americans were. All pupils had turned in their papers except for Britt. "Can't you finish your list, Britt?" asked the teacher.

"I'm still undecided," he replied, "about center."

187. A basketball coach giving final instructions in the locker room: "Remember, boys, basketball develops leadership, initiative, and individualism. Now get out there and do exactly as I told you."

188. One longtime basketball coach is thinking of becoming a track coach. "It's the easiest job of all," he says. "All you have to do is tell them to turn left and get back as quick as they can."

189. Winning basketball coach, talking about his top ranked team: "This is some bunch. I can't even show them game films of themselves. All they do is clap."

190. One college basketball coach was listening to a scout singing the praises of a certain high school prospect. "That boy doesn't care how tall, rough, or experienced the opposing team is," the coach proclaimed. "He takes that ball and goes. He doesn't know the meaning of 'fear'."

"That's true," said the coach, "and judging by his grades, there are a lot of other words he doesn't know the meaning of either!"

191. During a faculty meeting, several professors were discussing

a star basketball player who was on the verge of flunking out of college. "The boy is certainly a great player," commented one teacher. "He can do anything with a basketball . . . except autograph it."

192.   One university basketball team is going to try out the three-squad system this year. The first squad will be starting players. The second will be reserves. And the third squad will attend class.

193.   My neighbor says he'll be hearing any day now whether his son made the starting basketball five at State University or, "the coach intends to play favorites again this year."

194.   Our basketball coach has never gone in much for frills. "But," he says, "I'm thinking about wearing those headphones that the football coaches wear on the sidelines. You can't hear the crowd boo. . . ."

195.   Our basketball coach is a real winner and also a scholar with a Master's Degree. The subject of his thesis was, "What College Done For Me."

196.   A basketball official was jeered by a man in the crowd. He stopped the game, sat next to the man, blew his whistle, and yelled, "Play ball! If you can call 'em from up here, so can I."

197.   A coach, explaining why the team will not pray before games this year: "We've got so many things to pray for, we'd be penalized for delay of game."

198.   No basketball coach cares about the height of the players as long as their ears pop when they stand up.   DICK VITALE

199.   After a hotly contested basketball game, the referee was walking off the floor when a fellow came up and thrust a piece of paper into his hand. It read: "Matthew 27:5. Luke 10:37."
   When the ref got home that night, he picked up a Bible and looked up the references.
   Matthew 27:5: "And Judas . . . went and hanged himself."
   Luke 10:37: "Go, and do thou likewise."   JAMES DENT

Biologists/Scientists/Inventors

200.   Would it make your day to know that a hot shot biologist is trying to cross a pumpkin with a marijuana plant so he can grow a jack-o-lantern that turns itself on for Halloween?

201.   A biologist friend of mine loves to experiment with flowers. Like last year, he crossed a rambling rose with a pansy. Now the rose still rambles, but it takes very small steps and has limp petals.

202.   The University of Oklahoma biology department is trying to cross a pig and an octopus. The object is to develop a football that throws itself.

203.   Hear about the scientist who crossed a chicken with a silkworm? He got a hen that lays eggs with pantyhose in them!

204.   Hear about the biologist who crossed a pig with a giraffe? Says he's eating a lot higher on the hog.

205.   I'm constantly amazed by the progress scientists are making in cancer research. Seems every day they discover something else that causes it.

206.   Scientists now think that beer causes cancer. I've got 'em there . . . I don't smoke beer.

207.   Uncle Sylvester has had some strange inventions. His latest is a dictionary that is not in alphabetical order for people with time to kill.

208.   Science has proven man can live in outer space and at the bottom of the sea. It's the area in between that gives us trouble.

209.   Behavioral scientists tell us that the teens are a time of rapid change. Between the ages of 12 and 20, for example, a parent can age 30 years.

210.   Uncle Sam, the family inventor, developed a wrist TV. He's now trying to do away with the 30-foot whip antenna that straps around your waist.

211.   Scientists have discovered that a dollar bill carries germs, but there's no cause for alarm: even a germ couldn't live on a dollar today.

212.   Brunch was invented by a man who wanted to have champagne with his breakfast and needed an excuse.

213.   My grandfather invented the burglar alarm but someone stole it from him.   VICTOR BORGE

214.   Know what the biologist said when he crossed a violin with a turkey leg? "Oh, Fiddlesticks!"

Books/Magazines

215.   I just heard about the greatest book club. You send them $20, and once a month for the next 12 months . . . they leave you alone!

216.   Do you realize what would happen if Moses were alive today? He'd go up to Mount Sinai, come back with the Ten Commandments, and spend the next eight years trying to get them published!

217.   Sign in Doctor's office: "Please do not remove magazines—nurse will finish the article and call you in the morning."

218.   A writer who had written a number of undistinguished novels spent a weekend as a house guest of George S. Kaufman. When he was ready to leave, he wanted to show his appreciation of the playwright's hospitality.

"As soon as I get home," he promised, "I'm going to send you a copy of my latest book. It's the least I can do."

"It certainly is," Kaufman agreed. "I've read it."

219.   Ernest Hemingway once received a letter from a fan saying, "I understand you now charge one dollar per word. I am therefore enclosing a dollar and would like a sample."

Hemingway answered the fan's letter: "Thanks."

220.   I can't believe some of today's graduates. I asked a graduate if he ever read Webster's dictionary. He said he preferred to wait until they made it into a movie.

221.   This isn't generally known, but Webster is supposed to have written the first dictionary because of a nagging wife. That's right. Every time he opened his mouth, she'd say, "What's that supposed to mean?"

222.   Hear about the cannibal who wrote a cookbook? It's titled: "How Best To Serve Your Fellow Men."

223.   The advance proofs of a cookbook for gringos recently came our way. Wildest recipe is for a salad. You cut up lettuce, tomatoes, cucumbers, and green peppers. Then you add a dash of tequila and the salad tosses itself.   HENNY YOUNGMAN

224.   Did you hear about the man who bought a copy of Ernest Hemingway's *"Across the River and Into the Trees,"* but returned the next day and demanded his money back? He thought it was a book on golf.

225.   I wouldn't want to say that my wife always gets her way

and does everything that she wants to do, but she does write her diary a week ahead of time.   HENNY YOUNGMAN

226.   The Women's Book Club voted unanimously to have a review on *"The Charge of the Light Brigade."* Women always get interested fast when they hear the word "charge."

227.   A man who was very much interested in old books ran into an unbookish acquaintance of his who'd just thrown away an old Bible which had been packed away in the attic of his ancestral home for generations. He happened to mention it.

"Who printed it, do you know?" asked the book lover.

"Somebody named Guten-something," recalled the man with an effort.

"Not Gutenberg?" gasped the booklover. "You idiot, you've thrown away one of the first books ever printed. A copy sold at auction recently for over $400,000!"

The other man was unmoved. "My copy wouldn't have brought a dime," he announced firmly. "Some fellow named Martin Luther had scribbled all over it."

Born Loser

228.   Mud slides are a real problem out in California . . . you know you've bought a bad piece of land when Jacques Cousteau can stop in for dinner without leaving his boat.

229.   He has terrible luck. His best friend ran away with his wife. He says he's sure going to miss him.

230.   A group of wealthy businessmen were trying to help an old friend who had been persistently unlucky. Knowing that he was too proud to accept money as a gift, they rigged up a bogus raffle. Then they called at his dilapidated apartment and told him that they would all draw slips from a hat, and that the man who drew 4 would get $1,000. To make sure he would win, they wrote 4 on every slip. After drawing, the conspirators glanced at their slips, crumpled them up, and waited for their friend to announce that he had the lucky number. But the fellow never opened his mouth. Finally unable to bear the suspense, they asked him what number he had drawn from the hat. "Six and seven eights," he answered glumly.

231.   A guy stood in line over an hour at Disneyland and finally worked his way up to the ladies restroom.

232. I don't want to say he's a loser, but they threw him out of the library for being too quiet.

233. What a loser . . . he's the kind of guy who asks for a wine list at McDonalds.

234. If your nose runs and your feet smell, you've been built upside down.

235. Unlucky? You're looking at the only fella who ever found a four-leaf poison ivy!

236. He's so dumb. If you threw him into a think tank, he'd drown.

237. Once my parents played hide and seek with me. Ten years later, I found them in an abandoned shack in Cleveland.

238. Descriptions of an oddball:
He's not dragging a full stringer of fish.
His dipstick doesn't touch oil.
The butter slipped off his noodles a long time ago.
He's eating with one chopstick.
Her elevator doesn't go all the way to the top floor.

239. I remember once when my kid brother was lost, my parents sent me out to find him and take his place.

240. There's never a dull moment when you're around Charles. It lasts all night.

241. I'm not saying the woman is slow, but when she reads a STOP sign, her lips move.

242. He's a little on the dumb side. He never has to worry about being brainwashed . . . a light rinse would do it.

243. Two teenagers were eager to try the tunnel of love for the first time. "Shucks," the boy said later to a friend, "it was dark and we got soaking wet."
"How come?" his friend asked. "Did the boat leak?"
"There's a boat?"

244. A voice from heaven said, "Thou shalt fear no evil." Clyde asked, "Why is that?" The voice answered, "Because thou are a dummy."

245. He's so dumb, he once went to a drive-in in a cab. The movie cost him $112.

Boss

246. Boss: "Are you sure your wife knows you're bringing me home to dinner?"

Young man: "Sure, we argued about it for half an hour this morning."

247. I don't wanna say the boss is coldhearted, but in Alaska, they just named a glacier after her.

248. Boss: "Mary is right, Henry. She should be making as much as you are . . . so I'm cutting your salary in half."

249. Boss to efficient employee: "The other employees hate your guts, Mervin. Keep it up."

250. It must be getting close to payday. The boss is out front with a tin cup.

251. Boss to employee: "You can march to a different drummer, but I want the tempo speeded up."

252. A wise boss is one that recognizes that no response is necessary to 95% of all interoffice memos.

253. "Why did the foreman fire you?"

"Well, you know the foreman is the guy who stands around and watches the others work."

"Yes, anybody knows that. But why did he fire you?"

"He was jealous of me. A lot of fellows thought I was the foreman."

254. Sign on a boss' bulletin board: "TO ERR IS HUMAN, TO FORGIVE IS NOT COMPANY POLICY."

255. Secretary: "Your wife wants to give you a kiss over the phone."

Boss: "Take a message and give it to me later."

256. Boss' Creed: "Hiring people smarter than you proves you are smarter than they are."

257. The boss is definitely getting old. He hired a new secretary the other day and remarked that he didn't care what she looked like—as long as she knew how to spell.

258. When he got fired from his last place of employment, the boss told him: "You've been like a son to me—insolent, rude, and ungrateful."

259. The boss is so paranoid about being in charge that someone

told him to have a nice time and he snapped, "Don't you tell me what to do!"

260.   A company budget is what we all get along on until the boss needs more money.

261.   Inexcusable errors are made by employees. What the boss commits are "justifiable mistakes."

262.   Sayings from the Bible are very often proved out in business. For example, tell the boss what you think of him—and the truth will set you free.

263.   The boss likes dictating letters . . . that way he gets to use lots of words he can't spell.

264.   The boss may visit Panama. Especially since a lot of people offered to buy his ticket . . . one way.

265.   My boss has changed his religion. He no longer thinks he's God.

Brides/Grooms

266.   I'm not going to say she fooled around but her bridal gown was plaid and the wedding announcement was on the sports page.

267.   "Darling," said the new bride as they drove up to the motel, "let's try to act as if we've been married for years."

"Anything you say, dear," replied the groom, "but do you think you can manage all that luggage?"

268.   Kids are getting married so young nowadays. Like the wedding I went to last week. The groom was so young his mother wouldn't let him have any wedding cake until after he finished his vegetables.

269.   The first time my bride opened a can of sauerkraut . . . she buried it in the back yard.

270.   As Eugene and his new bride got into the elevator at their honeymoon hotel, the operator, a dynamite redhead, smiled at Eugene. She looked at him and said, "Hello, darling."

There was an icy silence until the newlyweds reached their room. Then the bride roared, "Who was that girl?"

"Look, honey," said the groom, "don't get excited. I'm going to have enough trouble explaining you to her."

271.   It was a teenage wedding for both bride and groom. The par-

ents of the boy were a bit unhappy about it but they attended the wedding. As their son repeated the vows and came to the part that says, "With all my worldly goods I thee endow . . . ," the mother whispered to the father, "There goes the motor scooter."

272. The bride said, "Are you going to love me when I'm old and gray?"

The groom replied, "Not only am I going to love you . . . I'm going to write to you every day."

273. It happened on the day of the big football game. The bride and groom stood before the minister. They hadn't yet said their "I do's," when the groom leaned over and whispered into the bride's ear.

Suddenly he pulled back. The bride had given him a sharp jab in the ribs with her elbow.

What happened? The groom had told his bride: "This is the happiest day of my life." After a pause, he added, "Auburn beat Alabama."

274. The honeymoon is over when the husband gets out of the car at a drive-in movie to wipe off the windshield.

275. A honeymoon is the period between "I do" and "You'd better."

276. The modern trend is toward shorter honeymoons—but more of them.

277. The honeymoon's really over when he phones that he'll be late for dinner . . . and she's already left a note that it's in the refrigerator.

278. A honeymoon is a short period of adjustment; marriage is a long one.

279. A Midwest preacher received this thank you note from a bridegroom he had married: "Dear Reverend, I want to thank you for the beautiful way you brought my happiness to a conclusion."

280. She: "You vowed to love, honor, and obey me. You don't love me."

He: "Two out of three ain't bad."

281. A sign on a Basin Street hotel reads: "Honeymoon Suite—$20 per night; $2 for each additional person."

282. The newlywed couple went to Washington and checked in at the Watergate hotel. The bride was upset. "Why did we come here?" she wanted to know. "You know the stories about this place.

Why, I'll bet there are hidden microphones, tapes, and bugs all over the place."

"Don't worry," the groom told her. He was an expert in these matters and he'd check it out. He went over the whole room, looking behind the pictures and the drapes, inspecting the lamps and the light fixtures. Then he moved the bed and looked under the carpet where he discovered a round metal plate held down by four screws. "Here it is," he said. "I'll just take these screws out and remove this and we'll be all right." So he did. And they got on with their honeymoon.

The next day, when he went down to check out, the clerk was quite solicitous. Had everything been all right, the clerk wanted to know. Had the champagne been properly chilled, the Tournedos Rossini correctly cooked, the flowers fresh, the maid service prompt and efficient? "Everything was fine, just fine," the groom replied.

"Oh, good," said the clerk. "Then you weren't disturbed by the noise?"

"What noise?" asked the groom.

"It was very strange," said the clerk, "and a most regrettable accident, but the couple in the room right below yours were injured about 4 o'clock this morning when the chandelier in their room fell from the ceiling."

283.   The honeymoon is over when you're no longer drinking to each other, but because of each other.

284.   Hippie to his bride: "Instead of a Niagra Falls honeymoon, we'll drive slowly through a carwash."

Business

285.   A couple of business partners had a serious quarrel, and one of them consulted a lawyer about dividing the business so that one could buy the other out. After several days, the attorney reported to his client: "I've finally talked your partner into seeing things your way and he has agreed to a settlement that is very fair to both of you."

"Fair to both of us!" exclaimed the businessman. "I could have done that myself. What do you think I hired a lawyer for?"

286.   A young man, tired of working for others, went into business for himself. A few months later, a friend asked him how it was to be his own boss. "I don't know," he replied. "The police won't let

me park in front of my own place of business; tax collectors tell me how to keep books; my banker tells me how much balance I must maintain; freight agents tell me how many goods must be packed; federal, state, county, and local agencies tell me how to keep records; the union tells me who I can employ and how and when; and on top of that, I just got married."

287. Know what happens to kids who take two hours to eat a meal? . . . They grow up to become advertising executives.

288. A druggist became so deeply in debt with his business that he was summoned by his banker. After quite a long talk, the druggist asked hopelessly, "Have you ever been in the drugstore business?" and the banker answered, "No." To which the druggist replied, "Well, you're in it now."

289. Ambition's a good thing, but Mafia graveyards are filled with men who wanted to go into business on their own.

290. That man started his business on a shoestring and in a few months had tripled his investment. What he's going to do with three shoestrings, I don't know.

291. "I can't understand why you failed in business," said the merchant.
"Too much advertising," replied the friend.
"What do you mean, too much advertising? You never spent a dime on advertising."
"That's true," said the merchant. "But my competitors did."

292. A shopkeeper put up this sign: "We require a 50% deposit from all customers we don't know, and a 100% deposit from some customers we do know."

293. Sign in a struggling new business: "CUSTOMERS WANTED—NO EXPERIENCE NECESSARY!"

294. Overheard between two business partners: "I think it's about time we taught that new secretary what's right and what's wrong."
"Okay," replied the other. "You teach her what's right."

295. Sign in a L.A. bakery: "LET'S PLAY STORE . . . YOU BE THE CUSTOMER."

296. Berger and Baum were partners. While they were having lunch, Berger shouted: "Oh, my God!"
"Whatsa matta?" asked Baum.

"We went away and left the safe open!" said Berger.

"What you worried about?" asked his partner. "We're both here."

297. Sign in shop window: "Do not be fooled by imitators. We have been going out of business in this location since 1948."

298. There is a sign in the window of a haberdashery that reads: "GOING OUT OF BUSINESS SALE." Underneath, in smaller letters, in an addendum: "We reserve the right to stay in business if this sale is a success."

299. Two businessmen discussing the state of the nation:

"The President says business is good."

"Yeah? But he's got a good location and he doesn't have to pay any rent."

Cars

300. After hearing about gasohol, a sports fan tried mixing gasoline with Gatorade. Now he says his car will only run a sideline pattern.

301. An automobile-fancier who claims they don't build 'em like they used to says: "We finally got the perfect second car—a tow truck."

302. An auto manufacturer, proud of his assembly lines, advertised that in a test one of his cars had been put together in exactly six minutes. The next day he received a phone call. "Is that advertisement about assembling a car in six minutes true?" a man's voice asked politely. "Yes, sir!" the manufacturer assured him. "An auto was actually turned out in precisely that time."

"Well, I just wanted to know," the voice said. "I think I'm the owner of that car."

303. In Hollywood, the big stars lead a much different life than most people. Recently, a well-known actor approached his seven-year-old son and said, "I'm sorry, son, but tomorrow morning I have to use the chauffeur and limousine for business."

"But Daddy," objected the boy, "how will I get to school?"

"You'll get to school like every other kid in America," answered his father angrily. "You'll take a cab."

304. The new gas-efficient, economy cars are a threat to romance. It takes them too long to run out of gas.

305. Now they have gasohol. A cop stopped one guy and made his car blow up a balloon.

The Henry lifestyle is family oriented. Robert shows off Patrick (left), Brent, and Merrilyn.

306. "It's scandalous to charge us $25 for towing the car only three or four miles," protested the grandmother.

"Never mind, dear," replied the second grandmother, "he's earning it . . . I've got my brakes on."

307. "Would the person who owns the Cadillac convertible with the cowhide seatcovers please report to the parking lot. There's a bull attacking your back seat."

308. The sports car owner was taking his friend for his first ride in his new low-slung car. The friend appeared to be puzzled, so the driver asked him what was wrong.

"I can't figure out where we are. What's that long wall we've been passing?"

"That's no wall," snapped the driver. "That's the curb."

309. It takes 2,875 bolts and screws to put a car together . . . but it takes only one nut to scatter it all over the road.

310. Man with car trouble on a country road: "How far is it to the next town?"
Farmer: "Two miles as the crow flies."
Man: "How far is it if the crow has to walk and roll a flat tire?"

311. I use gasohol in my car. Only problem is to keep it from leaning against lamp posts!

312. For a mechanic, Hell will be a place with grease everywhere, but no steering wheel or seat to wipe it on.

313. A teenager had an old car he wanted to sell and put this sign on it: "FOR SALE: $4,000. Rebate: $3,500!"

314. Did you hear about the guy who bought a used car recently with an old Cincinnati Bengal decal on the back window? The guy was so disgusted with the recent Bengal performances, he scraped the decal off and claims, "The car immediately began to run and pass better."

315. An American auto dealer ran into the recession and was forced out of business when foreign imports took over the field. His wife divorced him and his kids called him nasty names. He started drinking and became a bum. One day, while walking down an alley looking for a little wine left in a bottle, a Genie popped out of a bottle and thanked the ex-auto dealer for rescuing her. "For that, I'll grant you one wish," she told him.
"Hmmmmm," he thought. "Foreign car dealers are making all the money nowadays." "My wish is to be a foreign car dealer in a major city," he said.
Poof! When he awoke, he found he had become a Cadillac dealer in Cambodia.

316. Clyde's wife bawled him out for taking so long to choose a new car. "You married me only one week after you met me," she yelled.
"Yeah," he whined, "but buying a new car is serious."

317. A minister stopped by a car dealership to inquire about a new automobile. While studying a blue station wagon, the minister inquired, "What kind of gas mileage does it get?"
The salesman replied, "Thirty miles per gallon."

The shop foreman came running out and yelled, "It's the preacher!"
"Sixteen!" the salesman replied quickly.

318.   The biggest features on the new cars are airbrakes and unbreakable windshields. You can speed up to 100 mph and stop on a dime. Then you press a special button and a putty knife scrapes you off the windshield.   HENNY YOUNGMAN

Children

319.   A mother returned home from shopping and asked her 7-year-old who had stayed home, "What did you do, dear, while Mommy was gone?"

"I was a helper, Mommy," she said. "I helped the postman. I put a real letter in every mailbox on our block. I found them in your bottom dresser drawer all tied up in a blue ribbon."

320.   The young mother wanted to enter her 5-year-old daughter in a kindergarten, but the entrance age was 6 years. The teacher was discouraging. "But," the mother protested, "Anne can easily pass the 6-year-old test." The teacher turned skeptically to the little girl. "Say some words," she told her.

The little girl gave the teacher a dignified look. Then, turning to her mother, she inquired, "A purely irrelevant word?"

321.   Every family should have 3 children. If one turns out to be a genius, the other two can support him.

322.   I was laying on the discipline and my teenager shot back, "Did I ask to be born?"

I said, "If you had, the answer would have been 'No!' "

323.   I've got two boys, both of 'em training to be astronauts by correspondence. They're at home taking up space.

324.   Patrick's mother ran into the bedroom when she heard him scream and found his two-year-old brother pulling his hair. She gently released the babies grip and said to Patrick, "There, there. He didn't mean it. He doesn't know that hurts."

She was barely out of the room before the baby screamed. Running back in, she said, "What happened?"

"He knows now," replied Patrick.

325.   A little boy asked a little girl, "Are you the opposite sex or am I?"

326. I wonder if my kids are very smart. It's not that they don't know anything . . . they don't even suspect anything.

327. Raising children is like playing golf. You keep thinking you're going to do better.

328. A little boy, cornering one of his teenage sister's boyfriends, asked in all seriousness, "Why do you come around to see my sister every night? Don't you have one of your own?"

329. Why is it a preschooler will gag over oatmeal and hates his eggs, but will drink a dog's water and float a rubber ducky in the toilet?

330. Small boy to his mother: "Don't yell at me; I'm not your husband."

331. Many a small boy is the kind of kid his mother wouldn't let him play with.

332. Kids have lots of bias. Bias this! Bias that!

333. If you have good advice to pass on to your children, give it to them while they are still young enough to think you know what you are talking about.

334. Our minister was talking to the pint-sized members of the church's Sunday School class about things money can't buy. "It can't buy laughter," he told them. "That comes from the soul. And it can't buy love." Driving this point home, he said, "What would you do if I offered you $1,000 not to love your mother and father?"

A few moments of silence ensued while the boys and girls mulled this over and then a small voice demanded: "How much would you give me not to love my big sister?"

335. "Nancy, why did Mary and Joseph take Jesus with them to Jerusalem?"

The little girl shifted in her seat and said shyly, "I guess they couldn't get a babysitter."

336. The door-to-door salesman rang the bell in a suburban home and the door opened, revealing a nine-year-old boy who was puffing on a long, black cigar. Trying to cover his amazement, the salesman said, "Good morning, sonny. Is your mother in?"

The boy removed the cigar from his mouth, flicked off its ashes and replied, "What do YOU think?"

337. One child's definition of a pothole: "A hole is made when you take nothing and you bury it."

338. A 2-year-old was sitting in her mother's lap and they were looking at a magazine together. When they came across a picture of Jesus, her mother asked, "Do you know who that is?"

"Yes," the young daughter said matter-of-factly, "He goes to our church."

339. I got into my first fight when I was 11. This kid was blocking my way. He said, "C'mon, this is it." He wore glasses, and I saw him put them in his pocket. So I punched the pocket.

340. Good advice is what your own kids disregard but save to give to their kids.

341. One student's definition of a grandmother: "That's someone who comes to visit and keeps your mother from hitting you."

Clothes

342. Her clothes are designed to make her look younger, but she'll never fool a flight of stairs.

343. Now there's a new product to protect your clothes. Moth balls and marijuana. One whiff and the moths just stand around snapping their fingers.

344. A kindergarten teacher told a 5-year-old named Phillip that the boy had his shoes on the wrong feet. Phillip explained, "But they are the only feet I have."

345. An old-timer was sitting on the porch of a country store when a scantily clad young lady walked by. He said, "Her laundry sure ain't gonna break no clothesline!"

346. Sherlock Holmes met Dr. Watson on the street one misty morning, long ago. "Hi, Watson. I see you're wearing your plaid underwear," observed Holmes.

"How did you know that?" asked his astounded friend.

"Elementary, my dear Watson. You forgot to put on your trousers."

347. Sign in a woman's lingerie shop: "Just like the government, we give aid to the underdeveloped areas."

348. He says his wife always helps him pick his clothes—and then 10 years later, she won't let him wear them.

349. Self-confidence is walking around wearing a T-shirt that doesn't say anything.

350. Dress shop specializing in clothes for teenagers uses the ad: "Clothes your mother wouldn't like."

351. Most husbands would like to have their wives wear their dresses longer—about two years longer.

352. Overheard: "That's a great outfit if you're going to be selling little windup toys on the street."

353. You got on some nice threads. Too bad somebody had to go and make them into a bad suit.

354. A man who enjoys sitting on a bench in a shopping mall and people-watching has come to this conclusion: "On some women, stretch pants have no other choice."

Clubs

355. The guests at the club were chatting in little groups of two's and three's and seemed to be having a good time. The emcee turned to the first speaker and said, "Shall I let them enjoy themselves a little longer, or shall I introduce you?"

356. The secretary of a ladies luncheon club rose to present the speaker of the day. "Normally," she said with her brightest smile, "this honor would fall to our president, who has never missed hearing any of our speakers. But today she is in Atlantic City—and how we all envy her!"

357. You know how some service clubs don't pay speakers but give a gift like a pen or a mug? One group was so tough . . . the gift they gave was a tattoo. Then if they brought you back and didn't like you, they tore it off.

358. In my old neighborhood, even the Rotary Club wore black leather jackets. This particular Rotary had only one lawyer in it. His job was to get the other members out of jail so they could attend the meetings. Their biggest fund raiser was selling rotten tomatoes right before the guest speaker came on. That's why many times I'll work with a hand-held microphone. It's much easier to speak and duck at the same time.

359. The President of the Over-Eighty Club was challenged for admitting two members who were only seventy-eight and he explained, "Well, every organization needs some young blood."

360. Young Richard's father was a member of three lodges. "You

know," bragged Richard to his friend Bobby, "my daddy is a Lion, a Moose, and an Elk."

"Gee," said Bobby, his eyes wide, "if I give you a quarter, can I see him?"

361. How about that new order of bachelors called "Marriage Anonymous." When a member feels like getting married, they send over a woman with no makeup and her hair in curlers.

362. Wife: "I thought you were going to the lodge meeting tonight?"

Husband: "I was, but the wife of the Grand Exalted Invincible Supreme Potentate won't let him out."

363. During the local Men's Club meeting the other night, Charlie met a terrible bore. He says the fellow has quit smoking, his car gets 29 miles per gallon, and he's been eating tomatoes out of his garden for two weeks.

364. The president of an exclusive country club was watching golfers tee off on his first tee. He noticed a man addressing the ball ten feet in front of the markers.

"I say there," called the president, "you're supposed to put your ball behind those markers when you tee off."

The golfer ignored him.

"Don't hit the ball there," the president shouted. "Put it behind the markers!"

The golfer looked up and said, "Mister, I've been a member of this snooty club for 3 years, and you are the first person who's spoken to me. But if you're going to talk to me, I wish you wouldn't do it while I'm addressing the ball. For your information, although it's none of your business, this is my second shot."

365. Now there's a "Skier's Anonymous Club." If you have a craving to ski, you call them and they send a guy over to break your leg.

366. The president of a luncheon club says they've been having some difficulty lately with long-winded speakers. "I've been thinking," he said, "of posting a little sign on our podium. It would say, 'Nice guys finish fast.' "

367. Once there was a sad Texan whose greatest disappointment in life was that he couldn't become a member of the 50 Million Dollar Club to which all his friends belonged. It gave him a sense of frustration and a deep feeling of personal insecurity. On several occasions, he made up as high as $42,000,000, but then he would make a bad investment and could get no higher.

One day, he was lounging disconsolately against the solid-gold and diamond-studded lamp post outside the 50 Million Dollar Club, gazing longingly at his friends quaffing Napoleon brandy inside, when he suddenly remembered reading an article that said prayer would solve any problem.

So he went to the church around the corner and began praying: "Oh Lord, please let me get $50,000,000. . . ."

Just then a ragged figure knelt beside him—a man with hollow eyes, gaunt cheeks, a three-day beard. He began: "Oh Lord, help me. I've been out of work for a year. We're behind in the rent. My wife and children are sick. If maybe I had enough to get a bath and a shave and a clean shirt and pair of pants, I could find work. . . ."

The Texan reached into his pocket and pulled out a roll half the size of a hog, peeled off $800, handed it to the man and said impatiently: "Here. Don't be bothering the Lord with cotton-pickin' trifles!"

College

368. "Has your son's college education proved of any value?" the man asked a friend.

"Yes, indeed," the friend answered. "It cured his mother of bragging about him."

369. Couple applying for extension of son's college loan: "We had his board and tuition figured out right, but we didn't count on bail."

370. Is there any significance in the fact that dummy diplomas are handed out at commencement exercises?

371. At a college reunion, a genial professor was mingling with the crowds on the campus making an effort to recognize as many of his former students as possible. When a familiar face approached, he rushed up to the young man and expressed his delight at seeing him again after so long. "What are you doing now?" asked the professor.

"Well," stammered the young man, "this semester I'm in your 11 o'clock class."

372. Do you know why there's no medical school at our college? They dread the thought of scrubbing up before surgery.

373. One set of parents claims to have the only college student who can overdraw an unlimited expense account.

374. He's a college man. You've heard of the Ramblin' Wrecks from Georgia Tech. Well, he's a Total Loss from Holy Cross.

375. I'm glad to see our college emphasizing education over athletics. Our football team refuses to give a player a letter until they can tell which one it is.

376. I have a friend who, finding out about the expense of college, decided just to give his son the money and let him retire.

377. A college student left the library late one evening and when he got to his car in the parking lot, the battery was dead.

The nearest lighted building was a sorority house. He explained his situation to the young woman who answered the door and she permitted him to go inside and use the phone.

A voice called from upstairs: "Susan, you know you are not supposed to have any visitors on week days after 10 o'clock!"

"It's okay," Susan replied, "His battery is dead."

378. A boy was attending college.

His roommate told him: "I hear they have a new case of malaria in the dorm."

"Good," he replied, "I'm gettin' awful tired of that 7-Up."

379. It was graduation time at a medical school at a well-known college and one by one, the students visited the Dean's office to say good-bye. The last student to visit the dean had the lowest grades in the class. "Hopkins," the Dean said, "your grades show a complete lack of understanding of medicine and a general absence of knowledge about the human body. It is our recommendation that you consider becoming a specialist."

380. Excerpts from the college catalog, The Practical Student Survival Source Guide:

—Avoid bearded, pipe-smoking, liberal English instructors who make you drag your desks into a big circle.

—If you miss an exam because your grandmother died, say you were abducted by aliens—it's more believable.

—Don't try to get on your professor's good side. He doesn't have one.

381. A young agriculture student wanted to go to college and study to be a tree surgeon but had to give it up because he couldn't stand the sight of sap.

382. He graduated from college Magna cum loaded.

Committees

383.   Small towns have their problems, too. The program committee wanted to have a New Year's Eve party but couldn't agree on the date.

384.   An ideal committee consists of two, four, or six people who have no time and one person who likes to run things his own way.

385.   The credit manager was asked for some extemporaneous remarks regarding a certain matter during a board of directors meeting. He got up and said, "I feel like Marc Antony when he visited Cleopatra. I really didn't come here to talk."

386.   Critic: "What an odd posture for the statue of a General."
Sculptor: "It isn't my fault. I had the statue half finished when the committee decided it couldn't come up with enough money to put it on a horse."

387.   Chairman of the Board: "To insure your undivided attention, I'll announce who will write the minutes at the end of the meeting."

388.   A man bought some hot, sun-parched land with river frontage and planned to use it, with friends, for fish and game. But he was bothered by poachers. Finally, he solved his problem by posting this warning: "Anyone Entering This Property Without Protective Clothing May Sustain Radiation Burns."
The nearby city's Committee on Environmental Safety heard about it, discussed the possible ramifications, and decided it was a threat to life. They sent an investigator out.
"It means," he told him, "that anybody who comes on this property naked is liable to get sunburned."

389.   If Moses had been a committee, the Israelites would still be in Egypt.

390.   When all is said and nothing done, the committee meeting is over.

391.   If it weren't for business meetings, few people would be as advanced as they are in the art of doodling.

392.   Committee: "A group of people who, individually, can do nothing; but collectively can meet and decide that nothing can be done."

393.   For a number of years, Andrew Carnegie, whose wife loved classical music, made up the annual deficit of the New York Philhar-

monic Society. Then one year, at a committee meeting of the directors, he made the suggestion that the responsibility should not be his alone.

"From now on, I think the burden should be shared," he said. "You raise half the deficit from other donors, and I will give you the remaining half."

A few days later, the committee informed the philanthropist that his condition had been met. He was pleased by the news.

"I told you the money could be easily raised," he said. "Where did you get it?"

"We got it," they told him, "from Mrs. Carnegie."

394.   A committee is a group which succeeds in getting something done when, and only when, it consists of three members; one of whom happens to be sick and the other absent.

395.   Small typographical error seen in the church's bulletin: "The May meeting of the church finance committee will be hell as usual." After the typo was pointed out to the minister, he said, "I have to attend those meetings—and I don't think it's an error."

396.   Definition of "committee": "A collection of the unfit chosen from the unwilling by the incompetent to do the unnecessary."

397.   One basic rule of thumb: "If a sufficient number of committees are layered on top of each other, it can be assured that disaster is not left to chance."

Computers

398.   The most accurate computer ever made is the human digestive system. It never misses a calorie.

399.   One teacher moans that kids who used to "forget" their homework now claim it is lost in their computer.

400.   When the computer arrived at a large business concern, it was found too big for the elevator. "How am I going to get this thing to the fourth floor?" moaned the manager.

The deliveryman saw no problem. "Plug it in," he instructed, "and let it work it out for itself."

401.   A bachelor called a computer dating service and listed his specifications: He wanted someone who likes water sports, is gregarious, likes formal dress, and is small.

They sent him a penguin.

402.   There was this fully computer-automated bank in Miami. Seems somebody sent it a card saying, "THIS IS A HOLDUP," and the computer mailed the fellow $200,000 in unmarked bills.

403.   This is the age of tension. Almost everyone lives in fear of bending an IBM card.

404.   A computer performs complex calculations in one ten-thousandth of a second—and mails out statements ten days late.

405.   One business executive to another, talking about the office computer: "We can't sell it—it knows too much!"

406.   There's a new computer out that won't tell the IRS you cheated on your income tax if you promise to buy it.

407.   Remember the bookkeeper
       Perched on his stool,
       Green eye-shade tilted,
       Quill for a tool?
       He wasn't too fast,
       But nowhere in town
       Did you hear the excuse
       "Our computer is down."
                   R. S. SULLIVAN

408.   After you buy the offspring a brand new computer, how come they bring home the same old report cards?

409.   I finally figured out what to do with my home computer . . . I'm gonna trade it for an air conditioner.

410.   Computers are replacing everything. Saw one in the back of a pickup last night instead of a hound dog.

411.   Wife, sitting at home computer, excitedly tells husband, "I did it! I broke into the Fitzsimmons' computer and got Edith's recipe for lasagna!"

412.   To err is human—but to really screw up requires a computer.

413.   Go ahead . . . put it in the computer; at least you'll know where it is even though you can't find it again.

414.   The experts are telling us that eventually every home will have a computer.
   All this means is that our personal lives will be just as screwed up as things are at the office!

Congress

415. Congress is so strange. A man gets up to speak and says nothing, nobody listens, and then everybody disagrees. WILL ROGERS

416. There is someone else who spends money like a drunken sailor . . . a sober congressman!

417. In Congress, when the going gets tough, the tough call a recess.

418. The interesting thing about Congress is not that it does so many things that are questionable, but that it goes about its business of doing them with such grave, considered, and pompous indifference to good morals; like opening its sessions with a chaplain's prayer and then spending the rest of the day cutting throats.

419. Find out how Congress is spending your tax dollars. It's educational, enlightening, and probably the best cure for hiccups you'll ever find.

420. Why do you think some of our Congressmen go on overseas junkets all the time? In my opinion . . . they have to go somewhere and with their voting records, they're afraid to go home!

421. Congressional leaders are cautious about a tax cut. They say it's not something you rush into . . . like a congressional pay hike.

422. Transcendental meditation, by the way, consists of sitting down, closing your eyes, and letting your mind go blank. Congress has been practicing it for years.

423. The cost for sending congressmen abroad wouldn't be so bad, but those guys keep coming back home!

424. If you should meet up with a well-dressed stranger in Washington and want to know what he does for a living, ask him to show you the photos in his wallet. If the pictures are of a woman and children, the man could be unselfish, honest, and intelligent. If the pictures are likenesses of himself, then the bearer is undoubtedly a congressman.

425. How can we teach our kids the value of money when we can't even teach our Congressmen?

426. "Do you know how to save three Congressmen from drowning?"
"No."
"Good."

Cooking

427. You know the new casserole is a bomb when your guests say that it has an "interesting texture."

428. My wife's cooking is so bad we have the only garbage disposal in town that throws up.

429. How bad is her cooking? Well, at the covered dish supper, her casserole was the only one that didn't have flies on it.

430. Cooking was no problem for the bride. Cooking food that someone would eat was the problem.

431. Beverly Hills recipe for chicken soup: "First you boil the Perrier. . . ."

432. His wife dresses to kill . . . and cooks the same way.

433. My wife has only one problem with cooking . . . she burns things. Like we were married for three years before I realized there were other flavors besides charcoal.

434. A bride cooked her husband a nice meal. While eating, he asked, "Did you stuff the turkey yourself?"
"I didn't need to," said the wife. "It wasn't hollow."

435. Mom was a bad cook. She had a kitchen full of vending machines.

436. After 10 years, my wife's cooking never has improved. The veterinarian says our cat has only four lives left.

437. When a newlywed served a baked ham to her husband, he noticed she had cut the ends off and he asked her why. "That's the way Mother always did it," she replied with a shrug.
When his mother-in-law came for a visit, she asked her the same question, "That's the way my mother did it," she replied.
Finally, he asked the wife's grandmother, who answered, "That's the only way I could get it into the pan."

438. They say a woman's work is never done—and my cooking proves it.

439. Woman showing bandaged hand to a friend, "I hurt it while I was preparing dinner. It's frostbitten."

Cowboys

440.   There is the story about the cowboy who hurried into a strange Texas saloon one night, leaned over the bar, and whispered to the bartender, "Friend, where is the toilet?"

The bartender, being extremely busy, waved a hand toward the rear of the building, and said, "Go down that hallway and you'll find it."

So the cowboy did as instructed and came, finally, to two doorways on the left and two doorways on the right. He opened the first door on the left, stepped through it, and fell into a swimming pool, "ker-splash." He was flailing with both arms, gasping and gurgling, when an attendant heard the commotion and came running. "Can I help you?" he called out.

Whereupon the drowning cowboy, still struggling for survival, replied, "For heaven's sake . . . don't flush it!"

441.   The old cowboy and his son were sitting in front of the fire smoking their pipes, crossing and uncrossing their legs. After a long silence, the father said, "Son, step outside and see if it's raining."

Without looking up, the son replied, "Aw shucks, Paw, why don't we just call in the dog and see if he's wet?"

442.   My cowboy friend confesses that he was a late bloomer: "I rode a stick horse until I was 10."

He rode it to school one day, he recalls, and someone stole it. "I had to walk all the way home," he says.

443.   Ranches in some parts of the West are by no means always a paying proposition. At such a place, a traveler stopped, seeking a night's lodging.

Discussing with his host hard times in general, the stranger asked, "How in the world do you manage to make enough on this place to run it?"

His host pointed toward his hired man at the far end of the table. "You see that feller? Well, he works for me and I can't pay him. In two more years, he gits the ranch. Then I'm gonna' work for him till I git it back."

444.   Know what you call a Mexican cowboy on a white horse? . . . Roy Rodriguez.

445.   A rancher in Texas had to confront the new federal statute prohibiting job classification by sex. He finally ran the following

ad in the local newspaper: "Cowperson wanted. Applicant must use profanity and share a bunkhouse with four male cowpersons who seldom bathe."

446. A stranger walked up to a rancher and showed him his card. "I am a government inspector," he said, "and this card entitles me to inspect your farm and grants immunity from any interference."

A few minutes later, the rancher heard screams from his pasture, where the inspector was being chased by a bull. Leaning over the gate, the rancher yelled at the top of his voice, "Show him yer, card, mister! Show him yer card!"

447. Clyde Grump and his wife, Bessie, came to town on Saturday and decided they would eat at the town's new drive-in restaurant. One look at the menu and Clyde hopped from the table, dragged Bessie out of the restaurant, shoved her into the truck, and drove off full speed toward the ranch. "Clyde, what'n blazes are you doin'?" gasped Bessie.

"Did you see the price of that hamburger?" he asked, gritting his teeth and standing on the accelerator.

"Sure. A dollar eighty-nine. But what. . . ."

"That means we got a $48,000 cow standin' out in the south pasture without us there to guard her!"

448. A Texas rancher had some boots made, and they turned out to be too tight. The bootmaker insisted on stretching them.

"Not on your life!" said the rancher. "These boots are going to stay too tight. Every morning when I get out of bed, I got to corral some cows that busted out in the night and mend fences they tore down. All day long, I watch my ranch blow away in the dust. After supper, I listen to the TV tell about the high price of feed and low price of beef. All the time, my wife is naggin' me to move to town.

"Man, when I get ready for bed and pull of those boots—well, that's the only pleasure I get all day!"

449. A farmer took his first trip to the zoo. He saw a baboon. His grandson asked what it was. "I think it's a cowboy, the seat of his pants is worn out."

450. "I'm taking a shortcut through your field to catch the 4:45," said a tresspasser.

"If my bull sees you, you'll catch the 4:15!" replied the rancher.

451. One cowboy finally got real fed up with speeding cars which constantly scared his livestock and children. He erected a sign which

immediately began to slow down the motorists who were passing his place. The sign read: "Nudist Camp Crossing."

452. A Catholic bronc rider on his first ride was asked how long he hung on. "Exactly 14 Hail Mary's."

453. This dude asks a cowboy "how come that cow doesn't have horns?"

The cowboy explains, "Well, some cows have horns and some don't. Some are born with horns and we dehorn them. Some breeds aren't supposed to have horns. There are lots of reasons why cows don't have horns, but the main reason why that cow don't have horns is 'cause it ain't a cow. It's a horse."

454. A young cowboy was raised in a proper home and his mother had taught him the art of courtesy. Whenever he occasionally forgot his courtesy, he was able to develop a line of flattery that got him out of trouble. The cowboy happened to step on an elevator in which he and a middle-aged fussy socialite were the only occupants. He forgot to take off his hat. When the snobbish woman asked, "Don't you take your hat off to ladies?" He quickly replied, "Only to old ones, ma'am."

455. A cowboy fell off his horse and broke his leg. That smart horse grabbed his master's belt in his teeth, and dragged the cowboy home to safety. Then, the horse even went to fetch the doctor. An admiring friend praised the horse's intelligence to his owner. "Aw, he ain't so smart," said the cowboy. "He came back with the veterinarian."

456. A cowboy cornered a veterinarian at the local feed store and tried to get a bit of free advice.

"I've got a funny horse," he explained. "Sometimes he walks normally; other times, he has a bad limp. What should I do?"

The vet snapped, "Next time he walks normal, sell him."

Credit

457. Wealthy people miss one of the greatest thrills in life—paying the last installments.

458. Now some of you may be asking, "Why are you here, Joe?" I mean, we know why we're here . . . we're here because the club across the street wouldn't take Master Charge."

459. The people in Texas are so rich that instead of tossing coins, they throw credit cards in fountains.

460. My wife just bought $5,000 worth of furniture on the Lay-Awake plan. She spent the money and I lay awake wondering where it's coming from.

461. Sign on a gas station: "We honor Mastercard, Visa, American Express, Mobil, and Gulf. However, we only accept cash."

462. The average man now lives about 32 years longer than he did in 1800. It takes that much longer for a fellow to get his credit cards paid off.

463. Uncle Fred consolidated his debts. Now each month he has just one bill that he won't pay.

464. You can't buy happiness . . . but you can charge it.

465. "He's so heavily in debt that he's known as the Leaning Tower of Visa."

466. Two credit managers were comparing the credit ratings of their customers. "Oh, yes," said one, "what about this fellow Pickens. How trustworthy is he?"
    "We have no way of knowing," said the other. "He always pays cash."

467. With all the credit cards, the only one to still pay cash is the Tooth Fairy.

468. One definition of installment buying: "By the time you're sick and tired of the thing, you finally own it."

469. If you think nobody cares if you are alive . . . miss a couple of car payments.

470. The dream of the older generation was to pay off the mortgage. The hope of today's young families is to get one.

471. If you want to write something that has a chance of living on forever, sign a mortgage.

472. No need to go ahead with the neutron bomb. We already have something that destroys people and leaves buildings intact. It's called a mortgage.

473. A fellow says he has arrived at that point in life where he's "just about even" financially. When asked to expand on this statement, he says, "I figure I owe about the same number that I don't owe."

474. "I'm sorry," said Louie the Gyp, "but I haven't any money to pay for the meal."

"That's all right," said the waitress. "We'll write your name on the wall and you can pay the next time you come in."

"Don't do that. Everybody who comes in will see it."

"Oh no, they won't. Your overcoat will be hanging over it."

475. Just think, pioneers who crossed the country practically unarmed now have descendants who won't go downtown without credit cards.

Crime

476. Know how break dancing got started? Two street kids stealing hub caps off a moving car.

477. This fellow in his early 30's came steaming into his doctor's office one day. His doctor was his lifelong friend and old college fraternity brother as well as his physician.

"You've got to give me some arsenic or strychnine or something," the fellow demanded. "I can't give you anything like that," said the doctor. "That's poison. You could kill somebody."

"Exactly," snarled the fellow. "My wife is driving me insane. She won't even talk about a divorce and if I have to spend another six months with her they'll be carting me off to the booby hatch. I thought I could slip a little arsenic into her coffee. . . ."

"Listen," said the doctor, "if you did that, the police would be sure to find out and then you'd go to prison for the rest of your life. If you're determined to get rid of your wife—take this."

"What is it?" the fellow wanted to know.

"It's a powerful aphrodisiac," said the doctor. "Sprinkle it in your food every night. It will inflame your passions. Over the course of a month, you can love your wife to death and no jury in the world will be able to do a thing to you."

The fellow fell on the bottle with glad cries and carried it home.

So a little more than three weeks later, the doctor stopped by his friend's house. He noticed a bundle sitting on the front porch. Looking closer, he was shocked to see that the bundle was his friend, wrapped in blankets and sitting in a rocking chair. His hair had turned white. His cheeks were shrunken, he blinked constantly, and his head and arms and legs trembled uncontrollably. He drooled. Altogether, he was a miserable wreck. "John . . . ," said the horrified doctor. "John, is that you?"

"It's me," wheezed John feebly.

"What in the world happened?" the doctor asked.

"I've been following your advice," John replied. "I've been doing just what you told me to do. I've been using the powder."

Just at that moment, the front door flew open and out trotted the friend's wife, dressed in a jogging suit. She was the picture of vibrant health, rosy cheeks, shining hair, and pearly teeth. She waved a cheery hello to the doctor. "Got to do my daily three miles," she caroled. Bouncing down the steps, she did a few deep knee bends and then raced out of sight. The doctor was staring after her when he heard a strangled cackle from the bundle of sticks that was his friend.

"Hee, hee, hee," gasped the living skeleton. "Look at the poor fool. She doesn't even know she has only a few more days to live."

478.   Policeman: "What a mess this room is. Why didn't you report the robbery right away?"

Woman: "I didn't suspect a thing—I just thought my husband had been looking for a clean shirt."

479.   A man was walking down a street and at the corner, he was jumped by two young fellows with intentions of taking his money. This man was in good shape, and for 10 minutes, he gave them the fight of their lives. He fought, he kicked, he gouged . . . and when they finally subdued him, one of the fellows ran his hand in the man's pocket and all he found was a dime.

He looked at his friend and said, "You mean to tell me this man put up a fight like that and all he had was a dime?"

His friend said, "Baby, be thankful! If he woulda had $10, he'd have killed us!"

480.   Our corporate treasurer is shy and retiring. He's shy $200,000; that's why he is retiring.

481.   The only witness to a jewelry store robbery was an elderly lady. When the police officer asked her what the crooks looked like, she said: "All I know is a truck pulled up, an elephant got out from the back of it, broke the store window and took a trunk full of jewelry."

The policeman asked if it was an Indian elephant or an African elephant. The old lady said she didn't know one from the other. The policeman informed her that the Indian elephant had small ears and the African type had large ears, and asked her again which one it was. "I couldn't tell you," she said, "It had a stocking pulled over its head."

482. The hit-and-run victim slowly got to his feet. "My mother-in-law just tried to run me over," he gasped to the policeman.

"But how do you know it was your mother-in-law . . . you're blind," asked the officer.

The man answered, "I'd know that laugh anywhere."

483. A preacher of a little mountainside church ran off with the church funds. A deacon was sent to find him. When he returned, he was asked if he had found their preacher and filed charges against him. "I found him," he replied, "but he had already spent the money so I brought him back so we can make him preach it out."

484. Washington is the only city where you are never more than five miles from the scene of a crime.

485. I have an uncle who is with the F.B.I. They caught him in Florida.

486. A lawyer was questioning a witness in a murder case. "Did you say that she shot him at close range?"

"Yes."

"Were there any powder marks on him?"

"Yes. That's why she shot him."

487. A woman customer paid the proprietor of a nursery with a check. She asked: "Do you want identification?"

"It's not necessary," he replied. "Crooks don't buy peat moss."

488. In Oklahoma City, Pulliam was charged with shooting some pigeons that belonged to Long, a farmer. Pulliam's lawyer tried to frighten the farmer. "Now," said the counselor, "are you prepared to swear that this man shot your pigeons?"

"I didn't say he shot 'em," replied Long. "I said I suspected him of doing it."

"Ah, now we're coming to it. What made you suspect Mr. Pulliam?"

"First off, I caught him on my land with a gun. Second, I heard a gun go off and saw some pigeons fall. And third, I found four of my pigeons in his pocket and I don't think the birds flew there and committed suicide."

489. Sign on a gun shop door: "If you are interested in investigating life after death, just try robbing this place."

490. A would-be bank robber, after studying hundreds of newspaper accounts of bank robberies, decided to try one himself. Flourishing his pistol in a bank, he announced, "This is a stick up. I want an undetermined amount of cash."

491. And then there was the crook so dumb he stuck up a man who was coming home from Las Vegas.

492. A New York bank is giving away a set of china to anyone who agrees not to rob it.

493. An employee of a store got a phone call from a man who said his girlfriend had lost a valuable earring in the store. The employee searched for the earring but couldn't find it. Later, the man called again and offered a $200 reward. Shortly afterward, a woman walked into the store and told the employee she had found an earring in the restroom. The employee bought the earring from the woman for $75 and waited for the man to call back. He never did.

494. The lush was lurking on a dark and deserted street corner. An innocent stroller came walking by and the lush sprung out of the shadows, a gun in his hand.

"Shtay where you are," growled the drunk. Then he pulled a bottle out of his pocket. "Here," he ordered, "take a drink of thish."

Too terrified to resist, the poor man took the bottle and drank deeply. "Wow," he exclaimed, "that stuff tastes awful."

"I know," said the drunk. "Now you hold the gun on me and make me take a drink."

495. Prosecuting attorney ordered the defendant, "Tell the jury why you shot your husband with a bow and arrow."

"I didn't want to wake the children," said the woman.

496. Juvenile delinquents in Texas are so rich they slash their own tires.

Dancing

497. After months of taking ballroom dancing lessons, the happy couple was ready to show off their talents at the annual small town holiday dance. As the band began the first tune, he leaned over and whispered, "Is that slow-slow-quick-quick?"

498. If you're over 40, do yourself a favor and stay out of discotheques. At that age, it's no longer dancing. It's like committing suicide . . . one bone at a time.

499. A little boy who went to the ballet for the first time with his father was amazed watching all the girls dancing on their toes. He turned to his father and asked, "Dad, why don't they just get taller girls?"

500. Some of the dance steps are so wild at our favorite discotheque, they won't permit premarital dancing.

501. How about the belly dancer who got a stomach cold and couldn't shake it.

502. What's considered congestion elsewhere is successful atmosphere on the dance floor.

503. You probably know that belly dancing is the only profession where the beginner starts in the middle.

504. A man fell two-thirds behind in his payments for cha-cha-cha lessons at a dance studio. The studio sent a hypnotist to his house, and when he woke up, he only knew how to cha.

505. Men have given a lot of thought to the art of belly dancing among women and come to the conclusion that they would have been better off thinking about something else.

506. My lodge brothers took their wives to a New Orleans dance review. The girls objected to the fan dancers; the boys objected to the fans.

507. The best thing you can say for today's dance steps is that if someone makes a mistake, no one knows.

508. Grandpa said he knows why the kids don't touch nowadays when they dance, "You don't never touch nobody who's havin' a fit!"

509. Two dogs were watching a teenage dance when one looked over at the other and said, "You know, if we acted that way, they'd worm us!"

510. He held her close as the band played a slow dance. They didn't speak until the music stopped. Then she looked up and whispered: "This dance makes me long for another one."

He said, "Yeah, me too. But she couldn't make it tonight."

511. Some people age gracefully. Others attempt to learn the new dances.

512. Bumper snicker: "Hug a Musician—They never get to dance."

Daughters

513. A precocious seven-year-old asked her mother for a baby brother. Her mother was taken aback by the request but said in a

The life of a professional humorist consists of traveling 250,000 miles per year, making over 100 appearances annually, and living off of green peas and chicken. Here, Doc Blakely explains to this special interest group why he is so happy to get a bar-be-cue plate of beef and pork. "I've eaten so much chicken my feet are starting to curl," he quips here to an appreciative audience.

soothing tone, "I'm afraid that just isn't possible, darling. Babies cost a great deal of money, and Daddy and I just can't afford one right now."

"Mommy," said her daughter in a most exasperated tone, "women don't BUY babies. I think you and I should have a little talk!"

514.   Father welcomed his daughter's boyfriend at the door. "She will be right down. Care for a game of chess?"

515.   After the death of her father, a woman tried to persuade her 80-year-old mother to move in with her. The older woman was adamant: "No! Absolutely not! I've always said I'd never live with any of my kids. I've seen too many problems arise from that kind of situation."

The daughter said, "Yes, Mom, but you're different."

"I know I am," replied her mother, "but you're not."

516. You don't realize how many junk cars there are until your daughter starts dating.

517. Neighbor: "They say your daughter has made up her mind to marry a struggling young doctor."

Father: "Well, if she's made up her mind, he might as well stop struggling—it won't do him a bit of good."

518. Conversation overheard between two fathers: "What is your teenage daughter doing this summer?"

"Her hair and her nails."

519. The minister's wife was visiting a member of the congregation, and mentioned, with particular pride, that her daughter had won first prize in a music recital.

"I know just how you must feel," said her hostess understandingly. "I remember how pleased we were when our pig got the blue ribbon at the fair last year."

520. The clergyman's small daughter watched him preparing next Sunday's sermon. "Daddy," she asked, "does God tell you what to say?"

"Yes, He does, dear," he replied. "Why?"

"I was wondering why you cross so much of it out," she said.

521. "How is your daughter getting along in her bookkeeping class at school?"

"Terrific. Now, instead of asking for her allowance, she just bills us for it."

522. A five-year-old girl had just received two gifts for her birthday and couldn't stop telling about them. Finally her mother couldn't stand to hear about them one more time and said, "Now, listen, we're having company for dinner, and it isn't nice to boast about your belongings in front of people. Please don't mention your watch or cologne at the table."

The little girl sat squirming but quiet during the meal. But when her mother stepped out to the kitchen, the child said quietly, "If anybody hears or smells anything, it's me."

523. Daughter: "Is it true that Santa Claus brings us presents?"

Mother: "Yes, that's true."

Daughter: "And the stork brings us babies?"

Mother: "Yes, that's true."

Daughter: "And the Police Department protects us?"
Mother: "That's right."
Daughter: "Then what do we need Daddy for?"

524. My daughter doesn't think it's time to clean up her room until her phone rings and she can't find it.

525. The minister's daughter returned home at 3 o'clock in the morning from a dance. Her father greeted her sternly, "Good morning, child of the devil."
Her reply, "Good morning, Father."

526. My teenage daughter really gave us a time last night. She started to run away from home. Luckily, she never got beyond the front door. The telephone rang.

527. The mother of two daughters, ages 5 and 7, decided it was time to tell them about the birds and the bees. She sent off for a booklet recommended by the PTA and, having read it, called the girls in for a long chat.
When she finished, she said, with her heart in her throat, "You may ask me any question you want to."
The oldest said, "Anything?"
She said, "Yes, anything." Then took a deep breath, thinking, "Here it comes."
The little girl asked, "Can we have a new baseball bat?"

528. The sweet little girl had an awful fight with her friend. Her mother scolded her, saying, "It was the devil who made you pull Barbara's hair."
"That may be," answered the child, "but kicking her shin was all my idea."

529. Mother: "Did you say your prayers last night?"
Daughter: "Well, I got down on my knees and started to say them and all of a sudden I thought: I bet God gets awfully tired hearing the same old prayer over and over. So I crawled into bed and told Him the story of the three bears."

530. When asked what her father did for a living, one little girl replied, "He's a civil serpent."

531. Mom: "Don't play with boys. They're too rough."
Daughter: "What if I find a smooth one?"

532. Amelia (whose sunburn was in the peeling-off stage) said to her mother: "I'm only four years old and already I'm wearing out."

533. When a 5-year-old girl first saw her newborn baby brother—

wrinkled, red, bald, and shut-eyed—she remarked to her mother, "So that's why you kept him hidden under your coat for so long!"

534. The father was apprehensive about the date his daughter was getting ready for. "Are you sure he's a good driver?"

"Oh, yes, Dad. He has to be. If he gets arrested one more time, he loses his license."

535. Mother: "What did you learn in school today?"

Six-year-old daughter: "How to whisper without moving my lips."

536. A minister was explaining the facts of life to his daughter. The youngster listened attentively as her father told her about the birds and bees, then asked, "Does God know about this?"

Death

537. Our favorite moneybags says when he dies, he wants to be buried with his bankbook: "I've never been in a hole it couldn't get me out of."

538. I had an uncle who told a girl that if she didn't marry him he'd die. Sure enough, 62 years later, he died.

539. An old man, with only a few hours to live, said to his nurse, "Will you promise me something?"

She said, "Of course. What is it?"

"After the doctor pronounces me dead," he said, "get a second opinion."

540. A politician was musing on the hereafter: "I'm not too worried—seeing as how I've got friends in both places."

541. A doctor had just been laid to rest in the cemetery. When the last shovel full of dirt had been put in place a high pitched, muffled sound came from the grave. Several colleagues peered at the spot. Then one remarked, "I think it's his beeper."

542. If you don't think there's a divine plan, just read the paper and explain to me how come everybody dies in alphabetical order.

543. The will of the wealthy, but eccentric farmer was being read and the relatives all listened expectantly.

Finally the lawyer said, "And to my nephew, Charlie Jones, whom I promised to mention in my will . . . 'Hi, there, Charlie.'"

544. A friend of mine stopped smoking, drinking, overeating, and chasing women—all at the same time. It was a lovely funeral.

545. Three men who died were cremated. One from Nebraska,

one from Ohio, and one from Kansas. The Nebraska man was first. And when his ashes were removed, they were put into a quart jar. The Ohio man was next. His ashes were put into a pint jar. The Kansas man was last. At the end of 15 hours, the furnace door was opened. Out walked the Kansas man, mopping his face with his hankerchief and saying, "Boy, if we get two more days of this hot weather, it'll ruin the entire corn crop."

546.   "Hey, Clyde, how you been doing?"
"Not too good. Had to bury my wife."
"Aw, I'm sorry to hear that. What was wrong with her?"
"Well, she was dead."

547.   "You're all in black, Millie," said a friend. "Did your husband die?"
"No, not this one," Millie responded. "But he's been so impossible lately that I went back into mourning for my first husband."

548.   "How's your grandfather, the hypochondriac?" asked the doctor. "Does he still think he's sick?"
"Oh, no, Doc, now he thinks he's dead!"

549.   Eager job applicant: "Sir, I read in the newspaper that a member of your staff has died. I wonder if I might take his place?"
Employer: "Well, it's all right with me if it's all right with the undertaker."

550.   An old miser called his doctor, lawyer, and minister to his deathbed. "They say you can't take it with you," the dying man said, "but I'm going to try. I've got 3 envelopes with $30,000 cash in each one. I want each of you to take an envelope, and just when they lower my casket, you all throw in the envelopes."
At the funeral, each man tossed in his envelope. On the way home, the minister confessed, "I needed the money for the church, so I took out $10,000 and threw only $20,000 into the grave."
The doctor then said, "I too must confess. I'm building a clinic and took out $20,000 for it and threw in only $10,000."
The lawyer said, "Gentlemen, I'm ashamed of you. I threw in a check for the full amount."

551.   My bachelor friend Bill is quite a ladies' man, very conceited. He's the kind of guy who would like to die in his own arms.

552.   The business tycoon was dying, and the priest hadn't yet arrived. "John," he gasped to his partner, who was sitting by the side of the bed. "I want to confess to you. I stole $74,000 from the

safe. And I'm the one who told your wife about your mistress. And John . . . I sold our secret patents to our rivals for $200,000. And John. . . ."

"That's okay," John whispered. "I'm the one who poisoned you."

553.   A rather cynical fellow was told by his wife that she would dance on his grave . . . at which time he arranged for a burial far out at sea.

554.   One of the cardinal rules of having good sense when you are ill . . . is to never go to a doctor whose office plants have died.

555.   I'm reminded of the widow who said, "I had so much trouble collecting the money from my husband's estate—sometimes I wish he hadn't died."

556.   It is estimated that one person dies every ten seconds. We can't control death, but at least we have it timed.

557.   Some people say they'd like to go to bed at night healthy and wake up dead in the morning. Not me. I'd like to linger, to linger and suffer, and linger and suffer, and go to doctors, and bigger doctors who won't know what's keeping me alive, and then linger and suffer, and linger, and, then, the last minute, I get well.

558.   A rich doctor died and his friend became curious about the size of his estate. He phoned the widow and asked, "How much did he leave?"

   She replied, "All of it."

559.   Did you hear about the salesman who died and left an estate of 500 towels and 200 hotel keys?

Dentists

560.   "Open wide," said the dentist as he began examination of a new patient. "Good grief," he said, "you've got the biggest cavity I've ever seen . . . the BIGGEST CAVITY I'VE EVER SEEN!"

   "You didn't have to repeat it," snapped the patient.

   "I didn't," said the dentist. "That was the echo."

561.   My dentist is a strange doctor. I gave him $50 for an impression and he did Rodney Dangerfield.

562.   My dentist apparently reads only technical journals. I asked if he knew about Sherlock Holmes. He said no, but he was familiar with his brother, Mobile.

563. A dentist giving brushing instructions to a patient: "The best way to brush your teeth is to hold your brush in your right hand; hold your teeth in your left hand. . . ."

564. Medical tip: "Never go to a dentist who has his office sound-proofed."

565. Sign in a dentist's office: "COFFEE $25, TEETH CLEANED FREE."

566. Friend of mine thinks his dentist really charges too much: "Last week he put in a crown. I think it belonged to Queen Elizabeth!"

567. Sign in Dentist's office: "Smile . . . the sunshine is good for your teeth."

568. A police officer was about to ticket a car which was double-parked, when suddenly a woman approached excitedly. "Oh, please, don't give me a ticket, officer," she pleaded. "You see, I just visited my dentist to have a tooth pulled. I left my car double-parked so I'd have something to worry about to keep my mind off the pain."

569. We put all our money in precious metals . . . we got braces for all the kids.

570. Two friends, Herb and Jim, called their office one Monday to say they wouldn't be in to work that day. Each gave the same reason: That he had to have some dental work done. Later, one of the men in the office asked Jim for an explanation. "Herb and I went fishing," he replied. "When we were out in the middle of the lake, Herb took out his dentures and put them on the boat seat. I decided I'd play a prank on him. When he wasn't looking, I put his teeth in my pocket. Then later, when I got the chance, I took my dentures out and put them where his had been. We fished awhile, then decided to go to another spot. Herb picked up the teeth and tried several times to get them in his mouth. He got fiery mad and threw them as far as he could and said, 'That durn dentist never did git those dang teeth to fit me right!' Well, I froze because mine—the ones he just threw away—fit perfectly and cost me a bundle, besides. I sat stunned a few seconds, then reached in my pocket, got his teeth, threw them as far as I could and said, 'Mine don't fit, either.'"

571. A Texas oilman was told by his dentist that his teeth were in perfect shape. "Go ahead and drill anyway, Doc," he urged. "I'm on a lucky streak."

Divorce

572. Half of the marriages are now ending in divorce. Couples claim incompatibility, irreconcilable differences, desertion.

What's wrong with "I hate his/her guts?"

573. My wife and I broke up because of illness in the family. She got sick of me.

574. The woman, seeking a divorce, came before the judge and said she wanted her freedom on the grounds that her husband was tired of her.

"What makes you think he's tired of you?" asked the judge.

"Well," sighed the woman, "he hasn't been home in five years."

575. I knew a woman who had 16 children and was getting a divorce because of compatibility!

576. Wife in court during divorce settlement: "Heaven knows I've tried to make a good home for him, Your Honor. I've redecorated it 3 times during the last 5 years."

577. My wife didn't marry me for my money, but she sure divorced me for it.

578. There was only one good thing about our divorce. My husband got custody of his mother.

579. It's all right for a man to love you and leave you, provided he leaves you enough. ZSA ZSA GABOR

580. I ran into a guy who insisted he was always early with his alimony payments. He thought if he was late, she might try to repossess him.

581. A lady (82) wants a divorce from her husband (87) after 60 years. When the lawyer asked, "Why?" she said, "Because enough is enough."

582. Tom sued his wife for divorce because she was mean tempered, bossy, and had three straight sets of twins. Grounds: She was overbearing.

583. "I'm going to get a divorce," the man told his friend. "My wife hasn't spoken to me in three months."

"I'd think twice about that if I were you," his friend said. "Wives like that are hard to find."

584. My ex-wife was a great housekeeper—when we were divorced, she kept the house.

585. A husband told a judge that he wanted a divorce because his wife did bird impressions. "Your Honor," he explained, "from the day we were married this woman has watched me like a hawk."

586. He's divorcing his wife because she has a sobering effect on him . . . she hides the bottle.

Doctors

587. One doctor has as a patient a grumpy middle-aged man who didn't think much of physicians. The only reason the man had come to the doctor was because his wife was nagging after him ceaselessly. "Well," the doctor asked, "What seems to be the trouble?"

"Isn't that what you're supposed to find out?" the man demanded. "You're the one with all the diplomas and the expensive education. You're the one who knows it all. Earn your fee. You're so smart, you find out what's wrong with me."

The doctor looked at the stubborn fellow for a few minutes and then said, "I think I'm going to send you to Dr. Blank."

"What kind of specialist is he?" the man asked.

"He's a veterinarian," the doctor replied, "and he's the only doctor I know who can make a diagnosis without asking his patient questions. Besides, he probably treated your mother."

588. One busy morning, it took a long time for the doctor to see all of the patients in his waiting room. The last patient was an old man and the doctor apologized to him for the delay. "I don't mind the waiting so much," said the old man, "but I thought you would prefer to treat my ailment in its early stages."

589. Mrs. Brown complained to her doctor that his bill was unreasonably high. "Don't forget," he replied, "I saw your son nine times when he had the measles."

"And don't you forget," she retorted. "He infected the whole school!"

590. A nervous woman patient phoned her doctor at a late hour and said, "I now know exactly what's wrong with me! I've got hypoglycemia!"

"Yes, yes, I know," purred the medical man. "I was watching the same television show."

591. Question: "Do doctors make amnesia patients pay in advance?"

592. The next time you're lying on the operating table, remember

this: The guy that's about to cut you open for delicate surgery is the same klutz who only hours before missed a two-inch putt!

593.   There's a story making the rounds about a doctor who printed his prescriptions in large, perfect letters. No pharmacist could read them.

594.   I don't like smart aleck doctors who try to show off using their big medical words. Words like . . . liver . . . and gallbladder.

595.   A fellow was choking on a chicken bone in a swanky restaurant. A doctor leaped forward and removed the bone.
   The man said, "Gee, Doc, you saved my life. What do I owe you?"
   The doctor said, "Half of what you were willing to pay when that bone was still in your throat."

596.   Specialist: "A physician who has trained his patients to become ill only during office hours."

597.   A surgeon was making his hospital rounds and was chatting with a young lady he had operated on a few days earlier.
   "Do you think the scar on my stomach will show?" she asked the doctor.
   "That will be entirely up to you," he replied.

598.   The doctor got a little tired of midnight phone calls from people who didn't want to pay him for an office visit. At 2 o'clock in the morning the phone jangled and he answered.
   "Say," whined a voice, "what do I do for a broken leg?"
   "Limp," replied the doctor and hung up.

599.   I have a wonderful surgeon. One of the best. He's very concerned about health costs. He refuses to operate unless he really needs the money.

600.   A little old lady lay on her pillow, a comfortable look on her face. "I feel much better today," she said. "I don't think my appendix will have to be removed." With a big smile, she said, "It surely was nice of the new minister to call and see me."
   "Grandmother," said Mary Lou, "that wasn't the minister. That was the specialist from the city who examined you."
   Granny's brow wrinkled, "Well, I thought he was a little familiar for a minister."

601.   The doctor bent over the operating table and said to his patient, "I think it's only fair to tell you that only one out of every

four patients completely recovers from this operation. Before I proceed, is there anything you would like me to do?"

"Yes," replied the patient, "help me on with my pants and shoes."

602.   A really smart doctor is one who can still diagnose the ailment of a patient who doesn't smoke or drink or isn't overweight.

603.   About doctor's appointments: They give you an appointment six weeks ahead. Then ask, "Why did you wait so long to see me?"

604.   Remember that 50% of all practicing physicians today graduated in the lower half of their class.

605.   A doctor called Angus to tell him that his check had come back again. Angus replied, "So did my arthritis."

606.   "Is your nephew Irving a good doctor?"

"Good? He's such a lovely boy. Why, last year I needed an operation and I couldn't afford it. So he touched up the X-rays!"

607.   He won't take his doctor's advice to stop drinking. He claims there are lots more old drunks than old doctors.

608.   The doctor was invited to an elegant dinner party. The host, a braggard of the worst kind, carved the roast beef with a flourish. With nothing left to carve, he turned to the physician and loudly announced, "How's that, Doc? I'll bet I could be a surgeon, too."

The doctor replied, "You've done the easy part. The trick is to get it back together."

Drinking

609.   Walter Winchell once said that sophistication is the art of getting drunk with the right people.

610.   A doctor noticed a drunk holding a Bible in one hand and a bottle in the other sitting in a pool of spilled liquor. "My dear man," said the physician, "you evidently read the Good Book. How can you justify your present condition?"

"Listen, smartie," slurred the drunk, "I committed a sin last night and it says in here I oughta be stoned."

611.   Two friends promised to meet in the same bar and at the same time, ten years later. So ten years later, one of them walked in diffidently and sure enough there was his pal on a stool. "I never thought," he said, "that day when we left this bar that I'd really see you here today."

"Who left?" hiccuped his pal.

612. A doctor was quizzing a man at the end of a first aid course. "Suppose," he asked, "you saw a car accident and you found a man bleeding profusely in the arm. What would you do?"

"I'd give him some brandy," answered the man.

The doctor, wishing to give him a second chance, said, "And what if you hadn't any brandy available?"

The man thought a moment, "Then I'd promise him some."

613. A bartender looked up and saw a gorilla walk in the door. As he flattened himself against the back of the bar in horror, the gorilla put a $10 bill on the bar and ordered a martini. The bartender fled to the back room in a panic. "There's a live gorilla in the bar," he stammered to his boss. "He just put a $10 bill on the bar and ordered a martini."

"Serve him," said the boss, "and give him $1 in change. After all, he's a gorilla, what does he know?"

The bartender served the martini and put down $1 in change. As the gorilla sipped the drink, the bartender said, "You know, we don't get too many gorillas in here."

To this the gorilla replied, "I'm not surprised at $9 a drink."

614. "The last time I met you," said the social worker, "you made me very happy because you were sober. Today you have made me unhappy because you are intoxicated."

"True," replied the old soak with a beaming smile, "but today's MY turn to be happy."

615. They asked one guy to leave the bar last night. Claimed he was getting ahead of the ice machine.

616. "I left a bottle of Scotch on the train this morning," Jarvis told an acquaintance as they boarded the 5:15 for home.

"Was it turned in at the lost and found department?" queried his traveling companion.

"No," was Jarvis' glum reply, "but the fellow who found it was."

617. Despite the high prices for whiskey, a 75¢ drink is still available in the mountains of North Carolina . . . according to a recent autopsy.

618. A drunk stood looking at the reflection of the moon in a pool of water on the sidewalk. After staring at it for a while, he stopped a fellow and said, "Hey, is that the moon down there?"

The guy said, "Yeah, it sure is."

The drunk said, "Well, how the heck did I get way up here?"

619.   I tried the Drinking Man's Diet, but it was a disaster. I lost six pounds and three weekends.

620.   If it wasn't for olives in the martinis, he'd starve to death.

621.   He's thinking of quitting drinking. He's beginning to see the handwriting on the floor.

622.   A drunk, hanging on a parking meter, was approached by a sweet old lady who asked, "My good man, why don't you take a bus home?"

"Schno use," he replied, "my wife'd never lemme bring it in the house."

623.   Two drunks were weaving along the railroad tracks. One said, "I never saw so many steps in my life."

The other said, "It's not the steps that bother me; it's the low railing."

624.   The police found a fellow laying in the middle of the road. He had a bracelet on his arm with writing on it. It read: "If you find me unconscious, do not give me insulin. I am drunk."

625.   "All right," said the doctor, "now stretch your hands out in front of you." He was startled to see that his patient's hands trembled violently.

"Good Lord!" he said. "How much do you drink?"

"Not very much," admitted the patient. "I spill most of it."

626.   I don't mean to imply he drinks too much . . . but he's considered the Bourbonic Plague.

627.   That boy drinks like he expects Prohibition to come back on Thursday.

628.   That fellow drinks so much he's listed in Booze Who.

629.   That boy wasn't born . . . he was squeezed out of a bar rag.

630.   I don't mean to imply that he's a drunk, but he drinks like Jack Daniels needs his bottle back.

631.   Doctor: "I can't quite diagnose your trouble. I think it must be the drinking."

Patient: "Okay, Doc, I'll come back when you're sober."

632.   One drinking buddy to another: "A few drinks of that and you're nine feet tall and bulletproof."

633.   "Staggers" quit drinking. The first night he came home sober, his dog bit him. He didn't recognize the scent.

634. Show me a guy with a few drinks under his belt and I'll show you a guy with soggy shorts.

635. The tender young love of a beautiful girl
And the love of a strong young man,
And the love of a mother for her child
Have gone on since time began.

But the greatest love, the love of love,
Even greater than that of a mother,
Is the all consuming, infinite love
Of one Irish drunk for another.

636. I'm not saying he drinks a lot, but his idea of frozen food is bourbon on the rocks.

637. A guy who lives down the street used to drink two six-packs a day, but he quit when he had a spinal tap, and it had a head on it.

Driving

638. Bumper Snicker: "If you don't like my driving, stay off the sidewalk."

639. A guy whose wife threatened to slaughter him if he ever again called her a back-seat driver now refers to her as the "Chairperson of the Steering Committee."

640. Nothing confuses a person more than driving behind a teenager who does everything right.

641. I'll never forget the time I gave my 16-year-old driving lessons. It was like being navigator to a kamikaze pilot.

642. "My wife drives like lightning," said the first fellow.
"A fast driver?" asked his friend.
"No," said the fellow, "she hits trees."

643. The Sunday School teacher was describing how Lot's wife looked back and turned into a pillar of salt when little Cindy interrupted. "My mother looked back once while she was driving," she announced triumphantly, "and she turned into a telephone pole."

644. Little boy: "Dad, I wish you would let Mom drive. It's more exciting."

645. If you go by the book, the shortest distance between two points is a straight line; if you go by car, it's under construction!

646. Tailgaters make me mad. Look how close that idiot is driving ahead of me.

647. The trouble with a lot of Sunday drivers is that they don't drive any better during the week.

648. A man unexpectedly found himself at the Pearly Gates and asked St. Peter, "How did I get here?"

"Don't you remember?" St. Peter replied gently. "Your wife said, 'Be an angel and let me drive.'"

649. If your teenager wants to learn to drive, don't stand in his way.

650. "With all those bandages you got, you seem to have had a serious accident."

"Yes, I tried to climb a tree in my car."

"What did you do that for?"

"Just to oblige a lady who was driving another car. She wanted to use the road."

651. A woman explained that she flunked her driver's test because she couldn't do that thing called "paralyzed parking."

652. Drive as if you were early for an appointment with the IRS.

653. Drive like hell . . . and you'll get there.

654. I can't understand why motorists wear safety belts, when it's the pedestrians who aren't safe.

655. Mother of teenager: My 16-year-old just got his license and can drive as well as his father or I . . . and he can do it on either side of the road.

656. A lady from the South was riding in a taxicab in New York when the driver slowed up a little to miss a pedestrian. Apparently, figuring that his unusual courtesy called for an explanation, he turned to the passenger to explain. "If you hit 'em," the cabby announced, "you've gotta fill out a report."

657. When she went to driving school, she was so bad they had to hire a guy to sit in the back seat as a witness.

Economy

658. Some economists claim that women's hemlines go up when prices rise. This is a trend that bears watching.

659. Recession is when we have no money in the wallet; depression is when we also owe money on the wallet.

660. A student says his economics teacher was explaining some facts of monetary life to the class. "The tighter the money," said the professor, "the higher the interest." Then he added, "Just like jeans."

661. I'm classified as Middle Income/Upper Outgo bracket.

662. Economists are finding out that getting the economy straightened out is about as easy as putting socks on an octopus.

663. Only one man in the world understands the U.S. monetary system, and he's always standing next to you at a bar.

664. A study of economics usually reveals that the best time to buy anything was last year.

665. The secret of economy is to live as cheaply the first few days after payday as you lived the last few days before.

666. Isn't it strange? The same people who laugh at Gypsy fortune-tellers take economists seriously.

667. Prosperity: This is the time you are annoyed because the dog and cat won't eat whatever canned dog and cat food you buy for them.

Recession: This is the time you are secretly delighted that the dog and cat won't eat the canned food and you hope they remain finicky until the party in power gets out of office.

Depression: This is the time you begin to look thoughtfully at the dog and cat.

668. "You're going to have to be more economical. Do you know what being economical means?" said the father to his 6-year-old daughter.

"Yes," she said sullenly, "that means spending money without getting any fun out of it."

669. Well, here's the latest economic forecast: "We're starting to see light at the end of the gangplank." DOUG GAMBLE

670. Being a forecast economist is like searching in a dark alley at midnight for a black cat that isn't there—shouting all the while: "I've got it! I've got it!"

Electricity

671. First thing you learn in electrician school: If you wet your finger and stick it in a socket, you can set fire to your underwear.

672. If you are yearning for the good old days, just turn off the air conditioning.

673. Tip to homeowners: "Never hire an electrician with scorched eyebrows."

674. The local editor was talking to a class of bright elementary students. He declared with pride, "Our newspaper gives complete coverage."

In the question-and-answer period, a youngster asked, "What do you mean by complete coverage?"

The editor explained, "If a storm knocks down a power line and no one knows whether the wire is live, we send two reporters, one to touch the wire and the other to write the story. That, young man, is complete coverage."

675. It takes two bureaucrats to install a light bulb. One to insert it and one to screw it up.

676. During the power failure, he complained of having gotten stuck for hours on the escalator.

677. A downtown worker arrived home a couple of hours later than usual, tired, and hungry. He couldn't believe his eyes when he noticed his wife hadn't even started dinner. There'd been a thunderstorm, she explained. The electricity went off.

"We have a gas stove," he reminded her.

"Yes," she said, "but the can opener is electric."

678. We had a power failure last night. My wife lost her voice.

679. My electricity bill is very low. I have this one long extension cord . . . it runs from my house to George's outside outlet next door.

680. There is a new electronic game out called "Public Utility." Turn on a switch and it asks for a rate increase.

681. During an electrical storm lightening hit the house, shattering light bulbs and blowing out the electric wiring in the room air conditioner.

The man and his wife were standing in the room, looking at the smoke coming from the air conditioner, wondering what to do next.

Then his background as an administrator surfaced. He told his wife: "Touch it and see if it shocks you."

682. Sign at a generating station: "Touching Overhead Wires Will Result In Instant Death. Anyone Touching Them Will Be Prosecuted."

683. The light bulb that goes out the most often will be the one you can't reach.

Enemies

684. Love your enemies . . . It'll drive them nuts.

685. They say he doesn't have an enemy in the world. But he's making progress. None of his friends like him.

686. There's an old story about a powerful Shogun who saw one of his Samurai coming up the road. The Samurai was bloodied, battered, and beaten. The Shogun said, "My good man, what has happened to you?"

The Samurai answered, "Oh, my Lord, I have been robbing and killing your enemies to the East."

"But," said the Shogun, "I have no enemies to the East."

The Samurai paused for a moment and then said, "You do now."

687. A couple went to a marriage counselor. The counselor asked, "Don't you young people have anything in common?"

"Yes, we do," said the husband. "We hate each other's guts."

688. A way to drive your enemies crazy: "Send them a telegram and on top put 'Page 2.' "

689. A reporter was interviewing an old man who was celebrating his 100th birthday. "What are you most proud of?" he asked.

"Well," said the man, "I've lived 100 years and haven't an enemy in the world."

"What a beautiful thought. How truly inspirational," commented the reporter.

"Yep," added the centenarian, "outlived ever dang one of 'em."

690. Where did a soldier in Gaul place the catapult? Just a stone's throw from the enemy.

691. Always forgive your enemies; nothing annoys them so much.
OSCAR WILDE

692. An old Chinese proverb says, "If thine enemy has wronged thee, buy each of his children a drum."

Energy

693. They may have cars in the near future that run on solar energy. A guy's going to feel pretty stupid the first time he drives a girl to the lake and tries to convince her his car is out of sun.

694. Some guy claims he's learned to turn chickens into gas. I mean you'd look pretty dumb walking down the street carrying a 10-gallon chicken.

695. There are a lot of folks that can't understand how we ran out of oil here in the U.S. Well, here's the answer. It's simple . . . nobody bothered to check the oil. Didn't know we were getting low. And, of course, the reason for that is geographical. All the oil is in Texas and Oklahoma and all the dipsticks are in Washington, D.C.

696. "Is the jogging craze Mother Nature's way of preparing us for another gas shortage?"

697. There's a motorbike that runs on laughing gas—it's a Yamaha-ha-ha.

698. My wife went into a gas station the other day and asked for $5 worth. "Where you want it?" the attendant asked, "behind the ear or on your wrists?"

699. If God had wanted us to have gasoline, He would not have created the Department of Energy.

700. What America needs right now is a compact car which, in heavy traffic, will run on the fumes from other cars.

701. These days, by the time you get it all together, there's no gas to take it anywhere.

702. One of the new cars claims it gets such fantastic mileage they list the gas tank as optional.

703. I just found a gasoline substitute that really works! It's called feet.

Exercise

704. Everybody is trying some sort of physical fitness program. I know a wealthy guy in Texas who did not have the time to go on a fifty-mile hike, so he sent his butler. HENNY YOUNGMAN

705. "Have you ever tried jogging?"
"Heck, no! When I die I wanna be sick."

706. One fellow said he'd be willing to take a bike to work, but he can't get it into his Volkswagen.

707. You almost have to be a muscle-bound weight lifter to pick up either my wife . . . or her purse.

708. "The doctor said jogging would add years to my life," a middle-aged man said, "and he's right, I've been jogging for a week now and already I feel 10 years older!"

709. You've reached middle age when your weight lifting consists of standing up.

710. I have a brother-in-law who's so lazy, he teaches trampoline in a nursing home.

711. Everyone is into fitness these days. A friend took up weightlifting, got the broad shoulders, huge arms, muscular legs, rippling chest . . . she looks awful.

712. I can do anything today I could do on my 21st birthday. This gives you an idea of the ridiculous shape I was in when I was 21.

713. I joined a health spa. They said, "Come on down and bring some loose fitting clothes."
I said, "If I had any loose fitting clothes, I wouldn't need to join your health spa."

714. I believe in exercise. I do 45 minutes of exercise every morning, unless I do them very fast, then it takes less time.

715. If it weren't for giving directions, my mother-in-law wouldn't get any exercise at all.

716. Joggers make dependable husbands. In those outfits they wear, home is the only place they can go.

Experts

717. A man was drowned in the Jamestown Flood and went to heaven. St. Peter was directing the activities and explained, "Each Friday we have a get-together for the new members. To break the ice, every new member makes a speech to all the others here, on any subject desired."
"Well," said the man from Jamestown, "I think I'll talk on the Jamestown flood. That was some flood and I believe you would agree unequivocably that I'm certainly an expert on that subject."

Joe Griffith poses with Brice Likly, a member of the U.S. Ski team. Joe emceed the fund raiser for the U.S. Olympic Ski team.

"Well, that's good," said St. Peter, "but I better warn you. Noah will be in the audience."

718.   An expert is someone who makes his or her mistakes in private.

719.   Just think, if you follow the advice of the health experts and put on a clean pair of socks each morning, by the end of a week, you won't be able to get your shoes on.

720.   Psychiatric experts tell us that one out of every four Americans is mentally ill. Check your three closest friends. If they seem all right, you're the one.

721.   The government experts report that 20% of the population

is trying to live within their means. What are they trying to do—mess up our economic recovery?

722.   Experts who say we spend more for alcohol than for education just don't realize the things you can learn at a beer joint!

723.   Statistical experts show that YMCA members have 1.3 children, while YWCA members have 1.7 . . . which merely goes to show that women have .4 more children than men.

724.   The word "exspert" should be analyzed carefully. "Ex" means a has-been and "spert" is little better than a drip.

725.   An expert is someone who is called in at the last minute to share the blame.

Farmers

726.   The farmer down the road is such a hick that when he gets in the elevator and pushes a button, he waits for gum.

727.   The reason he hates city people is because he fertilized his yard with sewage sludge and his house disappeared under 12 tons of tomato plants.

728.   A hardware merchant, doing business in the middle of a drought stricken region, became curious when, week after week, the same farmer came in and bought several hammers. He asked for an explanation. "Oh," said the farmer, "I'm selling the hammers to the folks in my neighborhood for one dollar apiece."

But that doesn't make sense," protested the merchant. "You are paying me $1.50 each for the hammers."

"I know," admitted the farmer, "but it sure beats farming!"

729.   Two veteran farmers were being interviewed by a local newscaster. At the end of his interviewing, he posed this question to each: "What would you do if you were to inherit a million dollars tomorrow?"

The first allowed as how he'd quit working at once, fish, take life easy, and live off the income from his windfall. The second scratched his head, thought awhile, and answered, "I reckon I'd just keep on farming, 'til it was all gone."

730.   Q—On the livestock reports on radio, what does it mean when they say "slaughter cows are weak to steady?"

A—This means that some cows took it better than others.

731.   A motorist, after being bogged down in a muddy road, paid

a passing farmer $20 to pull him out with his tractor. After he was back on dry ground, he said to the farmer, "At those prices, I should think you would be pulling people out of the mud night and day."

"Can't," replied the farmer. "At night, I haul water for that there mud hole."

732.   What this country really needs is a seed catalog that would pass a polygraph test.

733.   Farmer (plowing with one mule): "Giddap, Pete! Giddap, Barney! Giddap, Johnny! Giddap, Tom!"

Stranger: "How many names does that mule have, anyway?"

Farmer: "Only one. His name is Pete, but he don't know his own strength, so I put blinders on him, yell a lot of names at him, and he thinks three other mules are helping him."

734.   What's the definition of a gentleman farmer? He's the one with white sidewalls on his manure spreader.

735.   A brand-new Ag graduate tried raising experimental flax on his father's farm. He succeeded, made linen from the flax, made a tablecloth from the linen, and entered the tablecloth in the local county fair.

"Did you make this yourself?" asked a tourist visiting the fair.

"Yes, I grew it myself."

"Oh, how remarkable," exclaimed the woman, evidently with no idea how tablecloths came into being. "How did you ever do it?"

The neophyte farmer motioned her to come closer, then whispered, "I planted a little napkin."

736.   Farming makes a Las Vegas crap table look like a guaranteed annual income.

737.   The Washington representative was sent out by the Farm Bureau to inspect some Midwestern farms. He knew nothing whatever about animals, and when he came across his first goat he just didn't know what it was. He wired his chief in Washington: "Have found an animal with a sad face, a long beak, chin whiskers, a skinny frame, and a bare backside. What is it?"

The reply came at once: "Animal you describe is a farmer. Be nice to it. It votes!"

738.   Two farmers were always trying to outdo each other regarding crops. One morning the first farmer said to his boy: "Go over to

Smith's and borrow his crosscut saw for me. Tell him I want to cut up a pumpkin."

On returning, the boy said: "Mr. Smith said he can't let you have the saw until this afternoon. He's halfway through a potato."

739.   Sign seen in front of an Oklahoma farm: "Bought and prayed for."

740.   Ad in paper: "Wife wanted, must have farm experience and own tractor. Please send picture of tractor."

Fashion

741.   It shows you how times have changed . . . On July 4, 1776, a group of men wearing wigs, ruffled shirts, silk stockings, and tight pants met in Philadelphia and it was called Independence Day. In San Francisco, it'd be called Saturday night.

742.   Great clothing salesman . . . he handed me a pair of those skinny legged pants the college kids wear and said, "It'll give you that sexy, ready-to-deliver look." He was right. I look like a stork!

743.   I sat next to this interesting brunette on an airplane a month or so ago. First thing I noticed about her was that she wore a fashionably large diamond on a gold necklace. The way it sparkled, I could tell it was genuine. Later, we got to talking, and she introduced herself as Mrs. Connor. I finally got up the nerve to ask her about the stone. "That's one of the biggest diamonds I ever saw," I told her. "Is it one of the big famous ones?"

"Well, it's not the Hope diamond," Mrs. Connor assured me, "but unfortunately, it does carry a horrible curse."

"What is it?" I asked.

"Mr. Connor."

744.   Many a woman shows a lot of style, and many a style shows a lot of woman.

745.   The latest swimsuit fashions are the bare minimum of material designed to show the bare maximum.

746.   A low neckline is about the only thing a man will approve of and look down on at the same time.

747.   "Peekaboo gown" is a dress that isn't all there for women who are.

748. A man fifty years old must feel quite reckless
To put on a flowered silk shirt and a neckless.

749. Fashion tips for the redneck:
Always buy your slacks to fit properly, so when you bend over, people won't be able to see the tops of your underwear.
Polyester anything is out, except for bingo night at the Lodge.
Don't wear bow ties if you are fat or if you have a square head.
Never buy pants that do not have back pockets. (See fruitcakes and movie stars.)
Socks should always match, or at least be the same length.
If you run across a shirt with pictures of exotic birds on it, buy two. I'll take your extra.

750. Some women's fashions remind me of a barbed wire fence: They appear to protect the property without obstructing the view.

751. The daily news is too depressing. So I turned to the fashion section where I thought I'd find something more cheerful. There I noted that there will be little change in pockets next year!

752. I know a man who is so old that he has lived through three revivals of the wide necktie.

Fathers

753. Did you hear the story about the two little boys who met at school and one kid turned to the other and said, "My father can lick your father." To which the other kid answered, "Don't be ridiculous. My father IS your father."

754. Two fathers of teenaged daughters were talking in their car pool. "What is the tactful way for a girl's father to let her boyfriend know it's time to leave?" asked one.
"The way I do it," said his friend, "is to casually walk into the room and set off an insect bomb."

755. A father is a banker provided by nature.

756. Just when you realize your own father was right, your own son says you're wrong.

757. "It's one o'clock in the morning," the angry father said to the young fellow keeping his daughter company. "Do you think you can stay here all night?"
"Gee, sir, I don't know," he replied. "I'll call home and ask."

758. My father's tip for the day: "Keep your nose to the grindstone,

your two feet on the ground . . . and you'll not only wear off your nose, but you've have a heck of a time getting your pants off.

759.   After waiting a long time for a man to get through with the phone directory, a frustrated waiter offered to help him find the number he wanted. "No thanks," he replied, "I'm just looking for a nice name for my baby."

760.   First father: "My three boys stick together. When one gets into trouble, neither of the other two will tell on him."
    Second father: "Then how do you find out which one to punish?"
    First father: "That's simple. I send all three to bed without supper. The next morning I spank the one with the black eye."

761.   My dad never did really like me much. He used to encourage me to practice my electric guitar . . . while I was showering.

762.   The fathers were talking and one said, "I finally taught my son the value of a dollar. So now he wants his allowance in Swiss francs."

763.   Oscar has a problem at his house. "I find it very difficult," he reports, "for a 5-foot, 10-inch father to get through to a 6-foot, 4-inch teenage son about the nutritional deficiencies of junk food."

764.   Triumphant father to mother watching teenage son mow the lawn: "I told him I lost the car keys in the grass."

765.   The father of new identical twins grew so disgusted with people making goo-goo eyes at the babies that he developed a perfect answer to the question, "Are they twins?" He would reply: "No, they're not twins. I have two wives."

766.   A Miami Beach doctor who has eight kids does all the mechanical work on the family cars. A neighbor asked him if he really enjoyed tinkering with the engines. He said, "No, but with eight kids and a wife, the only place I can be alone is under the car."

767.   The youngsters next door haven't been allowed to have jelly since the time their father went to work one morning with a doorknob in his hand.

768.   A fellow was lecturing his teenage son the other day and told him, "You've got to learn to take criticism. After all, you're going to be a husband and a father some day."

769.   "Maybe you don't like my boyfriend," said the daughter to her father, "but you notice he calls for me in a $20,000 sports car!"

"That's nothing," replied the father, "I used to take your mother out in a $35,000 bus!"

770. A six-year-old was telling her friends how to behave at her birthday party, which her father planned to host and chaperone. "He's okay if you do what he tells you and when he hollers at you to sit down, you'd better not wait 'til you can find a chair."

771. I finally found one thing I have in common with my son. He listens to rock groups, and I listen to economists—and neither one of us understands a word they're saying.

772. A teenager called home late at night. When his father answered the phone, the boy said, "Hi, Dad. Did I wake you up?"
Father said, "No, do you want to call back later?"

773. Meeting at lunch, two businessmen began to talk about world problems, high taxes, the cost of living, and finally their families. "I have 6 boys," one of them said proudly.
"That's a nice family," sighed the other man. "I wish to heaven I had six children."
"Don't you have any children?" the proud father asked with a touch of sympathy in his voice.
"Oh, yes," sighed the second man. "Twelve."

774. A father was upset because his wife gave permission for their 8th grade daughter to have a date for a school party. Naturally, he went around making noises as an irate father is wont to do. When the boy showed up, a full six-feet tall in height, good old dad went into orbit. He fumed and foamed all evening, uttering dire warnings to his wife about what he'd do "if anything happens." Finally, on the dot of 9:30 P.M., when the young Cinderella had been told to be home, there was a telephone call. Both mother and father raced to answer it. Dad won. "Daddy," the daughter blurted, "the positively worst thing has happened!"
"What did he do?" the father shouted.
"You'll have to come and get me," the daughter said. "His mother came and got him at 9 o'clock."

775. Two little girls were talking about Sunday school. "Do you believe in the devil?" one asked the other.
"Not really," the other little girl said. "It's just like Santa Claus and the Easter Bunny. It's your father."

776. Dealer: "I can let you have this car, complete with air conditioning, full power, and radio for $8,777."

Father of two teenagers: "Take out the radio and I'll give you $9,000."

Fire

777. You can figure your youth is gone beyond all doubt when you've got money to burn and the fire's gone out.

778. Yes, Tom is burning the candle at both ends, but his only worry at the moment is where to get more wax.

779. At his birthday, he went to blow out the candles on the cake and the heat drove him back.

780. The customer in the New Orleans restaurant was loud and rude. "What do you have to do to get a glass of water around this dump?"

A little old lady at the next table leaned over and said sweetly, "Why not try setting yourself on fire?"

781. It won't be long until we have money to burn. It's almost cheaper than fuel right now.

782. He had his car insured against fire and they tried to sell him some theft coverage, too. "That would be a waste of money," he said. "Who's going to steal a burning car?"

783. I have a friend who is so sneaky. He's the type who'll sneak into your bedroom, pull out the string on your pajama pants and then yell fire.

784. I won't say how old she is, but she had a hot flash that was so intense that it set her dress on fire.

785. Not all of his inventions turn out so well. He burned himself badly trying to invent the laser toilet.

786. A frantic caller called the fire house late at night. "Help, my house is on fire. Flames are everywhere!"

The chief said, "Have you put water on it?"

"Yes, but the fire is getting worse."

"Then there's no use in us coming over. That's all we'd do."

787. Old age is nice. That's the time of life when friends come to your birthday party just to stand around the cake and get warm.

788. A drunk staggered up to a hotel desk late one night and demanded another room.

"But you have the best room in the house, sir," answered the clerk.

"I don't care," said the drunk. "I want another room and I want it quick."

You can't argue with a drunk, so the clerk turned to the bellboy and said, "Move the gentleman out of 506 and put him in 508 right away."

Satisfied, the drunk started toward the elevator without a hint of explanation.

"Would you mind telling me, sir, why you don't like 506?" called the clerk curiously.

"It's on fire."

789.   I resent the implication that I was drunk and set the bed on fire. That bed was on fire when I got in it.

Fishing

790.   A new arrival was stopped at the pearly gates. "I'm sorry," explained St. Peter, "but you told too many lies during your time on earth. I'm afraid you'll have to go to you know where."

"Ah, come on now, St. Peter," begged the newly arrived one. "Have a heart. After all, you were once a fisherman yourself."

791.   One sad fishing story concerns a local sport who caught a 60-pound marlin off the coast of Florida and dislocated both shoulders describing it.

792.   A city man was trying to fish a small mountain stream but was having no luck at all. Just as he was about to give up for the day, a mountaineer came by. "What are you usin' fer bait?" he asked. The angler showed the man his minnows. Whereupon the native pulled a bottle of corn liquor from his pocket and poured a cupful or so into the minnow bucket. Then he took one of the minnows and put it on the fisherman's hook. "Now try it," he advised. Almost immediately, the fisherman felt a hard tug on his line. After a struggle that lasted fifteen minutes, the angler landed a 17-pound bass. But the fish wasn't on the hook; the minnow had the huge bass by the throat.

793.   A fellow was fishing in Eagle Lake. Drifting slowly, dragging his hand in the water. Suddenly, his wedding ring slipped from his hand and sank rapidly in the deep water.

Three years later, he went back and caught a tub full of fish in the same spot. At home, he was cleaning the fish in the kitchen and he cut into something hard. There was no need to ask. He knew immediately what it was. It was his thumb. Took six stitches to close it up.

794. I went fishing back in one of the stumpy bays of Lake Alice the other evening—one of those quiet evenings when hardly a ripple blemished the surface of the water. The fishing was slow, but I was enjoying the quiet and watching all of nature flourishing around me.

After half an hour or so, I noticed considerable activity near the shore. On the bank was a large tree with limbs that hung far out over the water and one reached very near a stump.

From that limb, a small gray squirrel was desperately trying to snatch something off the stump. Looking closer, I saw two large nuts lying on the stump and the squirrel obviously had a powerful hunger.

For nearly a quarter of an hour, I watched the squirrel try nearly every acrobatic gyration in a futile effort to reach the nuts. With one last mighty lunge, he tried to shake the limb to within reach of the nuts, but, unfortunately, he lost his grip on the slender twig and fell into the lake.

Instantly, there was a huge splash and the biggest catfish I've ever seen grabbed the squirrel and swallowed it in one swift gulp. Somewhat shaken, I sat pondering the old adage that, in nature, only the strongest survive and how the poor squirrel had only wanted to eat those two nuts—now at the bottom of the lake—and meant no harm to anyone.

The lake had returned to its glassy serenity when, to my amazement, the catfish rose up out of the water and put two nuts back on the stump. . . .

795. The main reason that comparatively few females go fishing is that women have more important things to lie about.

796. When three friends went fishing, they took along a cooler full of beer and proceeded to take a blood oath among themselves that they would not pop a top until they caught a fish. Thirty minutes later, they hadn't even had a nibble. But, there were nine IOU's in the cooler.

797. It's that time of year when fishermen get that faraway lake in their eyes.

798. Junior planned to go fishing until his mother insisted he take his little sister along. "No," Junior told her. "The last time she tagged along, I didn't catch any fish."

"I'm sure she'll keep quiet this time," Mother said.

"It wasn't the noise," said Junior. "She ate all the bait."

799. Since the earth's surface is one-quarter land and three-quarters water, it seems obvious that we are intended to spend three times longer fishing than mowing the lawn.

800. "Wait'll you see the big bass I caught!" exulted the happy angler. "It's a beauty! But, honey, although the fishing trip was fun, I really missed you. I'm so glad to be back home. I'm just not happy when I'm away from you, sweetheart."

The wife replied: "I'm not cleaning that fish."

801. Sunday school teacher: "Do you suppose Noah did a lot of fishing?"

Six-year-old: "What? With only two worms?"

802. A man spent two weeks fishing at an expensive resort and didn't get a bite. But on the last day of his vacation, he caught one fish. "See that fish," he said to a bystander, "it cost me $1,000."

"Ain't you lucky," said the bystander, "that you didn't catch two."

803. People living together without getting married is particularly disturbing to the guy who has just been arrested for fishing without a license.

804. There were two Sunday fishermen who heard bells ringing in the distance. One said, "You know, Al, we really ought to be in church."

Al rebaited his hook and answered, "Well, I couldn't go anyway; my wife is sick."

Food

805. Catholics have adopted some protestant ways. They can eat steak on Friday. If Friday is payday.

806. How did the guy who invented cottage cheese know when he was finished?

807. Have you ever tasted eggnog? It's like drinking milk from a smashed cow.

808. No man is lonely while eating spaghetti. It requires so much attention.

809. The eggplant diet. First you plant an egg. Whatever comes up, you can eat.

810. I think of a grapefruit as a lemon that had a chance and took it.

811. If Mother Nature had provided Coca-Cola as a natural drink, kids would go out and buy water.

812. The Saturday night supper consisted of cold cuts and the wife asked, "How do you like the potato salad?"

He said, "Delicious. It tastes like you bought it yourself."

813. You are what you eat. For example, if you eat garlic, you're apt to be a hermit.

814. Use your imagination. Don't think of it as hamburger meat, but as filet mignon that has come unglued!

815. There are 49 different kinds of food mentioned in the Bible. It will probably come as a shock to some teenagers that the pizza isn't one of them.

Football

816. We have a very ethical football recruiting program. We don't believe in buying football players. All we give is room, board, and $300 a week for books.

817. Football coach, on job security: "I have a lifetime contract. That means I can't be fired during the third quarter if we're ahead and moving the ball."

818. Our football team is having a drug problem this year, too. Every time they go on the field, they get drug from one end to the other.

819. "I'd love to come to the university and play for you," says the huge tackle.

"What's your I.Q.?" the coach asked.

"Perfect," was the immediate response. "20–20."

820. My husband doesn't really enjoy football. He just wants to see somebody getting $250,000 a year get smeared.

821. Football coach on his favorite play: "It's the one where the player tosses the ball back to the official after scoring a touchdown."

822. Former University of Texas football coach says he never worried about running out of timeouts during a game. He kept a dog on the bench and turned him loose if and when needed.

823. A football fan is a guy who yells at the quarterback for not being able to pinpoint a receiver 46 yards downfield, and then can't even find his own car in the parking lot after the game.

824.   One of the paradoxes of football fans: "They race to the stadium in order to get a good seat . . . and then stand up during the whole game."

825.   During a championship game, one All American tackle was hit and his glass eye was knocked out. The referee saw it "looking at him" from the Astroturf, picked it up, and held it while the doctor revived the tackle. After coming to, the tackle took his eye back from the ref, dropped it in a bucket of water, swirled it around, and slapped it back in his head. The ref said, "Golly, you got a lot of guts. What would you do if your other eye were injured?"

   The tackle didn't even crack a smile. He said, "I'd become a referee, just like you."

826.   Following a 34–27 loss to Cleveland, the Tampa Bay coach was asked about what he thought of his team's execution: "I think it's a good idea."

827.   Football isn't complicated. You push. The other team pushes back. The one that pushes hardest wins.   BUM PHILLIPS

828.   A small time football coach with a reputation for optimism came into the locker room to give his team a pregame pep talk. "All right, boys," he cried cheerfully, "here we are, unbeaten, untied, and unscored upon—and ready for the first game of the season!"

829.   After a resounding defeat, the coach of a professional football team said, "What we need is a 5' 6", 130 lb. fullback . . . because that's the biggest hole our offensive line makes."

830.   Grouch: "I hear that the football coach gets 5 times as much salary as the Greek professor. Isn't that quite a discrepancy?"

   Student: "Oh, I dunno. Did you ever hear 70,000 people cheering a Greek recitation?"

831.   The football coach recalled the exceptionally dumb tackle he had on his squad. Once, he named the guy Game Captain, hoping to inspire him. The tackle won the toss and didn't know what decision to make. He raced over to the coach and said, "Coach, nobody will tell me what to do."

   "Tell you what," the coach replied. "Go back and ask the referee to toss again. Maybe this time you'll lose."

832.   "What position does your son play on the football team, Mrs. Jones?"

"I'm not sure," replied Mrs. Jones, "but I think he's one of the drawbacks."

833. Beauty plus brains it did not take to be an Atlanta Falcon cheerleader. One young miss, describing her qualifications, proudly said, "I've spent a lot of time overseas in Japan and Montana."

834. A triple-threat in pro football today is the star who is equally at home running, passing, or endorsing products.

835. In the midst of a deluge of snow and rain, the football captain won the toss and bitterly stared out over the field that was covered with cold, gray slush.

"Do we have to play football in that fluid?" he demanded.

"Yes," was the implacable reply. "Which end do you want?"

"Well," said the player, "We'll kick with the tide."

836. A minister stopped John McKay, coach of the Tampa Bay Bucs, and said sternly, "Sir, don't you know that it is a sin to play football on Sunday?"

"Well," said McKay glumly, "the way the Bucs are playing, it sure is."

837. Two armchair quarterbacks were discussing how much their football watching on TV irritated their wives.

"My wife won't say much if I watch just one game on Sunday, but if I watch two, she hits the ceiling!" said one guy.

"Mine, too! Say, what's her hang time?"

838. Fans like to look up to the football coaches—either putting them on a pedestal or a scaffold. DEL BIXLER

839. A ticket scalper was trying to buy a ticket off a guy who had two 50-yard-line seats. The scalper asked, "Is your wife with you?"

"Oh, no," was the reply.

"Well, listen. I'll give you $150 for that extra ticket of yours."

"No way," the guy said. "I'm gonna go to that game and I'm gonna have a few drinks and I'm gonna yell like hell. And then I'm gonna have a few more drinks. And then I'm probably gonna get into a fight. And then they're gonna come and get me and throw me out of the stadium. And then I'm gonna need this extra ticket to get back in." JAMES DENT

840. The shivering wife was sitting in the stands with the screaming football maniacs all around her: "Tell me again how much fun we're having," she said to her husband. "I keep forgetting."

Friends

841. A woman telephoned a friend. "How are you, dear?" she asked.

"Simply awful," came the reply. "My migraine headache is back, my feet are killing me, my back is almost breaking in two, the ironing is piled to the ceiling, the house is a mess, and the children are driving me out of my mind."

"Now you listen to me," said the friend on the other end of the line. "You just go and lie down and rest. I'll be right over and cook lunch for you and the children, get your ironing done, whisk up the house a bit, and watch the children while you get a bit of rest. By the way, how is John?"

"John?" queried the complaining housewife.

"Yes, John," said the caller. "John your husband."

"My husband's name isn't John."

"My gosh," gasped the caller, "I must have the wrong number."

There was a long, stunned silence on the line. "Then you aren't going to come over?" asked the woman.

842. You and your friend are walking in the woods and your friend is bitten by a rattlesnake. What should you do? . . . Find another friend.

843. Charlie went back to his 25th high school reunion. He ran up to the first person he saw, slapped him on the back and said, "Jimmy Wexler, you ol' sunavagun. Look at ya'. You used to be a real skinny fellow; now your nice an' fat. You had a head full of hair; now you're bald as a cue ball."

The man said, "Friend, I'm not Jimmy Wexler. My name is Lonnie Ford."

Charlie said, "I'll be doggone. You even went and changed your name!"

844. You are the kind of friend I would never lie about. The truth is bad enough.

845. He was talking about one of his friends. "Every morning at 5 A.M., he jumps up, throws wide his bedroom window . . . and climbs in."

846. Summer Camp letter:

Dear Mom and Dad:

Here are the names of my best friends at camp. Steve, Carl, Roger, Howard, Michael, Jeffery, and Paul.

Your son, Louis.

P.S.: Please rip up the list of my best friends that I sent you last week.

847. I'd like to share some very personal things with you to develop a close friendship, to get you on my side, and to make you like me. Then, I'd like to borrow some money from you.

848. My wife and I received a note the other day from an 8-year-old friend. The neatly penned message: "Thank you for coming to my party. Thank you for my present. I have to go to the bathroom now, so goodbye."

849. Why is it your friends try to fix you up with people they wouldn't go out with?

850. Bumper Snicker: "Don't Lend Money To Friends. It Causes Amnesia."

851. For the friend who has everything, give the gift that keeps on giving: a pregnant guinea pig.

852. A patient came into the doctor's office for an examination the other day and, after it was over, the fellow said: "All right, Doc. Now I don't want you to give me a bunch of tongue twisting scientific talk. Just tell me straight out in plain English what my problem is."

"All right," said the physician, "you're fat and you're lazy."

"Fine," said the patient, "now give me the scientific terms so I can tell my friends."

853. We've got our guard up and it's kind of sad. It was different on the old frontier. Everybody was friendly then. If you weren't friendly, they shot you.

Gambling

854. A horse race enthusiast, when asked the results of his afternoon at the track, replied: "I broke even, and oh boy, did I need it!"

855. Walter Winchell is of the belief that the less you bet the more you lose when you win.

856. You can't help but like a good loser—unless you had a bet on him.

857. If the Lord didn't mean for us to gamble, He would never have invented matrimony.

858. Today, when Grandma sits at the spinning wheel, chances are she's visiting Las Vegas.

859. Man at racetrack: "I don't have a cent to bet. My wife blew it all in on the rent."

860. Hear about the tourist vacationing in Las Vegas? He didn't have any money to gamble so he just watched the games and bet mentally. In no time at all, he'd lost his mind.

861. Horse racing enthusiast: "I went to the track on the 11th day of the 11th month," he said, "arriving at 11:00. My son was 11 that day, and the 11th race showed 11 horses. So I bet all my money on the 11th horse on the card."

"And he won?" asked a friend.

"No," the gambler replied sadly, "He came in 11th."

862. My uncle just back from Las Vegas reports, "What a place! You can't beat the sunshine, the climate, or the slot machines!"

863. A friend asked Flossie, the waitress, how she picked a long shot winner. Flossie said, "I just stuck a pin in the paper, and there it was," she replied.

"But yesterday," asked the friend, "how did you get four winners?"

"Oh, I cheated a little," confessed the waitress, "I used a fork."

864. Two men were talking about a friend. "I can't understand why he loses so much money at the racetrack and yet he is so lucky when he plays poker."

"That's easy to understand," his friend said. "They don't let him shuffle the horses at the track."

865. In Las Vegas, money can be lost in more ways than won, yet most of us have two chances of becoming wealthy—slim and none.

866. A priest, a protestant minister, and a rabbi formed a clandestine threesome because they loved to play poker. The mayor of the town in which they lived had just made a promise to clean up gambling in the city. The trio met at the rabbi's house, as usual, feeling that this small infraction of the law need not apply to the clergy since all winnings were donated to some charity.

But somebody tipped off the sheriff who obtained a search warrant, kicked down the door, pistol drawn. Caught all three of them, red-handed, all wearing green eyeshades, cards in hand, money on the table.

The sheriff yelled, "Hold it right there. You're all under arrest. You have the right to remain silent. Anything you say may be used against you in a court of law. I'll now take a statement from each of you."

With that, he turned his pistol on the protestant and asked, "Brother, were you gambling here tonight?"

The preacher thought to himself, "Oh, Lord, forgive this little white lie," and then said, "No, sheriff, I was not gambling here tonight."

The sheriff swung his handgun toward the priest and asked the same question.

The priest thought to himself, "Oh, Lord, forgive me this slight deviation from the truth," and said, "No, sheriff, I was not gambling here tonight."

The lawman trained his pistol on the remaining member and asked, "Rabbi, were you gambling here tonight?"

The rabbi shrugged his shoulders, placed his palms up in front of his chest, and asked, "With who?"

867. The gambling boom in Las Vegas is incredible. One day a man went to the drugstore because he had a headache and wanted to buy some asprin. The clerk said, "Why not make it double or nothing?"

The gambler agreed, made the bet, and lost. He left with two headaches.

868. Sign for state legislators: "Legalize Bingo, Keep Grandmas Off The Street."

869. The trouble with hitting the jackpot in Las Vegas is that it takes so long to put it back in the machine.

Golf

870. A golf pro was approached by two women.

"Do you wish to learn to play golf, ma'am?" he asked one.

"Oh, no," she said. "It's my friend who wants to learn. I learned yesterday."

871. It was the beginning of a beautiful weekend, so the wife decided she would lay down the law immediately. "Listen," she told her husband at breakfast, "don't think you're going to sneak off and play golf and leave me here with all the work."

"Golf is the farthest thing from my mind," the husband protested. "And will you please pass me the putter."

872. The two ladies joined each other at the golf course. One of the gals stepped up to the first tee, pulled back her club, closed her eyes, and swung with all her might. The ball hooked to the right, ricocheted off several trees, took a fantastic bounce, and rolled

into the cup for a hole-in-one. Her companion turned and frowned. "Betty, you sneak," she said coldly, "you've been practicing."

873. "I'd move heaven and earth to break 100," the golfing duffer said as he swung at his ball.

"Concentrate on heaven," pleaded his friend. "You've moved enough earth already!"

874. Rule from a golf league for beginners: "If you have taken 15 strokes on one hole and missed the ball three times, you're allowed to throw it."

875. Golf is a lot of walking, broken up by disappointment and bad arithmetic.

876. Played golf today. Broke 70. That's a lot of clubs to break.

877. In the sports column of the newspaper: "Arnie Palmer is getting ready to putt. Arnie, usually a good putter, seems to be having trouble with his long putts. However, he has no trouble dropping his shorts."

878. A male foursome was being held up by two slow lady players, one of whom was searching in the rough. Growing impatient, one of the men called to the other woman as she rested casually in the middle of the fairway, "Why don't you help your friend look for her ball?"

"Oh, she didn't lose her ball," the woman explained. "She's looking for her club."

879. A fellow says a friend, a perpetual duffer, told him the other day that he had finally had a winning day on the golf course. "Did you break a hundred?" our man asked.

"No," said his friend, "but I found more balls than I lost."

880. "Why so late teeing off?"

"It's Sunday. Tossed a coin between church and golf."

"But why so late?"

"Had to toss 15 times."

881. Four men were enjoying a round of golf. There were two ladies ahead of them, but they never held the foursome up. At least, they didn't until the last hole. As the four men prepared to tee off on 18, they noticed one of the women walking toward the tee, waving them through. As they passed her on the fairway, one of the men asked if she had lost her ball. "No," she answered, "we were talking and forgot to drive."

882.   A dedicated golfing duffer finally made a hole-in-one. He came home and joyfully told his wife about it.

"What's so wonderful about a hole-in-one?" she sneered.

"Let me explain, honey. I usually make double bogeys, and that means on a par three hole I usually make a five—sometimes a six or seven. This time I only took one stroke."

"Then," said she, utterly unimpressed, "why weren't you home earlier for dinner?"   MICK DELANEY

Gossip

883.   Neighbor told woman: "I hear your husband is in the hospital. What happened?" and the other replied, "Knee trouble. I found his secretary sitting on it."

884.   Did you hear about the guy who had a complex since he was kidnapped as a child. After three days, his parents received a ransom note demanding "Expenses Only."

885.   Did you hear about the student who called the library to ask the capital of Alaska, she was told, "Juneau."

"If I knew," she retorted, "I wouldn't be asking you."

886.   Two businessmen were discussing a competitor who had once been an employee of one of them. His ex-boss said, "I happen to know that fellow is a con artist. He's not above lying and stealing when it's to his advantage."

"Do you know him personally?" asked the other businessman.

"Know him! Why, I taught him everything he knows!"

887.   If you can't get folks to listen to you any other way, whisper it.

888.   Two women at a health club noticed a mutual acquaintance across the gym. "Do you believe that vicious rumor that's going round about her?"

"Yes," said the other. "What is it?"

889.   Don't believe any rumor unless you get it from two sources . . . who haven't talked to each other.

890.   Gossip shouldn't be repeated . . . but then, what else is there to do with it?

891.   Overheard in the office coffee shop: "I wouldn't say that he's conceited, but he's absolutely convinced that if he hadn't been born, people would want to know why not."

892. My wife likes to spread her gossip early in the morning before she finds out it's not true.

893. Science may never come up with a better office intercom than the coffee break.

Government

894. A bureaucrat is a man who shoots the bull, passes the buck, and makes seven copies of everything.

895. One midwest state government has this law: "When two trains approach one another on the same track, both shall come to a full stop and neither shall proceed until the other has passed."

896. Many a government official has found it difficult to write out a resignation because his arms were twisted behind his back.

897. A Governmental diplomat is one who can tell you to go to hell so tactfully that you start packing for the trip.

898. The zip code in Washington will be changed to 00000. Nothing there adds up anyhow.

899. I know a guy who just retired from civil service after 40 years. As a kind of surprise, the government gave him a retirement banquet and told him what his job had been.

900. The government has invented a machine that will do the work of five people. It takes ten to operate it.

901. President Reagan on the growing government: "When you get in bed with the Government, you're going to get more than a good night's sleep."

902. Hear about the government official who took an I.Q. test and couldn't spell I.Q.?

903. The tourist insists that a sign atop Hoover Dam, which weighs 12 million tons, reads: "U.S. Government Property. Do Not Remove."

904. Two government employees were surveyed by a third government employee. "What do you do here?"
#1 answered, "I don't do a thing."
#2 wrote, "I help him."
The agent reported that although there was some duplication, these two employees provided a base for the survival of a critically needed job—his own.

905. The salesman waiting in line for his unemployment check complained, "It frightens me sometimes when I realize that this administration with its criminal irresponsibility is my sole means of support."

906. In Washington, they use the Seven Dwarfs approach to government. You go to any government agency and one out of every seven you meet is dopey. JOEY ADAMS

907. Washington is where they do badly that which doesn't need doing at all. MARK RUSSELL

908. The government can't understand how this country could have been formed in 1776 without federal matching funds.

Hair

909. I don't consider baldness a real problem until you have to give up on toupees . . . and go to astroturf.

910. "What's happened to you!" exclaimed my husband one evening when I came into the living room with my head bristling with curlers.
   "I just set my hair," I replied.
   "Well," he asked, "what time does it go off?"

911. Have you ever heard of a teenager talking to his barber? "Take a little off around the hips."

912. Did you hear about the teenager who spent two years trying to find himself? Got a haircut, and there he was!

913. Husband: "What's wrong with your hair, sweetheart? It looks like a wig."
   Wife: "It is a wig."
   Husband: "How do you like that—you never could tell!"

914. Overheard: "With that mop of hair, he looks like his head is unraveling."

915. My uncle knows that the Bible says even the hairs on his head are numbered but each year it gets a little easier for the Lord to take inventory.

916. His hair is so thin you can see when he has a dirty thought.

917. The office tightwad says he's sorry he bought a cheap toupee. Now he's losing hair that isn't even his.

918.   Men spend thousands on hair transplants and toupees when what is really needed is more women who like bald men.

919.   Freshman: "Hey, you got your long hair cut off. How much weight did you lose?"

Second Freshman: "About 200 pounds—I got my Dad off my back."

920.   Nothing makes gray hair look more attractive than being bald.

921.   Is there a child that doesn't wonder why Dad grows gray and Mom grows blonder?

922.   He's 75 and people wonder why he isn't gray. It's because he has more chemicals in his hair than Lake Erie.

923.   Two nice middle-aged ladies were discussing a dance to be held at the yacht club.

"The theme is to wear something that will match your husband's hair," explained one. "I'm wearing that gray silk dress of mine."

"Gracious! I don't think I'll go," said the second.

924.   Our barber looked at the young man's sleek hair and asked if he wanted it cut or just the oil changed.

925.   A friend of the barber's walked into the local barbershop and asked that he be given a particularly GOOD haircut. He explained, "I'm flying to England tomorrow to be introduced to the Queen."

The unimpressed barber said, "In the first place, English weather this time of year is terrible. Secondly, flying to England is an exhausting trip. Thirdly, there'll be so many people there that the Queen won't know you from Adam."

Nevertheless, the friend made the trip. Three weeks later, he was back in the same barber chair.

"In the first place," he reported, "the English weather was superb. Secondly, the flight went like a dream . . . a delight! Thirdly, only two other people were at the palace when I met the Queen. And do you know what she asked me? 'Who on earth gave you that horrible haircut?' "

Health/Safety

926.   Once we talked out our problems over coffee and cigarettes. Now, they are our problems.

927.   My wife is a health food nut. She said, "Drink carrot juice. It'll make your eyes very strong."

So I've been drinking it till it's coming out my ears. But it works. My eyes are very strong, just like she said. Only one problem, I can't sleep at night . . . I see through my eyelids.

928.   A serious illness is one that keeps you out of the office even after your sick leave has run out.

929.   My wife is on a health food kick. Whatever she gets her hands on, she throws into the blender. Last week I drank a chicken.

930.   A friend who drinks 25 cups of coffee a day says his doctor told him either to cut back or to have his heartbeat recorded and sell the tapes to discos.

931.   Kids were served health food years ago, too. If you knew what was good for your health, you ate the food!

932.   There's a town in Texas that's so healthy the Old Folks Home has 10-speed wheelchairs.

933.   There's one good thing about kleptomania—you can always take something for it.

934.   You may not know that the greatest cause for heart attacks in men over 60 is women under 30.

935.   With all the warnings we're getting from consumer reports about eating and drinking, it's obvious that the best way to remain healthy is to eat what you don't want, drink what you don't like, and be sure to do what you'd rather not.

936.   It would be a lot easier to quit smoking if they could prove that cigarettes have calories.

937.   A rum dandy's not bad. It's got sugar in it for energy, milk for pep, and rum gives you dandy ideas of what to do with energy and pep.

938.   Findings by the Surgeon General of the U.S. Government opened the door for development of a tasteless cigarette for people who know they shouldn't smoke and don't want to know about it when they do.

939.   It's hard to be fit as a fiddle when you're shaped like a cello.

940.   "What's the matter with you, Jack? Never saw you scowl so much."

"Got rheumatism. Doctor told me to avoid all dampness. You have no idea how uncomfortable it is to sit in an empty tub and go over yourself with a vacuum cleaner."

Holidays

941. Have fun on St. Patrick's Day, but if you drink be careful . . . remember what happened to my Great Uncle Daniel last year after he had a few too many? He caught his shillelagh in his harp and twanged himself to death.

942. Roses are red,
      Violets are bluish,
      If it wasn't for Christmas,
      We'd all be Jewish.

943. A guy with a wife and 10 kids was down on his luck. Somebody gave him a turkey 6 weeks before Thanksgiving. The kids chased it so much it lost 20 pounds and the family dinner on Thanksgiving consisted of a bird that looked "like a tall sparrow."   JACK INGLIS

944. A Santa Claus actor asked a 5-year-old boy if he would leave something by the fireplace for him to eat when he made his rounds on Christmas Eve. The kid asked, "How about a Big Mack and a 6-pak?"

945. The post office will be closed on Christmas. They practice all year for that.

946. Our neighbor says the most dangerous fight he ever had was when he and his wife agreed not to give Christmas presents and he didn't.

947. A neighbor says he didn't realize it was less than three months 'til Christmas until he made the final payment for last year's gifts.

948. Turkeys will be higher this Thanksgiving, except around Washington where there's a surplus.

949. "For Christmas," said the wife to her husband, "let's give each other sensible gifts . . . like ties and fur coats."

950. Americans are putting up Christmas decorations so early, I saw a turkey in a pear tree.

951. Husband: "I gave my wife two gifts for Christmas."
      Neighbor: "That was generous. Why did you do that?"
      Husband: "Well, she said she wanted something to protect her and something to drive. So I gave her a hammer and a nail."

Home

952.   But I think everyone should own his own home at some time in his life. I believe it is our God-given right to be able to stand in the middle of our very own yard and say, "I can't afford this!"

953.   I bought a guard dog, but it didn't work out. I wanted him to guard the entire apartment . . . he wanted to guard a small area underneath the bed.

954.   A long married couple was sitting in the living room. He was asleep in his easy chair and she was watching television. Suddenly, a violent tornado struck the house. It ripped off the roof, picked the man and woman up, swirled them into the air, and deposited them a mile from home. The husband, seeing his wife sobbing, said, "Stop crying, can't you see we're safe?"

She whimpered, "I'm just crying because I'm so happy. This is the first time we have been out together in ten years."

955.   Household Executive: "Thank God I don't have to go to work. I just get out of bed in the morning and there it is, all around me."

956.   Some sort of award for tact and diplomacy ought to go to the husband whose wife was giving a crucial dinner party at home and, while carrying the beautifully brown, 15-pound roast into the dining room, dropped it. The meat rolled off the platter and slid along the floor until it reached the opposite wall. The man of the house spoke up calmly: "My dear, just pick it up and carry it back to the kitchen. Then, bring in the other roast."

957.   Two housekeepers were talking over their problems of work. One said, "This lady I work for says I should warm the plates for our dinner guests, but that's too much work. I just warm her's and she never knows the difference."

958.   The middle-aged man was shuffling along, bent over at the waist, as his wife helped him into the doctor's waiting room. A woman in the office viewed the scene with sympathy.

"Arthritis with complications?" she asked.

The wife shook her head. "Do-it-yourself," she explained, "with concrete blocks."

959.   I'm a great handyman around the house. I'm one of the few men in the world that holds a black belt in screwdriving.

960.   We knew it was finally time to clean out the garage the day we lost the lawn mower.

961. Nothing makes cleaning out the attic such a long job as being able to read.

962. My wife is a cleaning freak. Lemon Pledge everywhere. When you walk into the house, your whole body puckers.

963. Did you hear about the guy who deducted $2,000 from his taxes because he had water in his basement? Then, the IRS found out he lived in a houseboat.

964. "Does your wife repaint the rooms very often?"
"Well," came the reply, "when we moved in, the guest room was 9 by 12, and now it's 8 by 11."

Hospitals

965. The beautiful girl had been prepared for the operation and left on a stretcher just outside the operating room. While awaiting the nurse's return, a young man in a white smock approached, lifted the sheet, peeked under, and left without comment. Another did the same thing. As a third young man approached, the patient asked, "What am I here for—operation or observation?"
"Search me," answered the young man. "You'll have to ask the doctor. I'm one of the painters down the hall."

966. No matter how much a private room in a hospital costs, they only give you a semiprivate gown.

967. "Do you mind telling me why you ran away from the operating room?"
"Because the nurse said, 'Be brave, an appendectomy is simple.'"
"So?"
"So, she was talking to the doctor who was going to operate!"

968. A hospital is peculiar for one thing. It is a place where it is perfectly all right to put a total stranger in the bed next to you.

969. "What sign were you born under?"
"Neon. My father said he knew the way to the hospital and my mother believed him."

970. A visitor in Dallas asked, "What's the quickest way to get to the hospital?"
"Say something bad about Texas!" came the reply.

971. Patient: "I'm so nervous. This is my first operation."
Doctor: "I know how you feel. It's my first one, too."

972.   More and more hospitals are running their businesses like an assembly line. One fella walked into the emergency room and the nurse asked him what he had. He said, "Shingles." So she took down his name, address, medical insurance number, and told him to have a seat. Fifteen minutes later, a nurse's aide came out and asked him what he had. He said, "Shingles." So she took down his height, weight, a complete medical history, and told him to wait in an examining room. A half-hour later another nurse came in and asked him what he had. He said, "Shingles." So she gave him a blood test, a blood pressure test, an electrocardiogram, told him to take off his clothes and wait for the doctor. An hour later, the doctor came in and asked him what he had. He said, "Shingles."

The doctor said, "Where?"

He said, "Outside in the truck. Where do you want 'em?"

973.   A doctor, rushing an expectant mother to the hospital, didn't quite make it. The baby was born on the lawn in front of the maternity ward. When the bill was received by the new father, he objected to one item: "Delivery room, $50."

He returned the bill for correction. The revised statement came back three days later. It read: "Green fees, $50."

974.   Then there was the hospital patient complaining about the cost of some minor surgery. "What this country needs," he griped, "is a good $50 scar."

975.   Statistics disclose that babies are born to every fifth person going into the hospital. If you've already been in four times, be prepared.

976.   After a patient underwent an operation at the local hospital and came out of the anesthesia, he asked a nurse, "How come all the shades on the windows are pulled down?"

The nurse answered, "The house across the street is on fire, and we didn't want you to wake up thinking that the operation was a failure."

977.   The top surgeon of St. Jobe's Hospital suffered a slip of the tongue yesterday. A patient asked if her operation would be dangerous and he told her: "Don't be silly. You can't buy a dangerous operation for $500."

978.   Nurse: "Did you drink the carrot juice after the hot bath?"
Patient: "I haven't finished drinking the hot bath yet."

979.   You know what bothers me about surgeons? Everyone wears

masks at the operation. If something goes wrong, you don't know who to blame.

Hunters

980. Two nature lovers were hiking through a wilderness area in the Rocky Mountains. They looked across a shallow canyon with a dry creek and saw a bear. It was a lean, hungry bear that had gotten a whiff of those two and was heading purposefully toward them.

The men were hikers, not hunters. They weren't armed.

One sat on a log and hurriedly pulled tennis shoes out of his back pack and began putting them on. "You don't expect to outrun that bear with those tennis shoes, do you?" his companion exclaimed.

"No," said the fellow with the sneakers. "I know neither of us can outrun that bear. I just want to make sure I can outrun you!"

981. As Uncle Willie used to say, "If God didn't mean for us to hunt, he wouldn't have given us plaid shirts."

982. Visiting in Australia, an executive from Texas decided to go on a kangaroo hunt. He climbed into his jeep and instructed his guide to proceed to the plains in quest of a kangaroo. No sooner had they reached the wide open spaces when they spotted one, and the driver drove the jeep in hot pursuit.

For sometime they went at breakneck speed without gaining on the animal. Finally, the executive shouted to his guide, "There's no use chasing that thing."

"Why not?" asked the driver.

" 'Cause we're now doin' 65, and that critter ain't even put his front feet down yet!"

983. Many people who are uninformed about outdoor sports are under the impression that all hunting and fishing consists of is hunting and fishing. The truth is that only 3% of hunting and fishing involves actual hunting and fishing. The other 97% is devoted to getting ready for hunting and fishing.

984. My hunting buddy, Tom, has been my friend for 15 years. He's never changed in all that time . . . and that's quite a savings on underwear.

985. It was a dramatic meeting in the jungles of Tanzania. The trails had crossed and two American explorers, with their parties, practically collided. As they sat around the campfire that evening,

one of the explorers explained his reason for being there. "The urge to travel," he said poetically, "has always surged through my veins. I'm the kind of a fellow who wants to see what's on the other side of the hill. City life nauseates me. The sounds, the filth, the man-made monsters—they're not for me. I seek the companionship of nature—the flutter of the birds, the prattle of the animals, the beauty of the verdant foliage. Ah, enough about me. Why did you come?"

The second explorer replied, "Creditors."

986.   "I got three deer and a pot fur."

"What's a pot fur?"

"To cooke the deer in!"

987.   A couple of novice bird hunters paid a high price for a pedigree bird dog and took him out for a field test. After an hour, one said in disgust, "This dog is no good. We might as well put him to sleep."

"Let's throw him in the air one more time," said the other. "If he doesn't fly, we'll get rid of him."

988.   A guy returned from Safari. He had a few trophies. His wife bagged a huge lion and has the head mounted.

"She got it with that new Enfield 447?" asked a friend.

"No, she got it with the front tire of a rented station wagon."

Husbands

989.   Two women were talking about their husbands. Said one, "I'm more and more convinced that mine married me for my money."

Replied the other, "Then you have the satisfaction of knowing that he's not as stupid as he looks."

990.   Man can climb the highest mountain, swim the widest ocean, fight the strongest tiger, but once he's married, he can barely take out the garbage.

991.   Then there was the man who took his wife to the psychiatrist and said, "What's-her-name here complains I haven't been paying enough attention to her."

992.   A minister concluded a sermon the other day with the request: "If anyone out there is perfect, please stand up."

One gentleman arose. Gimlet-eyed, the minister asked, "Are you saying you are perfect?"

"Oh, no, not me," said the parishioner. "I'm standing up for my wife's first husband."

993. A woman dropped her contact lens in a wastebasket that was filled to the brim. After she had searched diligently but in vain, her husband went through the trash and found the lens. "How on earth did you find it?" she asked.

"Well," he explained, "you were only searching for a tiny piece of plastic, but I was looking for $225."

994. My husband will never ever fall for another woman. He's too fine, too decent, (and) too old.   MRS. BOB HOPE

995. If he yawns, please understand. He may be a married man and it's his only chance to open his mouth.

996. During an attack of laryngitis, a woman lost her voice for 3 days. Her husband, wanting to help his wife communicate with him, devised a system of taps. One tap meant "give me a kiss," two taps meant "no," three taps meant "yes," and 95 taps meant "take out the garbage."

Indians

997. Weren't the American Indians dumb, using shells for money? We use plastic cards.

998. In Wisconsin, President Kennedy was made honorary chieftain of an Indian tribe. Donning the headdress, he exclaimed, "Next time I go to the movies to see cowboys and Indians, it'll be us."

999. I just met the world's dumbest bigot. He went up to an Indian and said: "Why don't you go back to where you came from?"

1000. Who can blame the American Indian for dreaming of warpaths. They're the only people ever to be conquered by the U.S. and not prosper because of it.

1001. When asked by an anthropologist what the Indians called America before the white man came, an Indian said simply, "Ours."

1002. The early settlers took the country away from the Indians who scalped some of us and turned it over to the politicians who skinned the rest of us.

1003. An Indian petitioned a judge in a New Mexico court for permission to change his name to a shorter one. "What is your name now?" asked the judge.

"Chief Screeching Train Whistle."

"And what do you wish to change it to?"

The Indian folded his arms and grunted, "Toots."

1004. After taking several snapshots of an elderly Indian chief, the vacationer asked, "Have you lived on the reservation all your life?"

The chief retorted, "Not yet."

1005. One day the Lone Ranger and Tonto rode to the top of a hill overlooking the plains. Peering around, the Masked Man said suddenly, "Tonto, there's a war party of Indians approaching from the south."

"We go north, Kemo Sabe," said Tonto.

The Lone Ranger then said, "Oh, my God, Tonto! There are Indians coming from the North. And look, war parties coming from the East and West. What are we going to do?"

As Tonto rode off, he called back over his shoulder, "What do you mean 'we,' white man?"

1006. Historians recently unearthed the very first treaty between white men and the Indians. It says the Red Man can keep his lands for as long as the river runs, the sun rises, and the grass grows . . . or 90 days, whichever comes first.

1007. A man returns from the North Woods with word that the Indians are predicting a severe winter. The prediction is based on the size of the white man's woodpiles.

1008. As the dark skinned young man came out of the receiving room at the Red Cross Blood Center, a lady in the waiting room asked, "Are you a full-blooded Indian?"

"No, ma'am," replied the Cherokee, "right now I'm a pint short."

1009. Have you noticed how popular Indian music has become? Indian music is sort of a cross between Lawrence Welk and static.

Inflation

1010. Investment people are telling the story of the fellow who bumped his head and went into a 20-year coma. Awaking refreshed and clearheaded in 2007, the first thing he did was to phone his broker. With the help of a computer setup, it took the broker only a few minutes to report that his 100 shares of General Motors were now worth 5.5 million, and his holdings in Xerox had increased to an amazing $15 million.

"Good Lord!" exclaimed the man. "I'm rich!" At which point the telephone operator came on the line and said, "Your 3 minutes are up, sir. Would you please deposit a million dollars?"

1011. Inflation is when you sock something away for a rainy day and the sock shrinks.

1012. This sounds impossible, but . . . I pulled a sticker off a can at the supermarket and the last price was higher.

1013. Inflation is when you have money to burn and can't afford matches.

1014. An economist trying to explain inflation: "Think of the price spiral as a corkscrew and think of yourself as the cork."

1015. It's inflation when you pay $10 for the $2 haircut you used to get for $1 when you had hair.

1016. Inflation hasn't ruined everything. A dime can still be used as a screwdriver.

1017. The best way to slow down inflation is to send it through the mail.

1018. The Government isn't ending inflation, so we must learn to live with it. The first thing we need is a 25-hour work week so that we can have three jobs instead of just two.

1019. Barney sold pencils in front of the courthouse. Attorney Spencer stopped, gave him a dime as he had done for 20 years, but didn't take a pencil.

"Say, Counselor," snapped Barney, as the lawyer started to walk away, "you've been doin' that now for years. You give me the money but you never take a pencil. How come?"

"I gave you the first dime 20 years ago," explained the barrister. "It brought me good luck. I'm successful, so I've been doing it ever since. Why do you ask?"

"Well," said Barney, "startin' tomorrow, pencils are a quarter."

1020. Remember the famous sign on Harry Truman's desk? It's been rewritten . . . "The Buck—or whatever is left of it—Stops Here."

1021. Inflation: "When everything that's in is out because it's up."

Insects

1022. A bee is never as busy as it seems; it's just that it can't buzz any slower.

1023. Making money is getting to be like bees making honey. You can make it, but they won't let you keep it.

1024. A fisherman returned from Texas with a report on this year's mosquito crop: "The mosquitoes are so big," he said, "I slapped one that had three woodticks on it."

1025. A most happy experience for ladybugs is to discover that not all ladybugs are ladies.

1026. I went camping in a place called Mosquito Creek. One mosquito was so big he showed up on radar. Not only did he bite me, but he left footprints on my arm.

1027. A bee has to visit 2,000 blossoms in order to make one tablespoon of honey. Fortunately, it has nothing else to do.

1028. Do you know what you call an insect that leaps over fourteen cans of bug spray? Weevile Knievel.

1029. Waterbeds are so popular, I saw some bedbugs taking swimming lessons.

1030. Daisy June: "Listen to them June bugs all snuggled down cozy in the grass, chirping away. Clem, why can't we do something like that?"

Clem: "Shucks, Daisy June, I can't rub my hind legs together to chirp like that."

1031. A single housefly can lay 30,000 eggs a year. There are no statistics on how many a married one could lay.

1032. If you want to rid your dog of fleas, give him a bath in alcohol and a rubdown with sand. The fleas get drunk and kill each other throwing rocks.

Insurance

1033. Insurance agent asked man, "Do you want a straight life policy?" and the man answered, "No, not exactly. I'd like to play around a little on Saturday night."

1034. You can't win. I knew a guy who took out a $1,000,000 life insurance policy . . . and he died anyway.

1035. "Don't you know you can't sell insurance without a license?"

"I knew I wasn't selling any but I just didn't know the reason."

1036. "I had a wonderful insurance policy on my first husband."
"What'd you get."
"My second husband."

1037. The insurance salesman was having trouble making himself clear to his prospective customer. "What is the maximum value of your husband's present policy?" he asked.
"What's that again?" asked the housewife.
"If you should lose your husband, for example," he explained, "what would you get?"
She stared at the ceiling for a moment, then answered, "A German Shepherd."

1038. This sounds impossible, but . . . I once met an insurance salesman who did not say, "God forbid."

1039. My insurance company has a great motto: "After you die, we'll still be here!"

1040. Another thing about old age is that insurance agents quit bothering you.

1041. I just got my TV set insured. If it breaks down, they send me a pair of binoculars so I can watch my neighbor's set.   HENNY YOUNGMAN

1042. A friend says he would have bought life insurance sooner if he'd known it would make his wife a better housekeeper. Now she's even waxing the bathtub.

1043. A fellow's barn burned. His insurance man said, "We'll pay off. Give you another one just like you had."
"In that case, you can cancel the insurance on my wife."

1044. To insurance man: "What would I get if this building burned down tonight?"
"About 10 years," came the reply.

1045. An insurance salesman was having no luck getting one of his clients interested in buying a life insurance policy. He kept calling the prospect at the office and at home. The client kept stalling, talking around the subject, and being unavailable whenever the salesman phoned. Finally, the salesman caught him with a late evening call to his home. "I don't want to frighten you into a hasty decision," he said. "Why don't you just sleep on it tonight. If you wake up tomorrow, call me."

Jails

1046. A political prisoner was about to be executed by the new dictatorial regime. He was blind folded by the captain of the firing squad and asked if he wanted a cigarette.

"No thank you," said the prisoner. "I'm trying to quit."

1047. Three inmates in a Peking prison asked each other how they had gotten into such a fix.

"I am here because I supported Deng Xiaoping," said one.

"I am here because I opposed Deng Xiaoping," said the second inmate.

The two looked at the third man who said, "I AM Deng Xiaoping."

1048. We're the only country in the world that locks up the jury at night and lets the prisoner go home.

1049. Most federal prisons now have daytime TV. That's part of their punishment.

1050. "I know a fellow who made over $50,000 and paid only $30 in taxes."

"Boy, I'd like to meet him."

"He's in the federal pen in Atlanta."

1051. Farmer down in the hills made some gasohol in his still the other day and got two years to the gallon.

1052. Warden: "What would you like for your last dinner?"

Condemned: "Steak and mushrooms. Before this, I've always been afraid to eat mushrooms."

1053. A new inmate was delivered to his cell. He saw that his cellmate was a grizzled, toothless old man. "To look at me now," the old one said, "you'd never believe that I once lived the life of Riley: Winters in the sun, deep sea fishing, fine cars, beautiful women, the best cuisine."

"Well, what happened?" the new con inquired.

"Riley reported his credit cards missing," the old one replied.

Jobs

1054. Samuel Goldwyn once said, "I don't want any yes men around me. I want someone to tell me the truth—even if it costs him his job."

1055. A profession is something you study years to get into and then spend the rest of your life trying to earn enough to get out of.

1056. Personnel manager to applicant: "What we're after is a man with drive, determination, fire; a man who never quits; a man who inspires others; a man who can pull the company's bowling team out of last place!"

1057. If supermarket clerks are so smart and can rattle off those prices so quickly, why do they have to wear their names on their shirts?

1058. An executive is someone who talks to visitors while the employees get the work done.

1059. It's okay for both husband and wife to work, but only until one or the other gets pregnant.

1060. Show me a Jewish boy who doesn't go to medical school and I'll show you a lawyer.

1061. Before he came here, he was doing well as a photographer . . . but his pony died.

1062. Uncle Marty says the good thing about being unemployed is when he wakes up each morning, he's already at work.

1063. An accountant is a man who solves a problem you didn't know you had in a manner you don't understand.

1064. "Have you been moved to a branch office?"
"It's not really a branch. It's more like a twig."

1065. Employer to accountant: "Do you know double entry bookkeeping?
Accountant: "Listen, I know triple entry. One for you, showing the real profit. Another for your wife, showing a slight profit. And a third for the IRS, showing a loss."

1066. Tom and Harry were partners in a profitable painting contracting business. Unfortunately, they weren't entirely honest because they mixed water with their paint. One day, Harry's conscience started to bother him as they painted a poor widow's house. The next day, Harry told Tom that he just couldn't be dishonest anymore.
"Don't quit now," Tom begged. "A few more jobs and we can retire."
Harry refused to change his mind. He said, "Tom, I just can't do it. Last night an angel stood by my bed and said, 'Repaint, you thinner.' "

1067. What kind of a man is it who can turn iron into gold? The plumber!

1068. My teenager took a job aptitude test and found out he was best suited for retirement.

Judge/Jury

1069. The prisoner faced the judge. "Tell me," said the judge, "have you anything to offer this court before it passes sentence?"

"No, your honor," replied the prisoner. "My lawyer took every last cent."

1070. Two hoboes were brought to court for vagrancy. The judge asked the more outspoken one where he lived.

"On the fields, the mountains, the countryside, and the beaches," said the man.

The judge shook his head and asked his companion, "And where do you live?"

"Next door to him," was the reply.

1071. The foreman of the jury reported angrily to the judge that no agreement on a verdict was in prospect.

"The jury will have to continue its deliberations," said the magistrate. "If you haven't come to a decision by seven o'clock, I'll have twelve dinners sent to you."

"If Your Honor doesn't mind," said the foreman, "I suggest that the order be changed to eleven dinners and one bale of hay."

1072. No wonder people are nervous about the U.S. court system. You would be nervous too if you were standing trial, about to be judged by 12 people who were not smart enough to get out of jury duty.

1073. The jury finally returned to the courtroom after deliberating three days.

"Have you reached a verdict?" the judge asked.

"Yes, we have, your Honor," the foreman said.

"Please tell us your decision," the judge said.

The foreman cleared his throat and declared, "We, the jury, have decided not to become involved."

1074. It was an outstanding case in a small Western mining town. Joe was brought in on an assault charge. The state presented the weapons he used: a huge telegraph pole, a dagger, a pair of shears, a saw, a gun, and a Civil War saber.

Counsel for the defense produced the weapons used by the alleged victim to defend himself: a scythe, a hoe, an ax, a shovel, and a pair of tongs.

After deliberating, the 12 men of the jury filed in slowly and the foreman read the verdict: "We the jury would give $500 to have seen that fight."

1075.   A no-nonsense elderly lady was on the witness stand. The prosecuting attorney, testing her mental capacity and eyesight, pointed to the defense and asked, "Can you identify that man?"

"Yes, he's one of the biggest crooks in the country."

Obviously pleased, he lowered his voice sweetly and asked, "Can you identify me?"

"Yes, you're a crook, too."

With that the judge banged his gavel and ordered the two attorneys to approach the bench. In hushed tones, he whispered, "If either one of you birds asks if she knows me, I'll hold you in contempt of court."

1076.   Mr. Goldberg was brought into traffic court for speeding. The judge was Jewish.

"But, your Honor," Goldberg pleaded, "I was just trying to get to the synagogue in time to hear the rabbi's sermon."

"Did you make it?" the judge asked.

"Yes, your Honor, I did."

"Case dismissed!" the judge said, banging the gavel. "That's punishment enough."

1077.   Judge told the defendant: "It's alcohol and alcohol alone that's responsible for your condition."

The defendant replied: "You've made me very happy, Judge. Everyone else tells me it's all MY fault."

1078.   Judge: "So you're a locksmith? What were you doing in that bookie joint when the police raided it?"

Prisoner: "I was making a bolt for the door."

1079.   Southern country judge: "What's the charge against this man, officer?"

Officer: "Bigotry, your Honor. He's got three wives."

Judge: "I'm surprised at yo' ignorance, suh. That's not bigotry. It's trigonometry."

1080.   The judge asked the defendant whether he knew the difference between right and wrong. "Sure I do, your Honor. It's simply that I hate to make decisions."

1081. A judge recalled the best alibi he ever heard during his term on the bench: "A man involved in an auto accident and charged with reckless driving testified: 'It was my wife's fault—she fell asleep in the back seat.'"

1082. An industrialist was fighting a case in tax court. He looked at the bench and told his Honor, "As God is my judge, I do not owe this tax."

The judge said, "He's not. I am. You do."

1083. Judge to drunk: "You've been coming to me for 10 years."

Drunk: "Can I help it if you don't get promoted?"

Kissing

1084. First Girl: "I'm tired of marriage. Bill hasn't kissed me since my honeymoon."

Second Girl: "Then, why don't you divorce him?"

First Girl: "Bill isn't my husband."

1085. There's a new toothpaste on the market with alum in it, called "Kiss Me Quick!," for those too pooped to pucker.

1086. After 40, many people think that kisses are like money— squandered when not wisely invested.

1087. Merle Oberon, the actress, visiting the wounded in London, asked one soldier, "Did you kill a Nazi?" The soldier said he had. "With which hand?" Miss Oberon asked. She decorated his right hand with a kiss.

Then she asked the next patient, "Did you kill a Nazi?"

"I sure did!" came the ready answer. "I bit 'im to death."

1088. The doctor's wife confided to her maid, "I caught my husband kissing the nurse."

"I don't believe it," the maid gasped, "You're only saying that to make me jealous."

1089. A fellow told a neighbor, "While you were away, I saw a tall dark man kissing your wife."

"Did he wear glasses, have a small moustache, and carry a cane?"

"Yeah, that's him."

"Oh, that's just my insurance man. He'll kiss anybody."

1090. Sex education has sure changed. In my day, kids weren't even permitted to talk about kissing. The only practice we got was drinking from a slow water fountain.

1091. The boss said, "Who said you could neglect your office duties just because I give you a little kiss now and then?"

His secretary said, "My attorney."

1092. On his 80th birthday, criminal lawyer Clarence Darrow confided to an equally aged friend that his memory was beginning to fail him.

"Mine is as good as ever," boasted the friend. "Why, I can remember the first girl I ever kissed."

"I envy you," sighed Darrow. "I can't even remember the last."

1093. Getting free advice is like getting kissed on the forehead: It doesn't hurt, but it doesn't do much for you, either.

1094. Whoever named it necking was a poor judge of anatomy.
GROUCHO MARX

1095. A 90-year-old woman was celebrating her birthday with an annual party.

"What would you like for a gift?" asked a devoted friend.

"Just give me a big kiss," replied the woman. "Then I won't have to dust it."

1096. No man should kiss and tell. It encourages the competition.

1097. She: "How does Paul kiss?"

Her: "You can define it as unskilled labor."

Landlords

1098. The landlord called the teenager in the next apartment and yelled, "If you don't turn your stereo down, I'll go insane."

"Too late," came the reply, "I turned it off an hour ago."

1099. When the tenant of a New York apartment complained that no water came through the faucet in the bathtub, the landlord said for a 10% increase in the rent, he would move the bathtub underneath the hole in the roof.

1100. "I have it on good authority," someone said of a ruthless landlord, "that actually he was abandoned by wolves as a baby and brought up by his parents."

1101. Once, when Honore Daumier was behind in his rent, his landlord threatened him with eviction. The caricaturist was incensed.

"You make such a threat to me!" he stormed. "The day will come when people will make a pilgrimage to this hovel and say, 'Daumier, the great artist, once lived here.'"

"If I don't get the rent by tonight," the landlord said, "they will be able to say it tomorrow."

1102. "Don't you ever do anything quickly?" I asked my landlord.
"Yeah, I get tired," he snapped.

1103. If it weren't for the pull tabs on beer cans, my landlord wouldn't get any exercise at all.

1104. I don't know what makes my landlord so obnoxious, but whatever it is, it works.

1105. My landlady feels it would be a disaster to get rid of her hostilities since she simply doesn't have time to be nice to everybody.

1106. My landlord is so coldhearted, he has to add antifreeze to his pacemaker.

1107. If my landlord ate his heart out, he would break a tooth.

1108. Told my apartment manager that the apartment had roaches—he raised my rent for keeping pets.

1109. Our neighbor says his landlord asks too much for the rent. Last month he asked four times.

1110. "One of my tenants told me recently that the couple living in the suite above him shouts and pounds on the floor until midnight nearly every evening," said a landlord. "When I asked him if he wanted to make a complaint, he said, 'Not really, I'm usually up practicing my trumpet until about that time anyway.'"

Lawyers

1111. Q. How many lawyers does it take to screw in a light bulb?
A. How many can you afford?

1112. King Tut was buried with millions of dollars worth of treasures which proves one thing . . . his ex-wife didn't have a good lawyer.

1113. A young man was arrested for murder. His lawyer bribed an Irishman on the jury to oppose the death sentence, and hold out for a verdict of manslaughter. The jury was out for a long time, and finally came in with a verdict of manslaughter. The lawyer rushed up to the Irishman and whispered: "My client and I are tremendously obliged and grateful. Did you have a hard time of it?"

"The devil's own time, me lad!" the Irishman said, "The other 11 all wanted to acquit your client."

1114.   A lawyer cross-examined a pathologist, trying to establish a time frame of the death and post-mortem. The pathologist said the examination took place in the evening. "And Mr. So-and-so was dead at the time, is that correct?" asked the lawyer.

"No," answered the pathologist straight faced. "He was just sitting on the table wondering why I was doing an autopsy on him."

1115.   Lawyer (to rattled witness): "Did you, or did you not, on the aforementioned day, Friday, November 4th, feloniously and with malicous forethought, listen at the keyhole of the 10th floor condominium, then occupied as a residence by the defendant in this action on 86th Street near West End Avenue, and did you not also, on the Wednesday following the Friday in November before referred to, communicate to your wife the information acquired and repeat the conversation overheard on that occasion with the result that the gossip of your wife gave wide and far currency to the overheard conversation before mentioned? Did you, or did you not."

The witness pondered for a little while and then said: "Did I or did I not what?"

1116.   Gifford, who shot a fellow in a barroom dispute, wired to Philadelphia for a lawyer to defend him. The answer came: ARRIVING BY PLANE TOMORROW. BRINGING TWO EYEWITNESSES.

1117.   "You say it was night time, you were at least five blocks away from the scene, and you still saw the defendant shoot Mr. Taylor. How far can you see at night?"

"I don't know . . . How far is the moon?"

1118.   "I'm beginning to think my lawyer is only interested in money."

"Why do you say that?"

"He sent me a bill for $30.00. Claimed he woke up at night and thought about my case."

1119.   A college was interviewing applicants for its presidency. The search committee reduced the contenders to a mathematician, an economist, and a lawyer. The committee decided to conduct a final interview with each, and to ask each the same question: "What's two plus two?"

The mathematician went first. He pondered the question for a

Robert Henry is available for unusual assignments. Don't hesitate to call with strange requests.

while, as mathematicians will. Then he said: "Speaking in real integers only, without logarithmic variables or square root factors, the answer is four."

The economist was next: "Within standard statistical deviation, based on the expected Dow Jones, the answer, plus or minus one, is four."

The lawyer was last. He got up from the table, walked over to the windows, and pulled down the shades. Then he made a dramatic turn toward the committee and asked: "How much do you want it to be?"

1120.   My uncle, the lawyer, got a client suspended. They hung him.

1121.   Lawyer conventions: "All the members come together to mourn their dear, departed brothers—who are serving in minimum security prisons doing three years at hard tennis."

1122.   "Gentlemen of the jury," said the defense attorney, now beginning to warm to his summation. "The real question before you is shall this beautiful young woman be forced to languish away her loveliest years in a dark prison cell? Or shall she be set free to return to her cozy, little apartment at 4134 Seaside Street . . . there to spend her lonely, loveless hours in her boudoir, lying beside her little princess phone, 926–7873?"

1123.   A lawyer and his wife were on a sailboat in the Gulf of Mexico. A sudden movement of the craft hurled the lawyer overboard into shark infested waters. Almost immediately, eight large maneating sharks swam to the lawyer, formed a protective circle, and escorted him safely back to his boat.

"It was a miracle," cried his wife.

"No," said the lawyer. "It was only professional courtesy."

Life

1124.   Two can live cheaper than one but very few people want to live that cheap.

1125.   A nervous passenger on an elevator asked the operator, "What would happen if the cable broke? Would we go up or down?"

The exasperated operator replied, "That, madam, depends on the life you've led."

1126.   Live each day as if it were the first day of your marriage and the last day of your vacation.

1127.   There must be something to reincarnation. I can't believe I could have gotten this far behind in only one life.

1128.   Life for a male is divided into three parts. The first childhood, when he doesn't know anything about women and doesn't care. The second is middle age, when he still doesn't know anything about women but wishes he did. The third is the declining years, when he knows all about women and the women couldn't care less.

1129.   The entire philosophy of life can be summed up in five words: "You get used to it."

1130.   During one boring day, I tried to recall the highlights of my life and fell asleep.

1131. One of life's biggest mistakes is to think that you are working for someone else.

1132. One of life's major mistakes is being the last member in the family to get the flu after all the sympathy has run out.

1133. Remember that the day after tomorrow is the third day of the rest of your life. GEORGE CARLIN

1134. Life is like a 10-speed bike. Most of us have gears we never use. CHARLES SCHULTZ

1135. "How old is your wife?"
"She's 87, and God willing, she'll live to be 100!"
"And how old are you?"
"I'm 87, too, and God willing, I'll live to be 101."
"But why would you want to live a year longer than your wife?"
"To tell you the truth, I'd like to have at least one year of peace!"

1136. It's awful to marry a man for life—and then learn he doesn't have any.

1137. The three greatest threats to life today are muggers, burglars, and the supermarket cart.

1138. Give me the luxuries of life and I will willingly do without the necessities. FRANK LLOYD WRIGHT

1139. One thing is certain: "If you had your life to live over, you couldn't afford it."

Looks

1140. He has an interesting physique. It's called Early Famine.

1141. I know a woman who has had so many face lifting operations that every time she raises her eyebrows, she pulls up her stockings.

1142. He was so ugly, he used to work part time as a lab animal.

1143. He looks like a poorly packed duffle bag.

1144. How is it that we can look through the family album and split our sides laughing . . . then look into the mirror and never even crack a smile.

1145. A young lady was asked if she liked a dashing young lawyer. She said, "I do and I don't."
"What don't you like about him?" asked a girlfriend.
"His conceit. He's conceited about his looks."

"What do you like about him?"

"His looks."

1146.   When the day comes that I need a face lift, I'll put a clothespin on the back of my head.   CLINT EASTWOOD

1147.   A very vain, but aging friend is trying to look younger. She had her dentist put make-believe braces on her false teeth.

1148.   In courtship, what counts is the way you look. In marriage, what is vital is the way you overlook.

1149.   What a loser! He looks like a professional blind date.

1150.   My wife's face is not her fortune . . . it's the beauty parlor's.

1151.   During my 20th high school reunion, I saw an old sweetheart who had aged so much, she didn't even recognize me.

1152.   A fellow went to a PTA meeting. He found that styles have changed so much that you can't tell the parents from the kids. Everyone has long hair and wear pants. He told a parent, "My, that's a lovely daughter you have there."

"That's not my daughter. That's my son."

"Oh, are you its mother or father?"

1153.   You know what I can't understand? Here's Adam and Eve. He's incredibly handsome and she's indescribably beautiful. So where did all the ugly people come from?

1154.   "John," sighed his new bride, "how did you first realize that you loved me?"

"It was easy," replied her tactless spouse. "I started getting mad when people told me you were dumb and ugly."

1155.   Childhood: "The time of life when you make funny faces at the mirror."

Middle Age: "The time of life when the mirror gets even."

1156.   Middle age lament: "It's tough to go through life looking like your contents have settled during shipping."

1157.   A young farmer attending a dance tried to make conversation with his attractive companion. Smiling, he said, "You look like Helen Brown."

She nodded her head. "Yes, I know," was her reply. "I don't look so good in yellow either."

1158.   I don't mean to imply that she's skinny, but if she shuts one eye, she looks like a needle.

1159. It was a joke on his wife, the guy said, "She had her face lifted and there was one just like it underneath."

1160. One lady says she finally arrived at the conclusion that it's better to admit her age than keep explaining why she looks so bad.

1161. I only hope I look as good as my mother does when I reach the age she says she isn't.

1162. When I say ugly, I mean you had to sit her in the corner and feed her with a slingshot.

1163. He's as ugly as four miles of bad road.

1164. Ugly? She was a cover girl for swine flu.

1165. Talk about an ugly woman, when she goes to the ladies' room, the attendant asks to see some I.D.

1166. Even as a kid, he was ugly . . . He asked his father why they never went to the zoo, and his father said, "If they want you, they'll come and get you."

1167. You don't see many hippie-type college kids like you used to. Oh, I did see one—long, dirty hair, filthy overalls, grimy sweatshirt, beard—I mean she really looked awful.

1168. A man told his friend that his wife had recently gotten a mudpack to improve her beauty and his friend asked, "Did it?"
   The man replied, "It did for a couple of days and then the mud fell off."

1169. A woman has her face lifted, her nose bobbed, her varicose veins rerouted, her knee caps tightened, wears wigs and uplifts, and then says, "You're not the same man I married!"

1170. Beauty is only skin deep, but ugly goes clear to the bone.

Mail

1171. The post office has announced plans to shorten lines at the counters. Everybody stands closer together.

1172. About an hour after a woman bought 200 stamps for her daughter's wedding invitations, she returned to the post office to exchange them. Her daughter thought the whooping crane on the stamps looked too much like a stork.

1173. If postal workers ever strike, America will be faced with 3 major problems: 1. How will we handle it? 2. How will we end it? 3. How will we know it?

1174. Young wife (at the post office window): "I wish to complain about the service."

Postmaster: "What's the trouble lady?"

Wife: "My husband is in New York on business and the letter he sent me is postmarked Miami Beach."

1175. Not all the Postal Service employees showed up at their annual masquerade party. Those who dressed as letters and postcards are expected in about three weeks or so.

1176. The way to handle nuclear waste is to give it to the U.S. Post Office. The half they don't lose, they'll destroy.

1177. You know what our big problem is? We've run out of slogans. REMEMBER THE ALAMO! REMEMBER THE MAINE! REMEMBER PEARL HARBOR! What have we got to remember today? Our zip code.

1178. There is a new kind of wine called "Post Office Red." You mail five pounds of grapes in a container and mark it "FRAGILE!"

1179. If the post office really wants to make money, it's easy. Charge $10 for the greatest status symbol of them all—an unlisted zip code!

1180. President Reagan on the Postal Service: "We'd get better service if they sent their own checks by mail."

1181. Of course, I can understand the post office's point of view. In the five months since the last increase, they say they have lost 126 million. I'm not sure whether that was dollars or letters.

1182. You can always count on the Post Office doing a bang-up good job on your Christmas packages.

Marriage

1183. My marriage had its ups and downs. It started up and then went straight down.

1184. A husband telephoned his wife. "I'd like to bring him home for dinner tonight."

"To dinner tonight?" screamed his wife. "You know I have a cold, the baby is cutting his teeth, and the house is as hot as an oven because you can't afford air conditioning, and my household money is gone, so we'll have to eat hash again."

"I know all that, darling," he interrupted quietly. "That's why I want to bring him. The idiot is talking about getting married."

1185. "For twenty years," mused the man at the bar, "My wife and I were ecstatically happy."

"Then what happened?" asked the bartender.

"We met."

1186. You can figure your marriage is on the rocks when your wife forgets to send your apron to the laundry.

1187. If you want to know how your girl will treat you after you're married, just listen to the way she talks to her little brother.

1188. Never marry a beautiful girl. She might leave you. If you marry an ugly girl, she might leave you too—but you won't care.

1189. "You know," said the lovely blonde to her handsome companion, "for months, I just couldn't figure out where my husband was spending his evenings."

"What did you do about it?" asked her friend.

"Oh, nothing. I just went home early one night, and THERE he was."

1190. How my parents ever stayed together is a mystery to me. Dad used to chew and spit, chew and spit, chew and spit. Mom was not a good cook.

1191. The man who marries "into a family" usually finds that his wife has never married out of it.

1192. The poor widow lay crying on the psychiatrist's couch. "We were married 30 years before he died. Never had an argument in all those years."

"Amazing," said the doctor. "How did you do it?"

"I outweighed him 40 pounds and he was chicken."

1193. Fellow sitting next to me on a plane said, "Say, friend, I notice you're wearing your wedding ring on the wrong finger."

I said, "Yeah, I married the wrong woman."

1194. "No one will ever know how much you mean to me," the wife told the husband, "that is, if you're smart enough to settle out of court."

1195. A man should always come home with a great big smile on his face. It makes his wife wonder what he has been up to.

1196. On my wedding night, I felt it was important that she know who was the boss. So I let her have it straight from the shoulder, looked her right in the eye and said, "You're the boss."

1197. I saw a sign at an antinuclear demonstration that said, "Make Love, Not War. I'm married . . . I do both."

1198. Both of my marriages have been unlucky. My first wife divorced me and my second wife won't.

1199. A kid asked his father how much it cost to get married. He replied, "I don't know, son. I'm still paying on it."

1200. Only someone you live with can make a complete and perfectly understandable sentence out of the word, "So?"

1201. An 81-year-old man was in the hospital, his wife was bedside holding his hand.
The old man said, "You know, Sara, I've been thinking. You've stayed with me through thick and thin all of our married life. I remember when the depression came and times were so hard, you were with me. And when the war came and I had to join the Army, you became a nurse. And when I was wounded, you came to my side. You were with me. I think of the many problems we've had through our lives together and that you've always been there. You know, Sara, I've been thinking. You're bad luck."

1202. Some men think marriage is a 50–50 proposition, which convinces us that they don't understand women or percentages.
HENNY YOUNGMAN

1203. She's two-thirds married . . . She's willing and so's her mother.

1204. You can learn almost as much from marriage as you can from school, and in marriage, you don't have to take notes during lectures.

1205. No matter how happily married a woman is, it always pleases her to discover that there is a nice man who wishes she were not.

1206. My wife and I have an understanding . . . I make all the important decisions and she decides whether or not we'll act on them.

1207. "How many years have Alice and Joe been married?"
"About 17, I think."
"Has she made him a good wife?"

"Not particularly, but she sure has made him an awfully good husband."

1208. Marriage is like friendship that somehow got out of control.
JAN MURRAY

1209. Engaged couples should realize that a marriage will never be as good as she hopes or as bad as he expects.

Medicine

1210. I never knew my wife was nearsighted until I took a look at the pill she was taking each day—M & M's!

1211. After giving the woman a full medical examination, the doctor explained his prescription as he wrote it out. "Take the green pill with a glass of water after getting up. Take the blue pill with a glass of water after lunch. Then, just before going to bed, take the red pill with another glass of water."
   "Exactly what is my problem, Doctor?" the woman asked.
   "You're not drinking enough water," the doctor replied.

1212. We used to take life with a grain of salt. Now we take it with 5 milligrams of valium.

1213. Modern medicine surely is wonderful . . . I just heard about this heavy drinker who had an elbow transplant.

1214. A teacher, who found herself simply unable to cope with one mischievous boy, finally went to see her doctor.
   "Never before have I had such an unresponsive student," she told the doctor. "I can't reach him in any way. It's driving me wild!"
   "You must calm down," the doctor said. He prescribed tranquilizers.
   Then after a couple of weeks, the doctor telephoned the teacher. "Have the tranquilizers calmed you down?" he asked.
   "Yes."
   "Well, how's the kid?"
   "Who cares?"

1215. There's a new medication called "Zip" that's popular with doctors. It doesn't cure anything but it's easy to spell.

1216. A physician's wife said, "My husband gave one of my friends so many iron tablets that the only time she feels really good is when she faces magnetic north."

1217. Dewey was having trouble sleeping, so he went to the doctor.

"I can straighten you out," the doctor said. "I've got some brand new medicine that's as strong as they come."

At bedtime, Dewey took the medicine and slept like a baby. Best sleep in years. He slept so well that he woke up before the alarm went off. He took his time getting to the office, strolled in, and said to the boss, "I didn't have a bit of trouble getting up this morning. Slept like a log."

"That's great," said the boss, "but where were you yesterday?"

1218. I know a woman who got hooked on the Pill. Used to eat them like candy. One day she sneezed . . . sterilized her whole bridge club.

1219. A young housewife was asked by her neighbor, "What is that you're taking, my dear? The Pill?"

"Don't laugh 'til I give the punch line," Jeanne tells a fella at the Kentucky Municipal League Convention.

"No," was the worried reply. "This is a tranquilizer. I forgot to take the Pill."

1220. If medical science has done so much to add years to our lives, how come you never meet a woman who's past 40?

1221. Uncle Fred has taken so many vitamins and iron pills, his heirs will be squabbling over mineral rights to his body.

Men

1222. Two men were seated on a crowded bus, and one noticed that the other had his eyes closed. "What's the matter, pal?" he asked. "You sick?"

"No, I'm all right. It's just that I hate to see women standing."

1223. Every man has a secret ambition: to outsmart horses, fish, and women.

1224. A man will laugh at women trying to put on eye makeup—and yet will take 10 minutes to make three hairs look like six.

1225. A well-adjusted man is one who can play golf as though it were a game.

1226. Someone once observed that a man with six children is better satisfied than a man with six million dollars. The reason: the individual with six million dollars always wants more.

1227. First man: "All men have peculiarities. What are yours?"
Second man: "I wasn't aware that I had any."
First man: "Do you stir tea with your right hand?"
Second man: "Well, sure."
First man: "That's your peculiarity. Most men use a spoon."

1228. When you see how some people work, you wonder what they'll do when they retire.

1229. The man who remembers what he learned at his mother's knee, was probably bent over it.

1230. Advice to men:
1. Never play poker with a man named Ace.
2. Never eat at a place called Mom's.
3. Never invest in anything that eats or needs painting.

1231. Married life in the old days was simpler. If a man had a fight with his wife, he just went out and got drunk. Today, if he has a fight, he checks with his lawyers, sees a psychiatrist, spends an hour with his marriage counselor—and then goes out and gets drunk.

1232. A man is never so weak as when a pretty girl is telling him how strong he is.

1233. They say no man knows his true character until he has run out of gas, declared bankruptcy, and raised a teenager.

1234. A preacher said, "A man in this congregation committed a terrible sin last week. To show God's disapproval, I'm going to throw my Bible at him."

The preacher drew back his arm and every man in the audience ducked.

1235. Man always has had trouble looking a woman in the eye, and these new swim suits aren't going to help matters.

1236. Grouch Marx says: "I'm an ordinary sort of fellow—42 around the chest, 42 around the waist, 96 around the golf course, and a nuisance around the house."

1237. A bit of graffitti, discovered on the wall of a university men's room: "You should realize these four walls are the last refuge of male privacy."

A rejoinder, however, was scrawled below: "Think again." (Signed) The Cleaning Lady.

1238. Isn't it funny that no one ever asks a man how he combines marriage with a career?

Middle Age

1239. Teenager: "I'll say this for my old man—he tells it like it used to be."

1240. A man has reached middle age when he's warned to slow down by the doctor, instead of the police.

1241. Middle Age: "By the time you can afford to lose a golf ball, you can't hit it that far."

1242. "It's a sobering time," said a 40-year-old at a surprise birthday party, "when you realize you are too old to die young."

1243. The good news is that a university survey indicates that college girls find middle-aged men most attractive. The bad news is that they regard middle age as 32.

1244. Middle age is when you know the answers but nobody asks the questions.

1245. Middle age is when you want to see how long the car will last instead of how fast it will go.

1246. Middle age is when you get out of the shower and you're glad the mirror is fogged up.

1247. Middle age is when you're faced with two temptations and you choose the one that will get you home by 9 o'clock. RONALD REAGAN

1248. One of the symptoms of middle age: "Furnituritus. That's when your chest slips down into your drawers."

1249. College age daughter: "I'm trying to find out who I am and what I'm made of."
  Mother: "When you get to be my age, you don't care what you're made of . . . you just want to loose 10 pounds of it."

Military

1250. The Neutron bomb doesn't destroy property which means even after it bumps you off, you still have to make payments on your car.

1251. Inscription on a monument in France marking the grave of an army mule: In memory of Maggie, who in her time kicked 2 colonels, 4 majors, 10 captains, 24 lieutenants, 42 sergeants, 432 other ranks, and one land mine.

1252. A selectee told members of his draft board, "They can't make me fight," and one of the board replied, "Maybe not, but they can take you where the fighting is and you can use your own judgment."

1253. A Navy admiral was attending a social function in full uniform when he was approached by a stranger who had had several cocktails too many. The man draped his arm around the admiral's shoulder and was saying that he too had been in the Navy when his eyes happened to drop to the admiral's sleeve and gradually focused on the mass of gold braid. He stopped in the middle of a sentence and exclaimed, "Gad! You're in this thing pretty deep, aren't you?"

1254. The veteran was telling his children about his combat duty. "One morning," he said, "was especially bad. Bullets were whistling by and shells were falling all over the place."

"Why didn't you hide behind a tree?" asked his son.

"A tree? Why, Son, there weren't even enough trees for all the officers!"

1255. For you women who have never been to a draft board, it's where you walk around barefoot up to your chin!

1256. There was a young man who got into West Point . . . just barely. The minimum height for West Point is five feet, two inches; he made it by wearing thick socks. Also, he only weighed 120 pounds . . . a little guy, but a brilliant scholar. As second lieutenant, he drew as his first command the roughest, toughest platoon in the entire Army. When he assumed command, he mustered the platoon to attention in front of him and said, "Men, there are two questions we must settle immediately! Question number one, is there anyone in this outfit who thinks he can whip me?"

The men stood rigidly at attention, giving no response, so he put them at ease and repeated the question. Finally, the regimental heavyweight champion, standing six-foot-seven and weighing 274, stepped forward and said, "I believe I can whip you."

"Good," responded the young lieutenant. "You're my First Sergeant. Now, question number two. Is there anyone here who thinks he can whip my First Sergeant?"

1257. The young Army doctor was stationed at a remote dispensary in the South Pacific. One day, he was puzzled about treatment for one of his patients. He radioed a base hospital: "Have case of beriberi. What shall I do?"

A prankster got hold of the message. This was the reply: "Give it to Marines, they'll drink anything."

1258. During World War I, when Harrigan was in France, his wife wrote to him: "There isn't an able-bodied man left in Ireland and I'm gonna have to dig up the garden meself."

Harrigan wrote back: "Don't dig up the garden. That's where the guns are."

The letter was censored and soldiers came to the house and dug up every square foot of the garden. "I don't know what to do," wrote Mrs. Harrigan to her husband. "Soldiers came and dug up the whole garden."

Harrigan wrote back, "Now, plant the potatoes."

1259. The military man had completed his tour of duty and was taking a brushup course in business administration at a university.

The woman instructor, annoyed because he was late for class

nearly every morning, finally said coldly, "I understand you were in the Army."

He nodded affirmatively.

"And what," she continued, "did they say when you came in late?"

"Well," he said, smiling, "it was usually, 'Good morning, Major.'"

1260. During the Trojan War, a handsome young soldier broke into a house where he found two luscious maidens and their Aunt Kate.

Chuckling with glee, he roared, "Prepare thyselves to be taken away as wives, my pretties."

The lovely girls fell to their knees and pleaded with him. "Do with us as you must, but spare our faithful old aunt."

"Shut your mouth," snapped Kate. "War is war!"

1261. My cousin, Hank, tried to enlist in the Green Berets. He passed all the physical exams and training programs, except one. He flunked the art of camouflage.

So Hank asked the top sergeant, "How come?"

"Absence," barked the sarge. "You missed all three camouflage sessions."

Hank asked, "How do you know?"

1262. Drunk (leaving restaurant): "Shay, call me a cab willya?"

Admiral Nimitz (who was standing at the entrance): "My good man, I'm not the doorman. I'm an Admiral."

Drunk: "Awright, then call me a boat. I gotta get home."

Money

1263. By the time most people discover that money doesn't grow on trees, they're already way out on a limb.

1264. Nowadays, a miser is anyone who lives within his income.

1265. "Doctor, you've got to help me," said the patient.

"What seems to be the trouble?"

"I have a couple of dimes caught in my ear and. . . ."

"Good Lord, man. How long have you had them there?"

"About a year."

"Why didn't you come and see me sooner?" asked the doctor.

"To tell you the truth, Doc, up until now, I didn't need the money."

1266. Money can be a curse, especially if your wife has it.

1267. The average woman would never dream of marrying a man

for his money—if she could find any other way to get her hands on it.

1268.   He made his money the old fashioned way . . . he inherited it.

1269.   I don't want my standard of living to improve next year. I can't afford the standard I have now.

1270.   Hoping to encourage his wife to economize by making her more aware of her expenditures, the husband bought her an account book, gave her $100, and explained: "Now, dear, on one side you write down the money you received, and on the other side, you put down what happened to it."

Several days later, he sneaked a peek at the book. On one side it said, "Received $100." On the other, "Spent it all."

1271.   The nicest thing about money is that it never clashes with anything you're wearing!

1272.   Leaving a plush dinner club one night, a miserly gentleman stalked right past the doorman without tipping him.

Nevertheless, the doorman helped the man into the car with a flourish and said pleasantly, "By the way, in case you happen to lose your wallet on the way home, sir, just remember that you didn't pull it out here."

1273.   Husband: "If we were rich we would spend 6 months a year in Florida, 6 months in California, and 6 months in Europe."

Wife: "But that makes 18 months in one year!"

Husband: "Ain't it grand what you could do with money?"

1274.   Not everybody was ruined in the 1920 crash. My uncle got lucky, borrowed $20,000 and invested it in the market the day before the crash. When he jumped out the window, he landed on the guy that lent him the money.

1275.   Three fellows went to church. When it came time to take the offering, they discovered they didn't have any money. So, to keep from being embarrassed, one fainted, and the other two carried him out.

Mothers

1276.   "Hello," answered the dulcet toned voice on the telephone. "This is the Divine House of Transcendental Thought and Meditation. My name is Omar, the humble servant of His Highness Swahiji, the omnipotent ruler of our spirtual domicile. Did you wish to consult with the mighty and benevolent Swahiji?" "Yeh, tell him it's his mother from North Carolina."

1277.   Mother and daughter were in the kitchen washing dishes while father and 7-year-old Johnny were in the living room. Suddenly, father and son heard a crash as a dish fell to the floor. "It was Mom," said Johnny.
   "How do you know?" asked his father.
   "Because," answered Johnny, "Mom isn't saying anything."

1278.   Mother to teenager: "Someday you'll be a mother, then YOU'LL be wrong."

1279.   September is when millions of bright, shining, happy, laughing faces turn toward school. They belong to mothers.

1280.   My children tell me everything. I'm a nervous wreck.

1281.   If evolution works, how come mothers still have only two hands?

1282.   Thing a parent doesn't want to hear: "Hey, Mom, did you know it's almost impossible to flush a grapefruit down the toilet?"

1283.   A little boy was asked to define a mother and said it this way: "A mother is someone who buys you underwear when you wanted a model airplane."

1284.   The teacher had just given her second-grade pupils a lesson on magnets. Now came the question session, and she asked a little boy: "My name starts with an 'M' and I pick up things. What am I?"
   The boy replied instantly, "A mother."

1285.   Grandma Stein was walking through the park with two little boys when she met a friend. "How old are your grandchildren?" asked the lady.
   "The doctor is five and the lawyer is seven!" Mrs. Stein proudly answered.

1286.   Weary of the constant disorder in her sons' room, a mother laid down the law: For every item she had to pick up off the floor, they would have to pay her a nickel.
   At the end of a week, the boys owed her 65 cents. She received the money promptly—along with a 50 cent tip and a note that read, "Thanks, Mom. Keep up the good work!"

1287.   The term "working mother" is redundant. ERMA BOMBECK

1288. The son of a strictly orthodox Jewish family told his mother that he was planning to marry Peggy Malone, a sweet Irish Catholic girl. When the mother regained her composure, she said, "That's for you to decide, Milton, my boy. But please for a while, don't say anything to your father. He has a bad heart, business is bad, and it would be too much of a strain. And for a while, say nothing to your sister Judith; you know how strongly she feels about religion. And your brother, Arnold, with his temper would probably smack you good if he heard about it. But me, you should tell. Anyway, I'm committing suicide."

1289. A proud, doting mother talking about her son: "My son goes to a psychiatrist 5 times a week. And who do you think he spends the whole time talking about? Me!"

1290. Mother (fondly watching her 2-year-old): "He's been walking like that for a year."
    Bored visitor: "Amazing. Can't you make him sit down?"

Neighbors

1291. Two neighborhood kids, a 4-year-old girl and a 3-year-old boy, walked hand in hand up to the front door of the house next door. Standing on her tiptoes, the little girl was just able to reach the doorbell. The lady of the house asked what it was she wanted and the little girl said, "We're playing house and we decided to go visiting our neighbors. This is my husband and I am his wife. May we come in?"
    Thoroughly enchanted, the lady said, "By all means, do come in."
    Once inside, she offered the children lemonade and cookies, which they graciously accepted. When a second tall glass of lemonade was offered, the little girl refused by saying: "No thank you. We have to be going now. My husband just wet his pants."

1292. A man grew so tired of his wife's constant nagging that he finally moved into the garage. He kept on mowing the lawn and doing odd jobs around the house, and she would bring him an occasional pie or bowl of soup, but otherwise, their meetings were kept at a minimum.
    An interested neighbor had watched the situation develop and believed that the blame lay entirely with the wife. One day he asked the husband, "Why don't you just leave? She's impossible!"
    "Oh, I don't know," the husband answered. "She makes a pretty good neighbor."

1293. Teenagers judge the worth of a rock recording by how many neighbors call the police.

1294. After a number of neighborhood robberies, one lady began posting the following sign on her doors when she ran errands: "Son, will be back in a few minutes. Keep doors shut. The boa constrictor is out. Love, Mom."

1295. The difference between a cute little rascal and a potential juvenile delinquent is whether he is your child or your neighbor's.

1296. The trouble with not having children is the worry that some-day the world will be run . . . by the neighbor's kids.

1297. A man came home from visiting his new neighbors, and shouted to his wife: "What do you mean by running around telling our new neighbors that I am deaf and dumb?"
  Shouted his wife, "I never said you were deaf."

1298. A neighbor was heard talking, across the fence, to himself. "Hey, why are you talkin' to yourself?" his friend asked. He replied, "First I like to hear a smart man talk. And next, I like to talk to a smart man."

1299. My neighbor's doctor told him what he needed was an exciting hobby. I suggested Russian Roulette.

1300. "The man upstairs doesn't like to hear Georgie's drum but he's subtle about it," said a young mother.
  "Why?" asked Georgie's father.
  "He gave Georgie a knife and asked him if he knew what was in the drum."

1301. A friend in the Bronx told me: "If Diogenes ever came through our neighborhood with his lamp—somebody'd steal it."

1302. "If it weren't for my wife," he complained, "we'd be one of the nicest couples in the neighborhood."

Newspapers

1303. A Chicago newspaper used to have so many typographical errors in its first edition that an irate reader once wrote to the managing editor, "Don't change a thing in your composing room," he demanded. "I've just broken your code."

1304. From the church section of a newspaper: "The minister was congratulated on being able to get his parish plastered."

1305.   Typo on society page: "Following the wedding, the deception began."

1306.   The following headline in a local paper threw City Hall into an uproar: HALF THE CITY COUNCIL ARE CROOKS.

A retraction in full was demanded of the editor under threat of a libel suit. Next afternoon, the headline read: HALF THE CITY COUNCIL AREN'T CROOKS.

1307.   I read in our local newspaper an interesting ad: "Anyone found near my chicken house at night will be found there the next morning."

1308.   A fellow downtown just passed 40 and got bifocals. Now he can't keep up with what's going on in the world. He can only read the bottom half of the newspaper.

1309.   Note in small town weekly paper: "Due to shortage of space, a number of births will be delayed until next week."

1310.   This item appeared in a box on the front of page one of a Kentucky paper: "The Times is late this week and we want to apologize. The trouble started in a cornfield several years ago. From there it grew, fermented, aged in wood, was bottled in bond, and last Tuesday, finally reached our linotype operator."

1311.   Malapropisms and scrambled language found in newspapers across the country:
   "This has all the earmarks of an eyesore."
   "I deny the allegation and defy the alligator."
   "Let's grab the bull by the tail and look the facts squarely in the face."
   "The roosters have come home to hatch."
   "You can't straddle the fence and still keep your ear to the ground."

1312.   A correction in a community magazine: "Mai Thai is one of the students in the program and was in the center of the photo. We incorrectly listed her as one of the items on the menu."

1313.   A middle age woman called the newspaper to complain of a story about her recent wedding.

The editor inquired, "What did we print that has upset you? Did we mention age?"

"No, but you said my husband was a well-known collector of antiques."

1314.   In the window of a small town newspaper: "Read the Bible to learn what people ought to do. Read this newspaper to learn what they really do."

1315.   The newspaper may not pay as much attention to our mayor as he'd like. But there's only so much space on the comic pages.

1316.   Anybody who thinks no news is good news isn't trying to get out a newspaper.

Nudity

1317.   Clothes make the man. Naked people have little or no influence over society.   MARK TWAIN

1318.   What a sensational idea for an art school. You don't paint the nude models—you trace them!

1319.   Superstitions are not altogether silly. For instance, in Spain, it is considered bad luck for a nudist to ask Zorro for his autograph.

1320.   A local reporter came back with this story about the nearby nudist colony. "Even the maid who answered the door was completely naked," he told his boss.
   "How did you know she was the maid?" demanded the boss.
   "Well," said the reporter firmly, "I knew darn well it wasn't the butler."

1321.   Confucius: "Girl who has tan all over may have done everything under sun."

1322.   A couple fought and argued all the way to Folly Beach, because she insisted she was going to wear a topless bikini into the surf. She simply couldn't be dissuaded, saying that if men could do it, so could women. He finally surrendered, but told her that he'd stay in the car while she made an exhibition of herself.
   She slipped out of the car, and he watched as she walked through the sand. Then a big tough guy intercepted her, and asked her something. She turned and ran back to the car—hastily donning the bikini top.
   "What'd he say?" demanded the husband.
   "None of your business."
   "It is too my business! Tell me what he said. I'll murder the bum!"
   "Don't get excited," she sniffed. "All he said was, 'Got a light, buddy?'"

Joe Griffith wins a golf trophy while playing at a tournament at the beautiful Pinehurst golf course in Pinehurst, North Carolina.

1323.   One of life's mysteries is what a nudist does with his car keys.

1324.   "My uncle is sure glad that the streaking fad is over."
"Really? He's a cop?"
"Nope—a pickpocket."

1325.   One of the health fads for the nudist colonies is to eat Kentucky Fried Chicken by the pool. What you don't eat, you rub on as suntan lotion.

1326.   The housewife next door complains her husband is dull and unimaginative: "Some topless dancers went on strike—and he was the only one who read their picket signs."

1327. You can usually tell the old-timer at a nudist camp. He's the one who brings along a TV set.

1328. I hate nudist colonies. I wouldn't go any place where every woman wears the same thing. ZSA ZSA GABOR

1329. The slowest thing in the world is a nudist going through a barbed wire fence.

1330. My wife isn't very good at choosing gifts. She once gave a pocket watch to a nudist.

1331. An ad in local newspaper: "Wanted: Go-Go Girls. No strings attached."

Optimists/Pessimists

1332. Our idea of an optimist is a man who marries his secretary and thinks he'll be able to continue dictating to her.

1333. Pessimist to optimist: "I'm broke, the bank is about to foreclose on my house, I owe every store in town, and I don't have a dime coming in. What do I have to be thankful for?

Optimist to pessimist: "Be thankful you aren't one of your creditors."

1334. An optimist is a man who talks about what a fool he used to be.

1335. No matter what happens, there's always some pessimist who knew it would.

1336. If you're going to borrow money, borrow from a pessimist. He doesn't expect to get it back anyway.

1337. A pessimist's opinion of reality is knowing that every silver lining has a dark cloud.

1338. Note from a middle-aged married man: "An optimist is a fellow who thinks his wife's telephone conversation is ended when he hears her say 'goodbye.' "

1339. An optimist is someone who hurries to be on time for an appointment because he thinks someone else will be on time and waiting for him.

1340. Daffynition of a pessimist: "One who gets a clean bill of health from his doctor—and then seeks a second opinion."

1341. A pessimist is one who is afraid that somewhere, somehow, someone is having a good time.

People

1342. A Peeping Tom is a guy who's too lazy to go to the beach.

1343. You can always tell the people who say: "Money can't buy happiness." They're the ones who usually have had very little experience with either.

1344. People will accept your idea much more readily if you tell them Benjamin Franklin said it first.

1345. The man who can smile when things go wrong has thought of someone else he can blame it on.

1346. Adam said to Eve, "Of all of the people I know, I like you best."

1347. Americans worry. Have you noticed that almost everything these days is wrinkle resistant . . . except people?

1348. He's an equal opportunity bigot. He hates everybody.

1349. Remember when you get into an argument, if the other fellow prides himself on being rational, it doesn't prevent him from being stupid.

1350. The trouble with the world is not that people know too little, but that they know so many things that ain't so.   MARK TWAIN

1351. If you really want people to know where you stand, wear the same pair of socks for two weeks.

1352. The most unpleasant kind of people to have around are those who insist on knowing the reasons why you did something when you really didn't have one.

1353. A conservative: "A person that puts on his seat belt when he goes through a car wash."

1354. A grouch is a guy who has himself sized up and is sore about it.

1355. Some people grow up and spread cheer. Others just grow up and spread.

1356. The middle class consists of people who are not poor enough to accept charity and not rich enough to donate anything. GENE BROWN

1357. His mind is very much like Alka Seltzer—it gives you the illusion that something's going on.

1358. "Early to bed early to rise makes a man healthy, wealthy, and wise" or "The early bird catches the worm" . . . But, have you ever noticed that all the people who get up early have to go to the people who get up late to get paid? IRWIN C. WATSON

1359. Any fool can tell the truth, but it requires a person of some sense to lie well. SAMUEL BUTLER

1360. A highbrow is a person who says he can listen to the William Tell Overture without thinking of the Lone Ranger.

1361. Human psychology is a funny thing. Everybody wants to be normal, but nobody wants to be average.

1362. Perhaps nothing makes a person think more seriously of birth control than driving the school bus.

Philosophy

1363. Junk is all that stuff that got in your way for 10 years, which you threw away two weeks before you needed it.

1364. To err is human. To blame it on someone else is politics.

1365. The man who can smile while everything about him is going wrong . . . was probably quitting anyway.

1366. The first sign of maturity in teenagers is the discovery that the volume knob also turns to the left.

1367. You can live happily ever after if you aren't after too much.

1368. It's not things you don't know that get you into trouble. It's the things you think you know for sure.

1369. Rule to live by: "If there's a better way to do it, you won't learn of it until whatever it is is done."

1370. Confidence is the feeling you sometimes have before you fully understand the situation.

1371. The main difference between genius and stupidity is that genius has its limits.

1372. When you hear someone start shouting, "What's that got to do with it?" bet even money that person is starting to lose the argument. BOB TALBERT

1373. The only thing about being imperfect is the joy it brings to others. DOUG LARSON

1374. Sometimes a man who thinks of himself as a wit may be only half right.

1375. Laughter is like a diaper change. Not a permanent solution, just something that makes life tolerable.

1376. One thing about stupidity is that you can be pretty sure it's genuine.

1377. Experience is a wonderful thing. It enables you to recognize a mistake when you make it again.

1378. Abstinence is a wonderful thing if practiced in moderation.

1379. He who thinks by the inch,
And talks by the yard . . .
Should be kicked by the foot.

1380. The Queue Principle: "The longer you wait in it, the greater the likelihood that you are standing in the wrong line."

1381. Just when you start winning the rat race, you run into faster rats.

1382. Never buy anything with a handle on it, 'cause it'll just run into work. ERNIE HOBERECHT

1383. Hindsight shows you how a mistake looks from the rear.

1384. I like the philosophy of the old country western song, "As you slide down the banister of life, may the splinters never point the wrong way."

1385. If you can't say somethin' good about somebody, carry a gun.

Police

1386. Gentleman (at the police station): "Could I see the man who was arrested for robbing our house last night?"

Desk Sergeant: "This is very irregular. Why do you want to see him?"

Gentleman: "I only want to ask him how he got in the house without waking up my wife. I've been trying to do it for 20 years."

1387.   Down south, a policeman pulled over an out-of-state driver. He said, "All right, speedy, where you from?"

The driver said, "I'm from Cincinnati."

The policeman said, "Don't you lie to me. I seen that Ohio tag."

1388.   I come from a town so small that the police sign off with "5–2" instead of "10–4."

1389.   A sheriff down home ran for reelection. He received only two votes against his opponent's 467. Next day, after losing, he walked down the street with two six-shooters on his hips.

A citizen spoke up: "You only got two votes. You ain't the sheriff no more. You ain't got no right to walk around with those guns."

"Listen here," he replied, "anybody that's as unpopular as I am has got a right to protect himself."

1390.   The man had been pulled over to the curb for speeding. The officer snapped, "Okay, what's your name?"

The driver replied, "Valdimarsky Ybanowitz Merkowtiskyavics."

The officer said, "Well, don't let me catch you speeding again."

1391.   A traffic cop stopped a lady. "Here's my driver's license and picture," said the lady. The officer looked and said, "I'm glad to see you ain't one of those women who have their photos retouched to get rid of all the wrinkles."

"Sir," said the lady, "you are looking at my thumb print."

1392.   A group of Boy Scouts visiting the FBI office stopped to view the pictures of the 10 most wanted men. One boy pointed to a picture and asked if that really was the photograph of the most wanted person.

The FBI agent in charge assured him it was.

"Then why," the Scout asked, "didn't you keep him when you took his picture?"

1393.   Spotting a woman driving and knitting at the same time, the traffic cop pulled along side her car and shouted, "Pull over!"

"No," said the woman with a sweet smile, "just a pair of socks."

1394.   A car going over 70 m.p.h. down the highway was spotted by the police helicopter patrolman flying overhead. He radioed his partner on the ground and the policeman in the car stopped the speeder and began writing a ticket. "How in the world did you know I was speeding?" the man asked.

The patrolman didn't say anything, but pointed skyward.

"Do you mean to tell me that He has turned against me, too?" the man moaned.

1395. Sign on bulletin board in police homicide division: "In God We Trust—all others we polygraph."

1396. A lady motorist from the hills of Arkansas was stopped by the local patrolman who accused her of doing 45 miles an hour.

"Forty-five miles an hour? That's ridiculous!" she said. "I just left home 15 minutes ago."

1397. An exhaustive study of police records shows that no woman has ever shot her husband while he was doing the dishes.

1398. A fellow paid a psychiatrist $50 to treat him for his inferiority complex and then was fined $25 for talking back to a traffic officer on the way home.

1399. The police chief heads up our canine corps. He not only trained his dog to find golf balls in the rough, but the pooch will kick the balls back onto the fairway if no one's looking.

1400. Drivers applying for a license in Massachusetts are asked to frown when their photo is taken. The picture on the license is for identification, and how many drivers are smiling when a highway patrolman asks to see their license?

1401. My neighbor explained why he prefers whiskey to vodka, which leaves no alcohol breath: "If I happen to punch a cop, I want him to know I've been drinking."

1402. Police Chief questioning an eyewitness: "How far were you standing from the deceased when he was shot?"

"86 feet, 6 ½ inches."

"How can you be so sure?"

"I thought some darn fool might ask me, so I measured it."

1403. Sign of the times department: "About 11 P.M. last Friday night, the police radio dispatched an officer with the following message, 'Investigate juveniles drinking, fighting, and having fun.'"

Politicians

1404. He was a little late getting here. He had to stop and have his promises rotated.

1405. The principal advantage of being a defeated politician is that you don't have to explain why you didn't keep your campaign promises.

1406. An honest politician is one who will fulfill his campaign promises, no matter how dishonest he has to be to do it.

1407. A politician is a man who approaches every subject with an open mouth.

1408. Politicians wouldn't promise the impossible, if people didn't expect it.

1409. A candidate for Congress was campaigning in a Minnesota farm district. He stopped at a barn where a young maid was milking a cow. In a few minutes, a voice came from the nearby house, "Who's there in the barn with you, Velma?"
"A man," replied the girl.
"What kind of a man?"
"A politician, Mama."
"Velma, you come right in the house this minute!" shouted the woman. "And bring the cow in with you!"

1410. "I just found out why the Democrats win in Jersey City all the time!"
"Why?"
"Yesterday, somebody broke into the Mayor's office and found next year's election returns."

1411. "We seem to be having some difficulty in obtaining straight answers from you, Mr. Congressman," chided one of the TV panel newsmen. "Perhaps if you gave us just one, it would set a precedent. Tell me then, what is your favorite color?"
"Plaid," said the politician.

1412. Question: If the leaders of the Republican and Democrat parties were all in a canoe going down the Potomac River and the boat capsized, who would be saved?
Answer: The United States.

1413. Remember when you were a kid, all the fairy tales began with "Once upon a time." Now the fairy tales are even more unbelievable and begin with "If I am elected. . . ."

1414. A politician is a person who finds out which way the crowd is going, then jumps out in front of it and yells encouragement.

1415. Why don't those big shot politicians in Washington give the little man what he really wants? A little woman!

1416. I wouldn't say my favorite politician is old but he ran on a platform of bringing our cavalry up to full strength.

1417. Politics is the art of making yourself popular with the people by giving them grants out of their own money.

1418. Members of opposing parties will always be fighting. It's part of politics. Once a Democratic congressman walked up to a Republican after hearing him speak and shouted, "You can go to hell!"

"Thanks!" replied the Republican. "That's the first time I was ever invited to the Democratic headquarters!"

1419. There are two things I don't like about that politician. His face. B. W. SWEET

1420. Senator Sam Higginbottom explained how he expects to be reelected: "I am going to speak my mind because I have nothing to lose."

1421. Holding public office is like trying to dance on a crowded floor. No matter what you do, you're going to rub somebody the wrong way.

1422. Soon we will be able to say this about many politicians: "He went thundering into the pages of history like an extra quart of water over Niagra Falls."

1423. All the candidates keep insisting they want to know what the people think and every one of them has an unlisted phone number.

1424. Our mayor always puts her best foot forward. It's getting it out of her mouth that's difficult.

1425. In my home county, we have a two-party system. While one party is in power, the other is in jail.

Poor

1426. Wife: "What do you mean your sermon about the rich giving to the poor was half successful?"

Minister: "Well, I convinced the poor."

1427. A very unattractive woman was approached by a man in rags. "Could you spare a quarter for something to eat?"

Why are you begging—a big, strong man like you? I should think you would be ashamed."

"Mademoiselle," he said, removing his hat and bowing low, "I'm an incurable romanticist. I have known few women with such loveliness and the wind has swept them away. And so I have turned to this profession—the only one I know in which a gentleman can approach a beautiful young woman without being formally introduced." He got a dollar.

1428.   My father grew up during the depression when nothing went to waste. The people in the neighborhood were so hard up that anybody who had garbage to throw out was considered well-to-do.

1429.   The government is finally getting closer to the people. It's going broke right along with them.

1430.   A man was making his way home late one evening when another man moved out of the shadows and said, "Please, sir, won't you help a poor, unfortunate fellow creature? I have no job, no home, no family."

The first man was just about to brush past the fellow, but this next remark stopped him cold: "As a matter of fact, sir, all I have left in the whole world is this gun."

1431.   There are two kinds of cattlemen: "Those who go broke and those who stay broke."

1432.   How about the Texan who was so poor the telephone in his Cadillac was on a party line?

1433.   When I was a kid, I was so poor . . . that in my neighborhood the rainbow was in black and white.   RODNEY DANGERFIELD

1434.   Children have become so expensive that only people on welfare can afford to have them.

Presidents

1435.   Ex-President Jimmy Carter spoke at the Economic Club luncheon and told the joke about three envelopes that each incoming president should have for guidance. If the going gets tough during the first year, the president should open the first envelope that says: "Blame the past president!" After the second year, if there is no improvement, he should open the second envelope that declares: "Blame Congress!" If things continue to get progressively worse, the President should open the third envelope. This one advises: "Prepare three envelopes."

1436.   History buffs probably noted the reunion at a Washington party a few weeks ago of three ex-Presidents: Carter, Ford, and Nixon—see no evil . . . hear no evil . . . and evil!

1437. Pity poor old George Washington. He couldn't blame his troubles on the previous administration.

1438. "I say that the President is doing the very best he can!"
"I'm sure he is. And that's what frightens me!"

1439. To give you an idea of what some people think of our Commander in Chief, they held a banquet for him one night in Washington and the chairman of the dinner didn't bother getting any food. He just ordered five loaves of bread and three fish, and expected the President to do the rest.

1440. I understand the President was supposed to fly in from Washington on Air Force One, but he couldn't remember the number of the plane.

1441. You have to have a license to hunt, fish, drive, or even own a dog—but anybody who wants to can run for President.

1442. President Reagan on a balanced budget: "It's like protecting your virtue—you just have to learn to say no."

1443. One example of President Reagan's ability to charm even political opponents came when he invited House Speaker Tip O'Neill over to the White House for the Democratic leader's 69th birthday party.
The two swapped Irish stories over a bottle of champagne and then Reagan offered this toast which stopped the show:
"If I had a ticket to heaven
And you didn't have one too,
I'd give mine up
And go to hell with you."

1444. Richard Nixon's tapes have revealed a lot about the man we never knew. Here's a conversation that was supposed to have taken place with Bob Haldeman.
"Bob, I realize that some day I'm going to pass on," said the President to his aide. "I'd like you to find a nice burial place for me."
Two weeks later, Haldeman returned and said, "Mr. President, I've found just the spot. It's on a hill overlooking a beautiful stream. And the sun hits it during the day almost as if you were being spotlighted."
"Sounds good," said Nixon. "How much?"

"Four hundred thousand dollars."

"What? Four hundred thousand dollars!" cried Nixon. "I'm only gonna be there three days!"

1445. In some countries, being President is just an honorary position—like being a husband in Hollywood.

1446. Nixon was out walking along the beach at San Clemente and decided to go for a swim. He got out beyond the waves and suddenly began drowning.

Three teenage boys happened along, dove into the ocean, and pulled Nixon ashore. When he had regained his breath, Nixon thanked the boys. "In appreciation," he said, "I'd be willing to use my influence to help you boys in any way I can. Is there anything special you want?"

"I'd like to go to West Point!" said one boy.

"I believe I can arrange that," said the ex-President.

"I'd like to go to Annapolis!" said the next.

"I'll see to it immediately," said Nixon.

"I'd like to be buried in Arlington Cemetery," announced the third.

"That's a very strange request," said Mr. Nixon. "Why would you want to be buried in Arlington Cemetery?"

"Well," said the youngster, "when I get home and tell my father who I saved from drowning, he's gonna kill me!"

1447. Despite what you read, I have the greatest respect for the President. In fact, I worship the quicksand he walks on! ART BUCHWALD

1448. Definition of a Vice President: "A guy who lets the President beat him at golf."

1449. Calvin Coolidge is probably best known for his reticence. In fact, he hardly spoke at all. However, one Washington matron once boasted she could make the Chief Executive talk. Cornering him at a dinner, she sought to make good her boast.

"Oh, Mr. President," she said, trying to disarm him with frankness. "I have made a bet that I can make you say at least three words."

"You lose," replied Coolidge.

1450. President Reagan turned 70. If he's anything like me, every now and then, he must walk into the Oval Office and say to himself, "Now what did I come in here for?" DOROTHY PFEIFER

1451. People accuse the President of being power hungry. I don't think that's true . . . and neither do his 12 disciples.

Psychiatrists

1452. Doctor: "What seems to be your problem?"
Bob: "I think I'm an umbrella."
Doctor: "If I'm to cure you, you'll have to be totally honest with me and open up."
Bob: "Why? Is it raining?"

1453. "Exactly how long has your husband thought he was the Lone Ranger?"
"About fifteen years now."
"Well, have no fear. I can cure him completely."
"I guess it's for the best . . . but Tonto is so good with the kids."

1454. In the waiting room of psychiatrist's office: "Oh, I feel some better this morning, but I always feel bad when I feel better because I know I'm going to feel worse."

1455. A man visited his psychiatrist to bare his soul about his insecurity about his height. He was very short. The good doctor reminded him that some of the world's greatest men were short: Napoleon, Rooney, Lautrec. The little guy felt completely cured after this good talk and left the office feeling elated and ready to take on the world. On the way home, a dog ate him!

1456. A patient was brought to a psychiatrist by his family. They explained that he was suffering delusions that a huge fortune was awaiting him. He was expecting two letters which would give him details on a diamond mine he would inherit in Africa and a rubber plantation in Sumatra. The doctor explained, "It was a tough case. I devoted many hours to the patient and just when I had him completely cured, the two letters came."

1457. It's great the way psychiatrists always throw those big words at you. I went to one and he said: "Yes, I see you're suffering from a Cashew-Maraschino Syndrome."
I said: "What's that?"
He said: "Nutty as a fruit cake!"

1458. A man walked into a psychiatrist's office with a fried egg on top of his head and a strip of bacon over each ear.
The psychiatrist looked at him and decided it would be best to proceed with a normal greeting. There was no point in getting the man upset.
"What can I do for you?" the psychiatrist said.
The man smiled pleasantly and said, "Doc, I'm worried about my brother."

1459. "I wish you'd examine my husband," said the woman to the psychiatrist. "He blows smoke rings from his nose and I'm simply terrified."

"That is odd," admitted the psychiatrist, "but it's nothing to be worried about. Many smokers blow rings."

"Very true, doctor," said the woman, "but my husband doesn't smoke."

1460. Psychiatrist to sad eyed patient: "My dear man, you have no inferiority complex. You ARE inferior."

1461. Psychiatrist: "I'm not aware of your problem, so perhaps you could start me at the beginning."

Patient: "All right. In the beginning, I created the heavens and the earth. . . ."

1462. Patient lying on psychiatrist's couch: "Doctor, nobody takes me seriously anymore."

Doctor: "You're kidding."

1463. Hear about the patient who visited his psychiatrist and was told, "You're insane."

"I want a second opinion."

"Okay, you're ugly, too!"

1464. The difference between a psychologist and a psychiatrist is simple. One of them drives you crazy and the other examines you to find out how far.

1465. Patient: "Nobody speaks to me."

Psychiatrist: "Next!"

1466. One definition of a Psychiatrist: "A Jewish doctor who hates the sight of blood."

1467. Did you hear about the psychiatrist who cleaned his own turkey? It was a case of a gobbledegooker degooking de gobbler.

1468. "Do you like conceited psychiatrists as much as the other kind?"

"What other kind?"

1469. The school psychologist told the third grade teacher that she didn't hold the interest of her pupils. "When they come in from recess, I'll prove to you that they are not paying the least attention to what is going on."

In a few minutes, the youngsters straggled in and sat down. The psychologist asked for a number, and a boy gave him "36." This the critic wrote on the blackboard as "63." He then called for another

number, and a little girl said, "81," which was chalked up as "18."
Several other numbers were given and treated in a similar manner
by the psychologist. Finally, there came a voice from the back, saying:
"88. See what you can do with that."

1470.   A fellow turned to the man seated next to him, a well-known
psychiatrist, and said, "Doctor, I had such a tragic childhood. I
just wish I had enough money to tell you about it."

Relatives

1471.   A sad fellow entered a bar and ordered a double scotch.
He downed it with a single swallow. "Give me a triple this time."
Another gulp and the triple was gone.

"Another triple," he demanded.

The bartender said, "Take it easy, fella. That stuff can ruin you,
drinking so fast like that."

"Listen," said the drinker, "I come from a family who believes in
living dangerously. Twenty-five years ago, my father was the first
man to jump from a plane at 1,000 feet without a parachute. Ten
years later, my mother went up to 4,000 feet and leaped without
a parachute. Five years ago, my sister was the first woman to jump
out of a commercial airliner without a parachute. And this afternoon
at 4 o'clock, I'm going up to 35,000 feet in a jet and jump without
a parachute."

The bartender said, "I think you're nuts! Don't you realize you're
going to kill yourself?"

"Sure," said the customer, "but what have I got to live for? I've
got no father, no mother, no sister. . . ."

1472.   If you cross my Uncle George with a groundhog, you get
six more weeks of boredom.

1473.   The rest of the family is mixed up, too. During the Civil
War, his great-grandfather fought for the West. . . .

1474.   I told my mother-in-law that my house was her house. Last
week, she sold it.

1475.   Misers aren't fun to live with . . . but they make wonderful
ancestors.

1476.   My uncle is so narrow-minded that he can look through a
keyhole with both eyes at the same time.

1477.   It's a wise child who resembles a wealthy relative.

1478. My cousin became wealthy in the gas station business but never developed any class. He still wears his tire gauge in the outside tuxedo pocket.

1479. His brother is out of control. His only hope is to be reborn again . . . as an only child!

1480. Our son and daughter-in-law came up with a foolproof way to save money on food. They bought themselves an economy car and began driving it to our house for dinner.

1481. We have yet to meet a kid stupid enough to show pictures of his grandparents to total strangers on an airplane, let alone repeat the clever things they say.

1482. Paul asked his cousin, "What's the best way to teach a girl to swim?"

"That's a job that takes great skill," answered his cousin, Bill. "You must be gentle and kind with her, having her walk out to water that's about waist-deep. Then you put your arm around her waist, gently encouraging her to lie down across it. With your other hand, you pull her ankles up onto the surface of the water, working her legs in a kicking motion. . . ."

"It's my sister," interrupted Paul.

"Oh," answered Bill. "In that case, just push her off the dock."

Religion

1483. A small country church was having money problems. Yet, at a meeting of the deacons, it was proposed to give the pastor a long, overdue pay increase in his salary. The preacher was opposed to the idea.

"Brothers," he said, "I don't want you to increase my salary anymore. I'm having too much trouble raising what you are already paying me."

1484. It was a long sermon on free salvation and when the preacher finished, he asked the deacon to pass the collection plate.

"Just a minute now, Preacher. You said salvation was free—free as the water we drink."

The preacher said, "My good man, it surely is . . . salvation is free and so is the water free. But, somebody's got to pay for the plumbing."

1485. "Grandpa," the little boy asked as he returned from Sunday School, "were you and Grandma in Noah's Ark?"

"Of course, not," replied his grandfather huffily.

"Why weren't you drowned then?"

1486.   Seems a grandmother and her 5-year-old grandson were taking a walk in the country just after the first heavy frost of the season had dyed the foliage and given it a brilliantly colored crazy quilt appearance.

"Just think," the grandmother marvelled, gazing at a scarlet and gold-tinted hillside, "God painted all that."

"Yes," the grandson agreed, "and He even did it with His left hand."

"What do you mean 'He did it with His left hand?'" she asked, somewhat puzzled by the remark.

"Well," the boy replied reasonably, "at Sunday School, they told us that Jesus is sitting on the right hand of God!"

1487.   A group of women was talking together. One lady said, "Our congregation is sometimes down to 30 or 40 on Sunday night."

Another said, "That's nothing. Sometimes our group is down to 6 or 7."

One elderly lady whispered, "It's so bad at our church on Sunday night that when the minister says, 'Dearly beloved,' it makes me blush."

1488.   Did you hear the story about Adam who began staying out late and sneaking back into the Garden of Eden in the wee hours?

Eve watched these goings on suspiciously for a while and then one morning, after Adam had crept in and fallen into a heavy sleep, Eve stole silently to his side and carefully counted his ribs.

1489.   Rabbi Birnbaum sat in a temple all alone, tears streaming down his cheeks. He just learned that his only son had deserted the faith of his forefathers and had become a protestant.

The rabbi was sobbing uncontrollably when suddenly he heard the voice of God: "What is troubling you?"

"I'm so ashamed," cried the Rabbi. "My only son gave up being a Jew and became a Christian!"

"Yours too?" replied the Lord.

1490.   Did you hear about the kid who asked: "Why do so many churches have plus signs on them?"

1491.   Minister to small boy: "Son, can you show me where the post office is?"

Boy: "Sure. As a matter of fact, you follow me and I'll take you there."

Minister: "You're very kind. Where do you go to Sunday School?"

Boy: "I don't go to Sunday School."

Minister: "Oh, my! Well, you certainly should. I'm a minister and if you come to my Sunday School, I'll tell you how to get to Heaven."

Boy: "Mister, how come you can tell me how to get to Heaven when you can't even find the post office?"

1492.   Seems to me that ministers in our church could let up on stressing sin so much these days. Most folks are too poor to afford it.   LOU ERICKSON

1493.   Some churches welcome all denominations, but most prefer fives and tens.   LARRY BONKO

1494.   The answer to a maiden's prayer sometimes makes you wonder if the Lord was paying much attention.

1495.   A newly converted protestant came out of church a bit confused. "The preacher kept warning us that the end is near—and he ended up by asking us to sign a 5-year church building pledge."

1496.   A preacher saw a group of little boys sitting in a circle with a dog in the middle. He asked them what they were doing with the dog. One little fellow said, "We ain't doin' nuthin' to the dog; we're just tellin' lies, and the one that tells the biggest one gets to keep the dog."

The preacher told them that he was very shocked, that when he was a little boy, he would never have even thought of telling a lie.

The little boy said, "Give him the dog, fellas."

1497.   An aging church custodian once said: "I've seen 12 preachers come and go and I STILL believe in God."   LARRY EISENBERG

1498.   Notice on a church bulletin board: "Work for the Lord. The pay is not much but the retirement plan is out of this world!"

Restaurants

1499.   I've eaten in one restaurant so many times I finally got my own coat back.

1500.   I ate at a real health food restaurant. Instead of waiters, they had nurses.

1501.   Two New York motorists were traveling down South and decided to have a cup of coffee in a truck stop. When the waiter came over, one ordered coffee with a little cream and heavy on the sugar. The other took a look around and said, "I'll have mine the same, but make sure it's in a clean cup."

Shortly, the waiter returned. "Which one," he asked, "gets the clean cup?"

1502. Tips for tourists: "Beware of the restaurant where the escargot crawls across your plate and eats the lettuce."

1503. This sounds impossible, but I once drove 28 miles without seeing a McDonald's.

1504. A customer said at a local dinette, "I've never been so insulted in all my life."

Flo, the waitress, told him, "You ought to go out and meet more people."

1505. It's a cheap restaurant. I asked for the menu and the waiter said someone else was using it.

1506. Some exclusive high-toned restaurants are places that have three waiters hovering over each table: One to give you the check . . . and the other two to pick you up off the floor.

1507. The service in that restaurant is terrible, but you don't mind the wait, because the food is so poor.

1508. Last night I ordered a whole meal in French and even the waiter was surprised. It was a Chinese restaurant. HENNY YOUNGMAN

1509. The food in that restaurant was so tough that our dog couldn't even chew the gravy.

Romance

1510. The instructor in a YWCA charm course urged her students to give their escorts every chance to be gallant. "Remain seated in the car until he has time to step around and open the door for you," she said. Then, bowing to reality, she added, "But if he's already in the restaurant and starting to order, don't wait any longer."

1511. I heard about this young couple who wanted to get married after they had known each other just a few days. He asked, "Do you think you could learn to love me?"

"I think so," she said timidly. "I learned shorthand in three weeks."

1512. In the old days, a boy would give his girl his class ring when they were going steady. Nowadays, he lets her use his hair rollers.

1513. A fortunate young man in New Jersey proudly showed his friends this glowing love letter from his old girl, Susan:

"Dear John, I have been unable to sleep ever since I broke our engagement. Won't you forgive and forget? Your absence leaves a void nobody else can ever fill. I love you. I love you. I love you. I love you. Your adoring Susan.

P.S.: Congratulations on winning the lottery."

1514. "I don't see why you're so mad at your ex-fiancee," said the friend. "After all, she returned your ring."

"That's right," replied the other. "But she didn't have to mail it back marked 'Glass, handle with care.' "

1515. When you're over 30, you don't have the "hots for each other," you have a "meaningful relationship."

1516. A flight attendant on a Chicago-Los Angeles flight had her hands full fending off two persistent drunks. The one seated in the front of the plane was doing his best to persuade her to come to his apartment. At the rear, the second drunk was trying to get an invitation to her apartment. As the plane headed for the runway, the front seat pest handed her a key and a slip of paper on which he had written his address. "Here's the key and my address," he whispered. "See you tonight?" "Okay," she said, smiling sweetly as she headed for the drunk at the rear. She handed him the key and slip of paper and said, "Don't be late."

1517. He had a sad romance as a child. He carved his girl friend's name on a tree and it fell on her.

1518. You can't win. My neighbor explained the facts of life to his son with the old birds and bees story. Now the kid thinks he's in love with a woodpecker.

1519. Love is a three ring circus: engagement ring, wedding ring, and suffering.

1520. Don't ever underestimate love at first sight. Many of us might not pass a second inspection.

1521. If a woman calls off the engagement, she should return the ring. She should keep the stone, but return the ring.   EVA GABOR

Jeanne . . . "pointing" something out during a presentation at the Grand Hotel in Point Clear, Alabama.

1522. She thought she was in love but found out it was malnutrition.

1523. After many months of courtship, a girl dismissed her suitor with the statement that she could not think of marrying him until he had a few thousand dollars. "I've got thirty-five dollars," he said.
   "Well," she replied with a blush, "I guess that's close enough."

1524. After the party, I took her home. Gee, it was romantic. Her head was on my shoulder . . . and somebody else was carrying her feet.

1525. I worship the ground she walks on and I don't mind the property she owns on the other side of town either.   RED SKELTON

Salespeople

1526.   A man, after seeing his insurance man driving an expensive new car, said, "Boy, you must be the world's best life insurance salesman!"

"No, I'm not," said the insurance man. "I just tried to sell a policy to the world's best AUTOMOBILE salesman."

1527.   Auctioneer: "A man who can sell nothing for something to a buyer who is looking for something for nothing."

1528.   Sales had been going down, down, down, until finally the manager summoned all salesmen to come to the home office for a meeting. "All right," he shouted at them, "we're all going to have a sales contest—and the man who wins it keeps his job."

1529.   A salesman mentioned he'd only had three orders all week: Get out, stay out, and don't come back.

1530.   And you think you got trouble. My uncle sells transistor radios and they just gave him a new territory . . . Japan.

1531.   Hear about the woman who, having trouble with her TV set, took it back to the store where she had bought it? The salesman told her, "This set was guaranteed for 36 months. Unfortunately, July isn't one of the months."

1532.   An elderly fellow says he bought an item the other day and, inspecting it closely, asked the clerk: "Does this have a lifetime guarantee?"

The clerk, sizing up the age and general condition of his customer, replied, "In your case, yes, it does."

1533.   A man applying for work was asked what his former work was:

"From time-to-time, I was a door-to-door salesman selling wall-to-wall carpeting and back-to-back tape on a day-to-day basis with a fifty-fifty commission in Walla Walla, Washington."

"How was business?"

"So-so."

1534.   Mr. Cheatham had a clothing store and he had a suit he just couldn't get rid of. Finally, he told his number one salesman, "Max, we've had this suit for 12 years. I'm going on vacation. When I come back, I want the suit gone. If the suit ain't gone, you're gone. Understand?"

He came back after a two-week holiday and the suit was gone.

He heard moaning from the basement. He went downstairs and there's Max, lying there all bloody, his clothes ripped, and his shirt hanging out. "Max, what happened?" he asked.

"Boss, I sold the suit."

"Congratulations," Cheatham says, "But what happened?"

Max said, "A blind man came in and I got him to take the suit."

"Okay, but what happened to you?"

"I never did convince his dog."

1535. The customer's sales resistance was high, and the salesman had tried nearly every angle he could think of.

"But it's a beautiful suit," he said. "Why, even your best friends wouldn't recognize you in that suit. Just take a walk outside and examine it in the light."

The customer went out, and when he returned a few moments later the salesman rushed up to him.

"Good morning, stranger," he beamed. "What can I do for you?"

1536. Man at the next desk says he knows a salesman called "The Musket." Why, you ask? Because he's been loaded and fired five times in three years.

1537. Once the customer thinks he understands how much he will have to pay, he resents being "bumped" to a higher price, whether through hidden extras, bait-and-switch, or any other technique.

That kind of selling is too much like the joke about the elderly optician who was teaching his newly graduated son how much to charge a patient.

"After you put their new glasses on them," the old man explained, "you say, 'That will be $55.' If the patient doesn't flinch, you add, 'For the lenses.' And if he still doesn't flinch, you add 'Each.'"

1538. A little boy walked into the bank to open an account for $25. The cashier smiled and asked him how he'd accumulated so much money.

"Selling greeting cards," answered the boy.

"Well, you must have sold them to lots of people."

"Nope," said the boy proudly. "I sold them all to one family, after their dog bit me."

School

1539. "How are your children doing in school this year?

"Well, I still go to PTA meetings under an assumed name."

1540. A high school guidance counselor advised a young student: "Your tests indicate that your chances for success are greatest in a field where your family has some influence."

1541. In the restroom of a local high school which had installed hot air hand dryers was a neatly taped message that read, "Push the button for a message from your principal."

1542. Sign on the high school principal's desk: "My job gives me what I need—an excuse to drink."

1543. There was a mother who was having a hard time getting her son to go to school one morning. "Nobody likes me at school," said the son. "The teachers don't and the kids don't. The superintendent hates me, the school board wants me to drop out, and the custodians have it in for me. I don't want to go."

"You've got to go," insisted the mother. "You're healthy. You have a lot to learn. You've got something to offer others. You are a leader."

"Give me one good reason why I should care," he asked.

"I'll give you two," replied the mother. "You're 49 years old and you're the principal."

1544. "I'm worried about you being at the bottom of your class," said the father to his son.

"Don't worry about it, Dad," assured his son. "They teach the same things at both ends."

1545. "When I go to junior high school," eight-year-old Susan announced, "I'm going to take shop."

"Girls don't take shop," her older brother snapped.

"Why not?" she queried. "Isn't that where you learn to buy things?"

1546. In the first place, God made idiots; this was for practice. Then he made school boards.

1547. A teacher was telling her class about the discovery of the law of gravity.

"Sir Isaac Newton was sitting on the ground looking at a tree," she explained. "An apple fell on his head, and from that, he discovered gravitation. Wasn't that wonderful?"

"It sure was," piped a small lad in the back, "and if he had been sittin' in a school lookin' at his books, he wouldn't have discovered nothin'!"

1548. An executive training school was held. A young man who had completed the course was asked by his boss what he had actually learned during the six-week course and he answered, "Well, I learned to say 'Incredible!' instead of 'Ah, nuts!' "

1549.   The 7-year-old was giving his little sister some advice before she started first grade. "Whatever you do," he said, "don't learn to spell 'cat!' After that, the words just get harder and harder!"

1550.   So many students are driving to high school these days, school administrators are talking about using the buses to pick up teachers.

1551.   On a school bulletin board: "Free! Wisdom on Mondays through Fridays. Bring your own container."

1552.   A man who has never gone to school may steal a freight car, but if he has a university education, he may steal the whole railroad.   THEODORE ROOSEVELT

Secretaries

1553.   One by one, the vice-presidents of a large corporation were called into the office of the president and questioned. Then the junior executives were summoned. Finally, the office boy was brought in. "I want the truth," the boss bellowed. "Have you been out with my secretary?"

"No, sir," the office boy stammered. "I—I'd never do anything like that, sir."

"That's wonderful," said the boss. "Then you fire her."

1554.   Young stenographer to boss: "Well, if you can't give me a raise, how about the same pay more often?"

1555.   My secretary has a mind like a steel trap. You can't imagine the blinding light of understanding that flashed on her face the day she discovered the dictionary was in alphabetical order.

Once she took three weeks to look up the word "zoological."

1556.   The secretary spoke right up to her boss. "I've taken all the criticism of my work I intend to. How do you spell 'quit?' "

1557.   I've got a new secretary. She's already a month behind in her work. And what makes it even worse, she's only been with me a week.

1558.   The boss asked the new secretary to fill out a questionaire for the insurance company. When she came to a question that asked, "Do you have any serious physical disabilities?" the young lady thought for a moment and then wrote, "Freckles."

1559. An insurance company secretary called in sick. When her supervisor asked what was wrong, she said, "It's my eyes."

"What's the matter with them?" said the supervisor.

"It's such a pretty sunny day," the secretary replied. "I can't see coming to work."

1560. Secretary to boss: "Certainly I have a good reason for being late every day. It makes the workday seem much shorter."

1561. Overheard in the secretarial pool: "It's discouraging to make a mistake, but it's humiliating when no one even notices it."

1562. There was an inexperienced girl who got a job as a medical secretary. She was having trouble with the boss's notes on an emergency case which read, "Shot in the lumbar region."

She brightened up shortly and typed in the record, "Wounded in the woods."

1563. My secretary told me the other day: "I've added up this column of figures 10 times, sir."

I said, "Good girl!"

She said, "And here are the 10 answers."

1564. A philosophical New Yorker, who gave up all hope of getting perfect letters from his office typist, now sends the letters out as they come from her mill—spelling errors, erasures, and all. He evens matters with a rubber stamp that he had specially made. In the lower left-hand corner of each letter he stamps: "She can't type—but she's beautiful."

1565. A wealthy executive honeymooning with his beautiful secretary was discussing her replacement.

"I've been thinking of that, too," said the ex-secretary and new wife. "My cousin would be just right for the job."

"Who is she?"

"Joseph David Smith," replied the bride.

1566. Boss: "Why aren't you busy?"

Secretary: "I didn't see you coming."

1567. Two secretaries sat discussing their bosses during the coffee break.

"He's in a bad mood again," one moaned. "All I asked him was whether he wanted the carbon copies double-spaced too."

1568. Secretary's Rule to live by: "If it's filed correctly, it won't be anything you're looking for."

Shopping

1569.   A 6-year-old boy was in a supermarket with his grandfather, and had both hands in his pockets to hold up his shorts.

"What's the matter, son?" asked a clerk. "Forget your belt?"

"Naw," the kid said, "Old Gramps takes it away from me before we come in here so that I won't be grabbin' candy or nothin'."

1570.   I won't say how long I've stood in front of department stores waiting for my wife to come out, but yesterday a motorcycle cop put a chalk mark on my leg!

1571.   A fellow says his wife came home from the supermarket the other day with five LP records, three paperback books, a set of encyclopedias, a barbeque set, six pairs of nylons, three potted plants, and a 24-piece luggage set. "What are we having for dinner?" he asked her.

"I don't know," she replied. "I ran out of money before I got any food."

1572.   Lawyer in expensive divorce case: "Boy, your wife spent a lot on clothes."

Husband: "Yeah, she has a black belt in shopping."

1573.   Saleswoman at a lingerie counter to a male shopper: "Could you be a little more explicit than 'big and fat?'"

1574.   The difference between female and male economics: "A man will pay $3 for a $1 item he wants. A woman will pay $1 for a $3 item she doesn't want."

1575.   Do you know why God created Gentiles? Someone had to buy retail.

1576.   I was shopping for a suit in Hollywood at an exclusive clothing store on famous Rodeo Drive. The price was $64.00. "That's not bad for a suit," I thought. But that wasn't for the suit . . . that was for the price tag!

1577.   New on the grocery shelves: "Generic cigarettes. They still give you a disease, but it has no name."

1578.   It's funny that wives aren't embarrassed when they buy men's pajamas, but a husband purchasing a nightgown for his wife acts as though he was making a deal with a dope peddler.

1579.   Definition of a husband: "A person who goes window shopping only when he wants to buy a window."

1580. The eye doctor patiently tried lens after lens on an elderly lady. Nothing seemed to be right for her. "Don't get discouraged," the doctor reassured her. "It's not easy to get just the right pair of glasses, you know."

"It certainly isn't," the woman replied, "especially when you're shopping for a friend."

1581. A woman will buy anything if she thinks a store is losing money on it.

1582. This rancher from Texas wanted to buy his wife a sexy nightgown for her birthday.

"What size?" asked the little lady at the lingerie department.

"I dunno," the cowboy admitted. "But she wears a size 30 chaps."

Show Biz

1583. A recently wed Hollywood star admitted his marriage is a flop. "I'd ask her for a divorce, but I don't know her that well."

1584. TV's Monty Hall participates in many benefit performances. Recently, he received a phone call from an organization in Chicago.

"Will you appear at this benefit for us?" he was asked.

"Sure," Monty said. "I'll try to get my friend, Bob Hope, to come along, too."

"Well," said the caller, "if you can get Bob Hope, you don't have to come."

1585. The people in Hollywood are like a bowl of Granola . . . What aren't fruits and nuts are flakes.

1586. The nice thing about being a celebrity is that when you bore people, they think it's their fault.

1587. A new motion picture company was formed. It was decided that it would be called the Miracle Film Company.

"We'll get a big sign," said the boss.

"We'll get the biggest sign in the world so it can be seen for miles. We'll spend five hundred thousand dollars for a slogan on it."

So, after half a million was spent on the sign, it read: "If It's A Good Picture, It's A Miracle."

1588. Once Mrs. Douglas MacArthur was asked if she had seen Gregory Peck play the part of MacArthur in the movie, "MacArthur."

Smiling, the general's widow said, "I have the greatest admiration for Mr. Peck. However, I have seen General MacArthur playing General MacArthur, so I don't need to see Mr. Peck playing MacArthur!"

1589. After viewing some of the new "adult" movies, Matilda asked her husband, Roger, why he never made love to her the way the men in those movies made love. "Are you serious?" replied Roger. "Do you know how much they PAY those guys to do that?"

1590. The movie makers have a good idea. Instead of middle age, they are going to call it "Youth . . . Part II."

1591. A farm boy and his pretty girl friend were visiting the county fair and they went into a side show where a mind reader was performing. They sat in the front row just as the performer started his show.

"Ladies and gentlemen," he began, "I can see through anything. I can tell you what's in your pockets, the number on the back of your watch, the dates on your coins. I can see through iron, steel, and concrete."

Without waiting for him to finish, the girl grabbed her boyfriend's hand and headed for the door. "Come on, Virgil. We're gettin' out'a here. This ain't no place for a girl in a cotton dress!"

1592. "I've got a great idea for a night club show. All the chorus girls are fully clothed, but the audience sits there naked."

1593. A theatrical agent phoned an unemployed actor at his hotel and offered him a thousand dollars a week to play the lead in a TV series.

"Not on your life," replied the actor, "I won't do it for less than five thousand."

"Come down and we'll talk it over," urged the agent.

"What," shouted the actor, "and take a chance on being locked out of my room?"

Signs

1594. That doctor has a sign on his office door reading "8 to 5." Those aren't his hours—those are YOUR odds!

1595. Sign seen in small town bakery: "The boss told me to change the sign, so I did."

1596. Bumper Sticker on a deluxe camper: "Spending the children's inheritance."

1597. Sign pinned to Army barracks door: "Shut the door, stupid! Not you, Sir."

1598. Bumper sticker on teenage boy's car: "Support your Girl Scouts—Today's Brownie is tomorrow's cookie."

1599. Sign in a Washington store window: "You can fool some of the people some of the time, and generally speaking that's enough to allow for a profit."

1600. A Charleston gent named Murphy has this sign displayed prominently in his store: "Murphy's Law: Don't Mess With Mrs. Murphy."

1601. I know a man who is so shallow that if it weren't for his bumper stickers, he wouldn't have any opinions at all.

1602. Sign in a battery shop: "You want to start something?"

1603. Service station sign: "To avoid complaints on free service, all free service has been discontinued."

1604. Sign in an optometrist's office: "IF YOU DON'T SEE WHAT YOU'RE LOOKING FOR, YOU'VE COME TO THE RIGHT PLACE."

1605. Sign on downtown elevator: "Button for 8th floor is out of order. Push 5 and 3."

1606. Bumper Snicker: "A truly wise man never plays leap frog with a unicorn."

1607. A bumper sticker on the back of a well-worn station wagon: "Get Revenge—Live Long Enough To Be A Problem To Your Children!"

1608. Sign on secretary's desk: "Don't rush me. I'm making mistakes as fast as I can."

1609. Sign in a needlework shop: "It's a crewel, crewel world."

1610. On a roadside sign: "PRECISION ENGINEERING COMPANY—103 yards, 2 feet, 9 inches Ahead."

Singers

1611. Famous singer: "Did you notice how my voice filled the building?"

Music critic: "I even noticed some people leaving to make room for it."

1612.   Not long ago, a Sunday School Superintendent was visiting the primary department opening in his church. He was pleased by the enthusiastic singing of the boys and girls. However, one little guy was just sitting in his chair, not making a sound. The Superintendent made his way over to the boy and asked, "Jim, why aren't you singing like all the rest?"

The boy looked up, smiled, and answered, "Somebody has to listen, don't they?"

1613.   The choir teacher asked some third-graders if they could sing the last line of "The Star Spangled Banner." Willie raised his hand and sang, "And the home of the brave . . . Play Ball!"

1614.   Star of the James Bond films, Roger Moore said, "I'll do a musical as soon as they can find someone who can write a song all on one note."

1615.   Show me a guy with a song in his heart and I'll show you an old geezer with his pacemaker turned to KABL.   JACK HAYES

1616.   I know only two tunes—one of them is "Yankee Doodle," and the other isn't.

1617.   The master of ceremonies was trying to introduce a singer at a noisy teamster's convention, but he couldn't get it quiet. Finally, one of the men, obviously an authority, shouted, "Okay, you guys, shut up. Let the man work."

Everyone quieted down. Suddenly, the singer came from a side entrance, singing at the top of his lungs. Without warning, a fist crashed into his face and an indignant trucker said, "You heard the boss. Shut up."

1618.   I'd rather hear that boy sing than eat. I say that because for the last 30 minutes, I've been listening to him eat.

1619.   I know a school teacher who says she is absolutely certain that during a school celebration of Christmas, one of the children sang: "God rest ye, Jerry Mendelbaum!"

1620.   Opera is when a guy gets stabbed in the back, and instead of bleeding, he sings.

1621.   Description of a rock group: They are so loud they make my ears water.   GEORGE GOBEL

1622.   The little boy punched his mother in church and asked, "What's the lady next to me singing?"

"Alto," whispered the mother.

"No wonder she sounds so funny," blurted out the lad. "We're singing 'Joy to the World.'"

1623. A true music lover can be defined as a man who puts his ear to the keyhole when he hears a girl singing in the bath tub.

1624. This sounds impossible, but I heard a rock song the other day and understood some of the words.

1625. A woman in a rooming house complained to the landlady that the man in the next room kept annoying her with indecent songs. "I am sure that you're mistaken," answered the landlady, "Mr. Brown never sings any songs."

"I know," replied the woman, "but he whistles them."

1626. Hear about the archaeologists who have just deciphered the ancient writing on the tomb of Montezuma? It says, "Please tell those Marines to stop singing in the halls."

Sleeping

1627. Joe just called. Said he slept on his face all night and he's too ugly to come to work.

1628. You know what puzzles me about the Frankenstein movies? The way the monster always walks around with his arms outstretched. I haven't seen anybody walk like that since my wife fell asleep under a sun lamp!

1629. "Last night I dreamed you gave me $200 for clothes," the wife said. "Surely you wouldn't do anything to spoil such a dream, would you?"

The husband answered, "Of course not, my dear. You can keep the $200."

1630. If we can develop some way in which a man can doze in public and still keep from making a fool of himself, we have removed one of the big obstacles to human happiness in modern civilization.

1631. Did you hear about Senator Brown's nightmare? He dreamed he was unopposed in the primary and came in third.

1632. The only trouble with Italian coffee is that a week later you're sleepy again.

1633. The lion and the lamb shall lie down together, but the lamb won't get much sleep.

1634.   My father thought nothing of getting up at 6 o'clock in the morning . . . and I don't think too much of it either.

1635.   I never liked to drink coffee on the job. I toss and turn at my desk all day.

1636.   A bachelor is a man who never knows whether he snores or not.

1637.   The unmarried guys have one advantage over married men: They can take a nap on top of the bedspread.

1638.   If anything makes a kid thirstier than going to bed, it's knowing that his parents have gone to bed, too.

1639.   Some mothers of school age children are having trouble getting the kids out of bed these summer mornings.
   One complained about her sleepyheaded child to another mother, who said she had no problem at all getting her son up in the morning.
   "I just open the door to his room and throw the cat on the bed," she said.
   "How on earth does that help?" the first demanded.
   "He sleeps with the dog."

1640.   He was worried about his little daughter getting up ill in the middle of the night. So he consulted one of his know-it-all friends. "Does she drink milk before she goes to sleep?"
   "Yes."
   "That's the trouble," said the wise guy. "If you feed a child milk before bedtime, she goes to sleep and tosses from side to side, milk turns to cheese, cheese turns to butter, butter turns to fat, fat turns to sugar, sugar turns to alcohol, and the first thing you know, the poor little thing wakes up with a hangover!"

1641.   This husband who was an amateur psychiatrist told his wife that, once the day was over, she should try to relax and should never take her troubles to bed with her at night. So . . . she made him sleep in the guest room.

1642.   There's nothing like the clanging of an alarm clock to remind you that the best part of the day is over.

1643.   A sleepyeyed ranch hand came to work quite late one morning. "Sorry," he apologized. "I had truck trouble."
   "What happened to your pickup?" inquired the boss.
   "I was late gettin' into it."

1644. A man was tormented by nightmares. Whenever he went to sleep, he dreamed that ugly animals came out from under his bed and rushed back under it again.

"I told my brother about it and he stopped it," he told a friend later.

"Is your brother a psychiatrist?" the friend asked.

"No, he's a carpenter," the man replied. "He sawed the legs off my bed."

Small Towns

1645. My town is so dull, if it wasn't for mouth-to-mouth resuscitation, there wouldn't be any romance at all!

1646. Our town is so small that if it weren't for bacteria, we wouldn't have any culture at all.

1647. Our town is so small that the 7–11 closes at 10:00.

1648. My hometown is so small, it classifies "soap-on-a-rope" as jewelry.

1649. A fellow says he comes from a very small town. He says it's so small that they had a four-way stop in the center of town, but only two of the ways went anywhere.

1650. I came from a small town. The first baby of the new year was born in April.

1651. I live in a town so small we don't even have penicillin. The doctor just gives you a piece of moldy bread and tells you to wait.

1652. Our small town has only one motel—no waterbeds, just damp sheets.

1653. A traveler stopped at a gas station in a small town to buy gasoline and asked if there was a place close by to get something to eat. The slow-moving attendant answered, "Naw. There's jus' the cafe down the road and it closes at 6 o'clock."

"What do you folks do around here for excitement?" the motorist asked.

"Well," he said, " 'round here, folks don't get excited."

1654. "Why do people in your town keep on buying your newspaper when they already know what everybody in town has done that week?" a big city reporter asked a small town editor.

The rural editor pointed out, "They buy the paper because they want to see which ones got caught."

1655. A sign on a wall at a tavern in the small town of Victoria, Minnesota proclaims, "We don't have a town drunk—we take turns." Understand there was a mixup last Saturday night and six guys thought it was their turn.

1656. Just got an unhappy note from back home . . . they had to close the zoo. The slug died.

Sons

1657. Husband to wife, who is taking a picture of him with college student son: "Wouldn't it look more natural if he had his hand in my pocket?"

1658. I have almost a Siamese twin relationship with my son. We're joined at the wallet.

1659. Letter from college freshman son: "Send food packages! All they serve here is breakfast, lunch, and dinner."

1660. My son has accumulated a nice little pile. Now, he's trying to get his girlfriend to wash it.

1661. My son said, "I'm worried. I'm beginning to like girls better than my lizzard collection."

1662. At the restaurant the other day, I overheard two men talking about their sons who were away at college. "What does your boy plan to be when he graduates?" asked the one.
"I'm not really sure," he said. "But judging from his letters, it appears that he aims to become a professional fund raiser!"

1663. If your son mows the lawn without being told, don't plan on using the car that night.

1664. A middle-aged fellow was asked by a jealous friend how he managed to keep his weight down.
"I eat very slowly."
"How does that help?"
"I have two teenage sons. By the time I'm ready for a second helping, it's gone."

1665. When a boy turns out great, it's heredity. When he doesn't, it's those kids he hangs around with.

1666. The garden was at its peak of production, and Mother was busily putting some of its fruits away for next season. As she opened the freezer to deposit a batch, she noticed a row of plastic freezer containers, each containing a fly that was frozen stiff. She was removing the containers and puzzling over them when her 8-year-old son bounded in.

"Mom! Please, don't throw those away. I made those TV dinners for my turtle."

1667. Small boy to mother: "Can I help Dad put on the snow chains? I know all the words."

1668. The young family was discussing the imminent arrival of the second child. The parents decided they would have to move to a bigger house. Their firstborn listened gravely, then shook his head. "That wouldn't work," he said. "He'd just follow us!"

1669. An 8-year-old boy objected to going to Sunday school. "Shucks," he griped. "I bet Dad never went to Sunday school when he was a kid." His mother assured him that Dad went regularly.

"Okay," the boy agreed reluctantly. "But I bet it won't do me no good either."

1670. After the mother had given birth to triplets, the father asked his 4-year-old son what he thought about the blessed events. "Well," the boy said as he looked his father in the eye, "you better start finding a place for them. They won't be as easy to get rid of as them kittens were."

1671. Mother: "Jimmy, there were two slices of cake on the table last night when we went to bed, and this morning, there is only one. How do you explain that?"

Jimmy: "I don't know, Mom. I guess it was so dark, I just didn't see the other piece."

1672. The father was telling about his sons: "The first one is a doctor—the second one stays out all night, too.

"The third one is a lawyer, and the fourth won't tell the truth either.

"The fifth one is a school teacher, and the sixth one is always broke, too.

"The seventh one is a preacher, and the eighth one . . . well, he won't work either."

1673. He calls his son "Vincent Van Gogh" because he listens to him with one ear.

1674. The youngster brought home a report card heavy with poor grades. "What have you to say about this?" asked his mother.

"One thing for sure," replied her son, "You know darn well I ain't cheatin'!"

1675.   Neighbor: "Have you got a bottle opener?"
Father: "Yeah, but he's away at college."

Space

1676.   You know what would stop all this moon exploration? If they found out that one of those craters five miles across wasn't a crater—but a belly button!

1677.   A small child asked about the stars and an amateur astronomer explained about stars, the moon, and comets. "Do you know what a comet is?" asked the grown-up.
"Sure," said the kid, "like when they ask a question on TV and the guy says 'No comet.'"

1678.   "What are you going to talk about at the meeting tonight, Ralph?"
"I thought I'd talk about my trip to the moon."
"But you've never been to the moon," exclaimed his friend.
"Don't worry about a thing," he replied. "Neither has the audience."

1679.   A night parachute jumper missed his mark and landed in a remote parking lot. With lights still flashing, flares still burning, and crash helmet turned crossways, he asked, "Where am I?"
A woman swallowed hard and timidly said, "Earth."

1680.   An expert says: "Sagittarius is surrounded by a huge ring containing 40,000 trillion fifths of alcohol at 100 proof." The bad news is it is 2,000 light years away. The good news is that it's moving our way at 60 miles per second.

1681.   Where else but America could they send men to the moon, machines to Mars, and my luggage to Saginaw, Michigan?

1682.   Two monkeys were in a space capsule on their way to the moon. One complained about the situation. The other said, "Well, it's better than working in the cancer clinic."

1683.   The fact that the planets in our solar system have never been rearranged is sufficient proof that God is not a woman.

1684.   A NASA scientist says he is sure there are women on Mars. "NASA shot a communications satellite up there and got a busy signal."

1685. I'm proud to say my kids are studying to be astronauts! Their teachers told me they're both taking up space.

1686. You only go around once in life . . . unless you can catch a ride on one of the space shuttles.

1687. Deep Space . . . where the hand of man has never set foot.

1688. Do you know why they don't launch the astronauts from the Space Center in Houston? They'd have to change planes in Dallas-Ft. Worth!

Speakers

1689. Will Rogers was emceeing a banquet at which a speaker talked for too long. Said Rogers after the bore finally quit, "Ladies and Gentlemen, you have been listening to the famous Chinese statesman, 'On Too Long.' "

1690. The World's Best After Dinner Speech—"Waiter, give me both checks."

1691. The wife of one of our Presidents accompanied him on one of his European goodwill trips. Back at the White House, her daughter asked her, "What did you eat down there?"

She answered, "Lots of beef, spicy side dishes, and 7886 green beans."

"Quit kidding me, Mom," protested the daughter. "How would you know exactly how many beans you ate?"

"Young lady," answered the President's wife, "How do you suppose I occupy my time while your father's speaking?"

1692. The late Jack Benny once remarked, on accepting an award, "I don't deserve this, but I have arthritis and I don't deserve that either."

1693. Before I begin my speech to this illustrious audience, I would like to remind you that we are gathered in an auditorium and I presume that you all know the meaning of the word auditorium. It is derived from two Latin words: audio, to hear; and taurus, the bull.

1694. Of course, in my neighborhood, I used to work some pretty tough audiences. If they liked you, they didn't applaud, they let you live.

1695. You know you're in trouble when the program chairman advises you not to wear your good clothes.

1696. Applause before a speaker begins his talk is an act of faith. Applause during the speech is an act of hope. Applause after he has concluded is an act of charity. BISHOP FULTON J. SHEEN

1697. Victor Borge, in Flint, Michigan, played to an audience only one third of the hall's capacity. He remarked, "Flint must be a very rich town. I see each of you brought two or three seats with you."

1698. Doc told Uncle Lyndon to cut down on his political speeches for health reasons. Put him on a low podium diet.

1699. As the banquet was about to begin, the chairman realized no minister was present to give the invocation. He whispered to the main speaker, "Sir, since there is no minister here, will you please ask the blessing?"

The speaker arose, bowed his head and with deep feeling said, "There being no minister present, let us thank God."

1700. My congressman's speeches are getting much shorter. He's only talking about the issues he knows something about.

1701. There's no trick to being a humorist when you have the whole government working for you. WILL ROGERS

1702. Definition of a "roast": A phenomenon in which a noteworthy individual sits and listens as friends, business associates, and often part-time enemies stand up and say things about him/her that they've probably been saying behind his/her back all along.

1703. He's so dumb. He spent $2,000 to go to a speaker's school and tried to shave with the microphone.

1704. The luncheon speaker was obviously very nervous as he struggled with his notes and the microphone and his glasses. "I hope you will forgive me for being a bit nervous," he said. "I must confess that this is only the second time I've ever spoken in public. The first time was in Louisiana some years ago when I proposed to my wife over a rural party line."

1705. Since Grandpa had only a little formal education, he enjoyed ribbing the college people. Because of his uniqueness, he was invited to speak at a large college gathering. He congratulated the institution on its vast storehouse of knowledge, and told them he had figured out how they had collected so much. He said, "From my observation, this laudable accomplishment has been achieved because the freshmen bring in so much learning and the seniors take out so little."

Sports

1706. When a giant Italian boxer first came to the U.S., won all his fights, he began to think he was pretty good. One day on the West Coast, someone asked him how he liked Los Angeles. "Me knock him out in two rounds," he replied confidently.

1707. Do you know why mountain climbers rope themselves together? To keep the smart ones from going home.

1708. As a people, we certainly love pro sports. What else gives you a chance to boo a bunch of millionaires to their faces?

1709. He was not much of a prizefighter. In his first four fights, he never got to use his stool.

1710. John Wayne: "Before I got sick, I was getting exercise occasionally from bowling. But there weren't many alleys that would let me come back a second time. They didn't like my style. I have an overhand delivery."

1711. A lady told a friend her husband spoke three languages— golf, football, and baseball.

1712. They say they climb mountains because they "are there."
 I wonder if it would astound them
 To know that the very same reason is why
 The rest of us go around them!

1713. The International Chess Championship proves at long last that there is something more boring than watching paint dry.

1714. A 6′10″ college basketball player applied for a summer job as a lifeguard. When asked if he could swim fast, he said, "I can't swim."
 "Then how could you be a lifeguard?" asked the swimming coach.
 "I'm a heck of a wader," he replied.

1715. Stanley's father was distressed to find out that his son was planning to take up sky diving. "Are you sure you want to do it, son," he reasoned with the lad. "Why go into any sport where you have to do it right the first time?"

1716. There's a form of Russian Roulette where you put six cobras in a room and play the flute. One of the cobras is deaf.

1717. Seems a man had a terrible night with pins and told his buddy he was going to throw his bowling ball into the river that

Doc Blakely and Michigan's Secretary of State Richard Austin prove the point that head table chatter doesn't have to be dull. Listening and laughing with other good story tellers is what Doc calls "research."

night. The next evening, however, the disgruntled bowler was out on the lanes again, rolling them in the gutter. "I thought you said you were going to throw your ball into the river?" asked a friend.

"Yeah," replied the bad bowler, "I tried but I missed."

1718. A skiing enthusiast from the snow slopes of Colorado came up with a great idea: "A pair of skis that converts into a pair of splints."

1719. One of the advantages of bowling over golf is that you very seldom lose a bowling ball. DON CARTER

1720. Bench warmers: Every team needs huggers. Those are the guys you sign so you can hug 'em after you win, instead of having to hug the guys who play and sweat. TOMMY VARDEMAN

1721. A guy on my bowling team is so competitive he wears a tear away shirt.

1722. The Baptist, Methodist, and Presbyterian preachers joined a bowling league. Called themselves the Holy Rollers.

Stocks/Bonds

1723. A stockmarket analyst was asked how to become a millionaire in the bond market. He answered, "Start with two million."

1724. Don't gamble! Take all your savings and buy some good stock and hold it 'til it goes up, then sell it. If it don't go up, don't buy it. WILL ROGERS

1725. Talk about things going up . . . if forty years ago, you had invested in taxes, today, you'd be rich!

1726. A Methodist is not a thing in the world but a Baptist who made good on his stock investments.

1727. One businessman to another: "I used to be bullish, then I was bearish, now I'm brokish."

1728. They say stocks are a good buy . . . and they are. Last year mine were goodbye $5,000.

1729. He says the stock market is the only place he knows . . . where you can lose your life savings on something called securities.

1730. You'd be surprised how many people drive to their stockbrokers in a Mercedes to get financial advice from people who came to work on the bus.

1731. My Uncle Wilbur brags he has 50,000 shares of Xerox. He really only has one share; he xeroxed the rest.

1732. A businessman wanted to make a killing in the market. His broker knew this, called him and said, "I have a wonderful new issue for you."
The man said, "Okay, how much?"
"Five dollars a share." So he bought 10,000 shares.
Later in the month, the broker called him again and said it looked like the stock might hit $10 a share. So he bought 10,000 more shares.
In a couple of months, the broker called to say chances looked good for the stock to reach $20 a share and was told: "Get me 10,000 more shares."

Six weeks later, the man had to raise some money and he called his broker and told him to sell half his holdings.

The broker said, "You can't sell."

"Why not?"

"You are the only stockholder," said the broker.

1733.   A pretty blonde sat down next to a man sitting in the lobby of a hotel and whispered, "Are you looking for some company?"

He said, "Yes."

So she sold him ten shares of General Motors.

1734.   If you make money at poker, that's gambling. If you make it playing bridge, it's social activity. If you make it by outguessing the stock market, that's a miracle.

1735.   Two stockbrokers were lunching . . . "Let's talk about something besides stocks and bonds," said one.

"Suits me," agreed the second. "Let's talk about women."

"Good idea—common or preferred?" quipped the first.

1736.   The stock market is like a woman. Sometimes it's good, sometimes it's bad, but it's always fun to speculate.

Students

1737.   Teacher (to student): "Your theme on 'Our Dog' is identical to your sister's."

Student: "Yes'm, I know . . . it's the same dog."

1738.   Do you get the feeling that the world is being run by "C" students?

1739.   Sometimes the student misunderstands a slight bit as illustrated by answers given to test questions:

"Matrimony is a place where souls suffer for a time on account of their sins."

"Where was the Declaration of Independence signed? At the bottom."

"Where is Cincinnati? First place in the American Football League."

"Denver is located just below the O in Colorado."

"The soil of Prussia was so poor, the people had to work hard just to stay on top of it."

"The climate of Bombay is such that its inhabitants have to live elsewhere."

1740.   "Who discovered America?" the teacher asked. When one pupil answered, "Ohio," she said: "Ohio! Goodness, no! America was discovered by Columbus."

The pupil replied, "Oh, yeah, I just forgot his first name."

1741.   After the students had been photographed, the teacher tried to talk them into purchasing a copy of the group picture. "Just think how nice it will be to look at it when you are all grown up and say, 'There's Rose; she's married,' or 'There's Billy; he's a sailor.' "

From the back of the room came a voice, "And there's teacher; she's dead!"

1742.   Some students drink from the fountain of knowledge, others just gargle.

1743.   The Student's Psalm:

The monster is my teacher, I shall not pass.

He maketh me face the blackboard,

He destroyeth my love note,

He maketh me put my gum in the trash can,

He maketh me quiet and taketh away my candy,

He waketh me from my sleep and leadeth me to the office for conduct's sake.

His face hardens before me,

He maketh me write 600 words,

He filleth the blackboard with homework.

My notebook runneth over.

Yea, though I walk through the Valley of the Shadow of discipline,

I shall fear no evil.

For I am the meanest little devil in the valley.

1744.   A dedicated student is a boy who has discovered something more interesting than girls.

1745.   The English teacher was trying to break her class of the "I seen" habit.

"You should never say 'I seen him do it,' " she sternly admonished.

"Yeah," piped up a voice from the rear. "Specially if you ain't sure he done it."

1746.   The fourth grader returned the report card to his teacher after the parents had reviewed it. He said, "Mrs. Darling, I ain't trying to scare you, but my daddy said if this report card doesn't improve, somebody is gonna get a whippin'."

1747.   First grader: "We learned to say, 'Yes, Sir' and 'No, Sir' at school today."

Father: "You did?"

First grader: "Yeah!"

1748. The 6-year-old returning from his first day at school told his mother: "I'm not going back. I can't read and I can't write and they won't let me talk."

1749. Son to father examining his report card: "I'm not an under-achiever. My teacher is an over-expecter."

1750. The new (and pretty) schoolteacher stepped out of the room for a moment and while she was gone, someone scrawled on the blackboard: "I am the world's greatest lover!"
When she returned, she asked, "Who did that?"
"I did," a student confessed.
"For that, you stay after school," the teacher said.
The lad whispered to his buddy sitting next to him: "What'd I tell you—it pays to advertise."

1751. Teacher asked the fourth grader, "Can you name two famous brothers who made it possible for mankind to fly?"
He replied, "Ernest and Julio Gallo."

1752. "Where's your pencil, Hershel?" the teacher asked.
"I ain't got no pencil," Hershel said.
"How many times have I told you not to say that? Now listen. I haven't got a pencil. You haven't got a pencil. We haven't got a pencil. They haven't got a pencil . . ." explained the teacher.
Hershel said, "Well, what's happened to all the pencils?"

1753. In an adult education class out in the boondocks, a middle-aged woman enrolled and said she wanted to learn to write her name. She might have been a little slow, because it took her a month to master the course. Then she quit.
The next year, she was back again, though, and again told the teacher that she wanted to learn to write her name.
"But you learned last year, remember?" asked the teacher.
"Sure I remember, but I been married since then."

1754. What a small boy wrote about what he had learned about the human body: "Our body is divided into three parts, the branium, the borax, and the abominable cavity. The branium contains the brain, if any. The borax contains the lungs, lights, and heart. The abominable cavity contains five bowels—a, e, i, o, and u."

1755. Little Mary came home from school and said to her mother, "I wish you would let me take a bath in the morning before I go to school instead of at night before I go to bed."
"What difference does it make?" her mother asked.

"Every day at school," the little girl said, "Miss Taylor tells ever-body to stand up who had a bath today. And I haven't been able to stand up one time since school started."

1756.   A teacher asked her kids, "Where does the Lord live?"

A kid in the front row said, "I know where the Lord lives, Teacher. He lives at my house in the bathroom."

She said, "Johnny, why would you say such a thing?"

"Well, every morning, my father gets out of bed, goes to the bath-room door, and shouts, 'Good Lord, are you still in there?' "

1757.   Teacher: "Who can spell 'straight'?"

Small boy: "S-t-r-a-i-g-h-t."

Teacher: "Correct. Now, what does it mean?"

Small boy: "Without water."

Success

1758.   Ability is what you need to succeed if the boss doesn't have a daughter.

1759.   The doctor asks, "Shall I give your wife a local anesthetic?"

Husband replies, "No, I'm rich. Give her the best—something imported."

1760.   If you really want to impress people, a Ph.D. isn't worth half as much as being greeted by name and getting a little salute from the cop on the corner.

1761.   He's semisuccessful. Has his own parking place. Doesn't have a car, just goes out and lies down there at lunchtime.

1762.   He is a born executive . . . his father owns the business.

1763.   If at first you don't succeed, deny you were even trying.

1764.   I know a fellow who's so rich he doesn't know his son is in college.

1765.   "I made it on my own," he said, which proved to me that he was really not too smart to begin with.

1766.   Country Music has made it possible for a man to sing, "Gonna Catch a Freight Train—Don't Care Which Way It Goes" and he goes out and gets in his Cadillac and heads for the Waldorf Astoria.

1767.   It's the old story. Climb the ladder of success, reach the top, and you find you're over the hill.

1768. A friend believes that determination is the key to success. He makes it a point to finish something every day of his life. Yesterday it was a six-pack.

Talking

1769. A wise man once said: "Blessed are they who have nothing to say and cannot be persuaded to say it.

1770. He's the kind of person that approaches every subject with an open mouth.

1771. A tourist saw a beautiful display of dried flowers in a country store window. She went in and asked the owner how he preserved them so nicely.

"You just put 'em in a box with cornmeal and borax and barium," drawled the storekeeper.

"Equal parts, right?" said the lady. "Equal parts of cornmeal and borax and barium?"

"Yes, Ma'am," said the storekeeper.

"And that's all there is to it?"

"Yes, Ma'am. Jest be sure you don't barium too deep."

1772. A man purchased a parrot and, for 5 years, tried in vain to get him to talk. He read books on the subject, bought tapes for the bird to listen to. Nothing. Disgusted, he decided to take him back to the pet store. As he crossed the street, a car was coming right at them. The parrot yelled, "Look out!" The car hit the guy, knocking him to the ground. Only slightly bruised, the man got up muttering about "that dumb bird causing all his troubles."

The parrot looked at him and said, "Who's dumb? For five years, you try to get me to talk, and then when I do, you won't listen!"

1773. Hear about the new Howard Cosell doll everybody's crazy about? You wind it up and its batteries run down in 3 minutes. And they can never be replaced.

1774. Then there's the politician who is so adept at talking out of both sides of his mouth that he can give himself mouth-to-mouth resuscitation.

1775. There are people so addicted to exaggeration that they can't tell the truth without lying.

1776. An embarrassing thing happened to our state representative yesterday. He opened his mouth and a foot fell out.

1777. A farmer drove his team of mules into town and was very late returning home. "What took you so long?" asked his wife.

"Well," the farmer explained, "on my way, I had to pick up the preacher, and from there on, them mules of ours didn't understand a word I said."

1778. The judge eyed the man at the bar sternly. "Your wife charges you with not having spoken to her in five years," he said. "What is your explanation?"

"Well, your Honor," replied the man, "I didn't think it was polite to interrupt her."

1779. Sam was a very religious man. While visiting a cousin, he said to him, "Our rabbi is so holy that he talks with God."

"Talks with God?" said the relative. "How do you know that?"

"He told us so himself!" replied Sam.

"But maybe he lied."

"Dumbbell! Would a man who talks with God tell lies?"

1780. Since they have started giving men's names to hurricanes, I would like to suggest "Herbert." That's the name of my brother-in-law, who's the biggest blowhard in the country.

1781. A customer walked into a pet shop and spied a parrot. He ambled over to the bird and said, "Hey, can you speak, Stupid?"

The bird answered, "Yes. Can you fly, Dummy?"

1782. Trying to teach his parrot to talk, the bird owner said, "Good Morning" to it upon arising each day for several months. The parrot refused to cooperate, and said absolutely nothing. One morning, the man, out of sorts, walked right by the bird without his usual greeting. The parrot eyed him coldly and said, "Well! What's the matter with you this morning?"

1783. First man: "My boss can talk for hours on any subject."

Second man: "You're lucky. My boss doesn't need a subject."

1784. To make a long story short, there's nothing like having the boss walk in.

1785. My wife was getting after our son for using a four-letter word. He said, "But, Mom, Tennessee Williams uses that word all the time."

She said, "Well, you can't play with him anymore, either!"

1786. I have a speech impediment . . . my wife.

1787. Husband answering telephone: "She's out. Whom shall I say was going to listen?"

1788. A fellow in the dress business called a friend also in the dress business and asked him how things were going.

"Couldn't be better," said the friend. "Even with the recession, our sales are up 40%. We just landed Bloomingdale's. My wife is more in love with me than ever. My son, the lawyer, just won a personal injury case and his fee is one million dollars and my other son, the surgeon, was nominated for a Nobel Prize in medicine."

The caller finally got a word in edgewise: "I'm sorry, I'll call you back later. I didn't know you had someone with you."

Taxes

1789. Front license plate on a pickup truck: "Born Free—Taxed to Death."

1790. The most marvelous rumor of them all—Form 1040 has been found to cause cancer in laboratory rats.

1791. "Is this the first time you've been called down for an income tax audit?"

"Well, yes, it is. How could you tell?"

"You don't have to put your hands against the wall."

1792. A representative for IRS phoned the head of a large charitable organization. "I see here that a manufacturer named Fred Brown reports that he donated $10,000 to your charity last year. Did he?"

"Not yet," was the jubilant reply, "but he will!"

1793. A taxi driver who won $50,000 in a state lottery was asked if he was going to report it to the IRS.

"No, sir," the cabbie replied. "And I'm not going to report it to the MRS either."

1794. The so-called "simplified" tax return only has four questions on the form: "How much did you make? How much did you spend? How much is left? How soon can you send it in?"

1795. There is one difference between a tax collector and a taxidermist—the taxidermist leaves the hide.

1796. Reading tax guides makes an enjoyable pastime. Every once in a while you learn that something you've been deducting for years really IS deductible.

1797. They say George Washington never told a lie, but he never had to fill out an income tax form, either.

1798. Tax collector: "A guy who tells you what to do with the money you've already done something with."

1799. The other day I went down to the IRS. Thank heavens! I'm all paid up until 1947. HENNY YOUNGMAN

1800. The IRS should print income tax forms on Kleenex, so we'd have something to dry our eyes with, as we pay through the nose.

1801. Would I like to see my taxes lowered? Does the florist stay open on Mother's Day?

Teachers

1802. Do you know what you get if you cross a teacher with a rock . . . a rock that doesn't make enough money.

1803. Discipline in schools is a problem these days. Teaching today is like jungle warfare with lesson plans.

1804. Filling out a series of reports at the end of the school year, one tired teacher came upon this line: "List two reasons for entering the teaching profession." Without hesitation, she filled in: 1. July, 2. August.

1805. The Rotary Club gave a banquet for the teachers in the school system. As the affair came to a close, an official arose and proposed a toast. "Long live our teachers!" he shouted.
    Suddenly a voice from the back of the room inquired: "On what?"

1806. It was the first day of school and the teacher was getting the names of the pupils: Billy, James, Tommy, Shirley. One boy said, "My name is Dammitt."
    "That," said the teacher, "is a most unusual name."
    "Oh," said the boy, "it's a family name; we're proud of it."
    All went well until one day the principal came to see the class in action. He asked some questions, and finally, "Who can spell the word 'encyclopedia?'"
    Dammitt raised his hand. "Dammitt," said the teacher, "You know you can't spell 'encyclopedia.'"
    "Aw, hell," said the principal, "give the kid a chance."

1807. Teaching is . . . being sad when you learn that a student of yours is dropping out at the age of 16 . . . feeling relieved when you learn the dropout has found a job . . . becoming sad again when you learn that the dropout is making more than you are.

1808. A little girl at school ran up to her teacher sobbing bitterly. "What in the world is the matter, Mary?" asked the concerned teacher.

"I don't like school and I just found out that I have to stay here until I'm 18."

"Don't let that worry you," said the teacher. "I have to stay here until I'm 65."

1809. Confession of a distraught teacher: "It's not that my kids are unruly students, but I go to PTA meetings wearing a flack jacket."

1810. It is said by the old-time experts that the secret of successful teaching is to appear to have known all your life what you have learned this afternoon.

1811. They haven't really taken the prayers out of public schools. You should hear the teachers before they open the doors.

1812. A sign above a teacher's desk: "God loves you . . . and I'm trying."

1813. Teacher to class of small children: "Will all those who think they are stupid stand up." For a moment, no one got up and then one little fellow stood up. "Johnny," said the teacher, "do you think you are stupid?"

"No, Ma'am," said Johnny. "I just didn't like to see you standing up all by yourself."

1814. Teaching kindergarten must be like trying to keep 30 corks under water at the same time.

1815. My English teacher graded my first theme and remarked, "He should never write anything more ambitious than a grocery list."

1816. The teacher explaining to her third graders the importance of penmanship: "If you can't write your name, when you grow up, you'll have to pay cash for everything."

1817. Bumper snicker seen on a car: "If You Can Read This, Thank A Teacher." (It was on upside down).

1818. Sign seen on the wall of a third-grade classroom: "Your

Mother Does Not Work Here. You Will Please Pick Up After Yourself!"

Teenagers

1819.   A tourist in New York stopped two young girls in blue jeans and headbands and asked the way to the Empire State Building. Pointing down the street, one of the girls said: "You can't miss it. It's across the street from the record shop."

1820.   Teenagers don't trust anything over 30 unless it's on their speedometer.

1821.   Mother: "My teenage son pays $3.50 to see a 3D movie in which he claims 'things jump out at you.' I get to experience the same thing for free by just walking into his room."

1822.   Mother of a teenager: "I'm a little tired of those bumper stickers with 'Do you know where your children are?' I may not know exactly, but I'll guarantee my son is near a refrigerator."

1823.   There are now one billion teenagers in this world. Now you know why our Father art in Heaven!

1824.   One thing about discussing the facts of life with your teenagers is you'll probably learn some you didn't know.

1825.   The average income of the modern teenager is about 2 A.M.

1826.   It isn't what a teenager knows that worries his parents. It's how he found out!

1827.   They say that sound travels much slower than light—and that's so. Sometimes the things you say to your teenager won't get to him until he is in his forties.

1828.   Two fathers of teenagers were out walking. One pointed to the other's house and jokingly asked, "I wonder who lives there?"
    "Nobody," said the other glumly. "They just come and go."

1829.   Your teenager is growing up when he stops asking where he came from and refuses to tell you where he's going.

1830.   I have found that the best way to give advice to your teenager is to find out what he wants and then advise him to do it.

1831.   We adults do have something in common with today's teenagers. They listen to rock groups and we listen to economists. None of us understands a word they're saying.   JEAN STAPLETON

1832. Everybody's shook up these days. Teenagers are upset because they're living in a world dominated by nuclear weapons . . . And adults are upset because they're living in a world dominated by teenagers!

1833. A 13-year-old girl was talking to a friend about a new pop singer she'd heard. "I know he's going to be a big star," she said confidently. "My father can't stand him."

1834. Nowadays, young people think the straight and narrow is a style of jeans.

Telephones

1835. Two cleaning ladies were cleaning up an airline ticket office at 4 A.M. One of them said, "You better check the switchboard. There are usually 2 or 3 people on hold."

1836. A "professional telephoner" passes on this great tip for getting rid of some of those people who never seem to end telephone conversations: "Start a sentence and hang up," she says. "No one on the other end will ever believe you hung up on yourself."

1837. He's so dull his answering machine says, "Hi, I'm in right now, but you probably don't want me to answer the phone."

1838. The telephone solicitors in Miami are at it again. You know the type . . . the phone rings and a woman's voice asks. "Are you the man of the house?" Then she goes through her speel . . . "You will receive a free membership to the Rev. Leon Goforth's Spiritual Health Spa, including one free consultation with Rev. Goforth, himself, who will tell you how you can find salvation through deep knee-bends . . . You will also receive the Encyclopedia Britannica, volumes 'A' through 'M' . . . For one payment and one payment only all this and more, including a free estimate from your Roto-Rooter, a package of Velveeta cheese, a road map of Idaho, and a Shetland pony named 'Arnold.' "

1839. There is a new Dial-a-Prayer number for atheists. You call a certain number and nobody answers.

1840. I know a guy who has such a nasty disposition that he had a phone installed just so he could hang up on people.

1841. A friend tells about the family dog that got restless when it was left alone in the house. The owner discovered that by phoning the house now and then while she was away, and letting the phone ring a few times, it had a calming effect on the dog. One of the neighbors who knew about the situation, happened to be in the house checking up when the phone rang several times. He lifted the receiver, panted several times, barked into the phone, then hung up.

1842. Voice: "How do you feel this morning?"
Second Voice: "Great! Never been better!"
Voice: "I must have the wrong number."

1843. A mother was teaching her six-year-old to use the telephone. With much careful instruction, he dialed his grandmother's number. After about 12 rings, it was evident that no one was going to answer. So, mother said, "Go ahead and hang up. I guess she's not home."
Eager to make his first telephone call a success, the little boy said, "Not yet. Not yet. I think I hear somebody coming."

1844. Almost 100 years ago, Alexander Graham Bell, working with Thomas Watson on experiments that were to lead to the invention of the telephone, excitedly listened to the first sound over their experimental wire: "We're sorry, the number you have dialed. . . ."

1845. Prestige is when you are in the Oval Office talking to the President and the phone rings. He picks it up, listens for a minute, and then says, "It's for you."

1846. Beverly Hills: "The only city with unlisted phone booths."

1847. Crazy things seem to happen on New Year's Day. At ten in the morning, the information desk at the phone company got a ring and a voice said, "Operator, would you mind tracing this call?"
The operator replied, "Why should I trace this call?"
The voice said, "To tell me where I am."

Television

1848. A man needs a roof over his head . . . where else is he gonna put his antenna?

1849. Before television, no one ever knew what a headache looked like.

1850. It's funny, isn't it? Many of the coaches seem to get more upset when the television cameras are going.

1851. Talk about a loser . . . he got cable TV for the 24-hour weather channel.

1852.   Television is educational, teaching you the easiest way of wasting your time.

1853.   I asked him how much it would cost to fix my TV. He said what's the matter with it? I told him I didn't know. He said, "In that case, about $68.95."

1854.   The average family consists of a father, mother, two children, and a television repairman.

1855.   TV Announcement: "The problem is not with your set. We're having a little transmitter problem. But the engineer is putting more tinfoil on the aerial."

1856.   Soap operas prove it takes some women two years to have a premature baby.

1857.   The person who says crime doesn't pay never wrote for television.

1858.   Maybe one reason the Russians are getting so confident is they've been watching our TV programs and figure all Americans have tired blood, indigestion, and nagging backaches.   BOB GODDARD

1859.   Television is the device that acquaints you with all the things going on in the world that you could be a part of if you weren't sitting there watching television.

1860.   I'll say this for television. The more unsuitable the program, the quieter it keeps the children.

1861.   Little Betsy's grandmother told her they didn't have television when she was a little girl. So, the four-year-old queried, "Then what did they turn off when you were bad?"

1862.   At the El Cheapo Motel, the TV has only one channel—in black.

1863.   Television gets worse every year. Right now, it's five years ahead of schedule.

Tennis

1864.   "I sent my tennis racquet manufacturer a photo of me serving, for his advertising."
  "Any reply?"
  "What's an 'injunction?' "

1865. Wife: "Why don't you play tennis with Ed anymore?"

Husband: "Would you play tennis with a man who doesn't call lines and poaches all the time?"

Wife: "I certainly would not!"

Husband: "Well, neither will Ed."

1866. A short heavy fellow discussed his tennis game with a friend. "When my opponent hits the ball to me, my brain immediately barks out a command to my body: 'Race up to the net'—it says. 'Slam a blistering drive to the far corner; jump back into position to return the next volley.'"

"Then?" asked his friend.

"Then," sighed the rotund one, "my body says, 'Who, me?'"

1867. A wife described the progress of her husband's tennis game: "I can tell he's getting in shape. He's turning purple much later in the matches now."

1868. Three dressing rooms are needed for tournament tennis players these days. His, hers, and who knows.

1869. Do you know what women playing tennis remind me of? Take away the rackets and the balls, and they look like mothers trying to keep the kids in the yard.

1870. Our tennis fans are so tough that if a match is rained out, they go to the airport and boo bad landings.

1871. Brad Dillman, actor, explaining why he prefers golf to tennis: "All tennis courts look alike."

1872. "There's nothing boring about winning," says tennis teacher, Vic Braden. "In 40 years of tennis, I've yet to hear anyone say, 'Nuts, I won again.'"

1873. A reporter asked a priest, "What would the Lord do if two tennis players prayed for victory with exactly the same fervor?"

The priest's eyes twinkled. "I imagine," he said, "that He would just sit back and enjoy a whale of a game."

1874. It was the year when one of the top tennis pros made more money than any other player on the circuit. A friend remarked to him, "You made more money this year than the President of the United States."

"I should," replied the pro, "he had a bad year."

1875. "Does your husband play tennis?"

"No, but he just can't give it up."

Texas

1876. Texas would not be the great state it is today if it weren't for cotton . . . they use it to mop up the oil.

1877. Bachelor: "Just call me 'Tex.' "
Girl: "Are you from Texas?"
Bachelor: "No, I'm from Maryland, but I don't like being called Mary."

1878. I just had an unusual experience. Met this fella, 6 feet tall, wearing a 10-gallon hat, cowboy boots, lots of money, owns oil wells, and a cattle ranch. What makes it so unusual? . . . He's from Vermont.

1879. It's one of those typical Texas homes. Even the kitchen has seven rooms.

1880. Parts of Texas are so flat you can look farther than you can see.

1881. In Texas, even Oil of Olay is sold by the barrel.

1882. A Texan heard about a car pool so he had one installed in his station wagon.

1883. A rich oil magnate had descended on one of New York's big hotels. Irritated by the indifference of the staff on his great wealth, he determined to give them something to talk about. At breakfast, the following morning, he said to the waiter: "Just bring me $20 worth of bacon and eggs." The waiter shook his head. "Sorry," he replied, "but we don't serve half portions in this hotel."

1884. One Texan's formula for success: Get up early, work late, and strike oil.

1885. A rich Texan bought his kid a chemistry outfit—DuPont.

1886. A Texas newspaper conducted a contest. They offered a prize for the best essay on "Why I Am Glad To Be A Texan"—in 500,000 words or less.

1887. One of "them liars" is a man down in West Texas who told about the winter it got so cold that all the rattlesnakes froze up straight and solid.
He said he picked them up and hammered them into the ground for fence posts, and it was the biggest mistake he ever made.
When spring came, those snakes thawed out and crawled away with 57 miles of barbed wire.

1888. California is too far from Texas for it to ever amount to much.

1889. The tall Texas tycoon dashed down the hotel steps and flopped down in the back seat of a cab. "Where to?" the driver asked over his shoulder.
 "Anywhere!" said the Texan. "I got business everywhere."

1890. One Texas rancher was talking to another. "What's the name of your spread?" asked the first.
 "The XWK Lazy R Double Diamond Circle Q Bar S," replied the second.
 "How many head do you have?"
 "Only a handful. Not many survive the brandings."

1891. How about the Texan who boasted he had 5,000 head of cattle.
 "Is that a lot?" a visitor asked.
 The Texan answered, "In the freezer?"

1892. A friend of mine says he never realized how big Texas is until he tried to unfold a map of the state in his car.

1893. A preacher in the Bible Belt of Texas had performed so many shotgun weddings, he renamed his church "Winchester Cathedral."

1894. An early Texas settler wrote, "The rain is all wind, the wind is all sand, I'm 4,000 miles from nowhere, and one-half mile from Hell. The only way things could be worse is if I had to go home to live with my mother-in-law."

1895. I've got a Texan friend who is so wealthy he has a walk-in wallet.

1896. Where I come from in Texas it's so tough that any boy with two ears is a sissy and any cat with a tail must be a tourist.

Time

1897. "I got up at dawn to see the sunrise," said the tourist.
 "Well," said his friend, "you couldn't have picked a better time."

1898. A passerby asked a hippie on Boston Common what time it was.
 "Twelve o'clock," replied the hippie.
 "Goodness," said the man, "I thought it was later than that."

"Man, it never gets later than that around here," said the hippie. "Like when it reaches 12 o'clock, we start all over again!"

1899. How do you explain counterclockwise to a youngster with a digital watch?

1900. Time is money . . . especially a good time.

1901. He has such a relaxed attitude . . . it takes him an hour and a half to watch "60 Minutes."

1902. A consultant is a man who borrows your watch to answer your question of what time it is.

1903. A farmer was asked how he harvested apples in his orchard. He explained that he was trying out a new method—feeding apples to hogs—since the price of apples was down and the price of hogs were up. Said he held the hogs up and let them eat, moving from tree to tree until they got full.

Asked if that wasn't awfully time-consuming, the farmer said, "Yeah, but shoot, what's time to a hog?"

1904. Drunk to stranger on street: "What time is it?"
Stranger: "It's 11 o'clock."
Drunk: "I must be going crazy. All day long, I keep getting different answers."

1905. A friend of mine said: "Times are shore gettin' hard. Pinto beans are up 45%, smokin' tobacco is a buck a pack, and the fish won't bite. If things get any worse, I'm gonna have to line up a few more lawns for my wife to mow."

1906. Times have gotten hard when you go to the bank to withdraw your life savings and the teller asks if you want it heads or tails.

1907. An elevator operator complained that he was getting tired of people asking him for the time. A friend suggested that he hang a clock in his elevator. A few weeks later, the friend inquired as to how things were going. "Just awful," declared the elevator operator. "Now, all day long, people ask me, 'Is that clock right?' "

1908. There was a time when a fool and his money were soon parted. Times have changed . . . now it happens to everybody.

1909. Never put off until tomorrow what you can put off until the day after tomorrow.   MARK TWAIN

1910. Boss to retiring employee: "We wish you a pleasant retirement, Clarence. We wanted to give you a gold watch, but this company can't afford it. However, here's a phone number that gives the correct time."

1911. "Young man," said the angry father from the head of the stairs, "didn't I hear the clock strike four when you brought my daughter in?"

"You did," admitted the boyfriend, "It was going to strike 11, but I grabbed it and held the gong so it wouldn't disturb you."

Traffic

1912. It was a gorgeous day, and we were trapped in bumper-to-bumper traffic. We couldn't help hearing a woman shout at a man, at the wheel, "I told you it was too nice a day to go anywhere!"

1913. One advantage of a mobile home is that you have a place to live while you're looking for a place to park.

1914. Where else but in America could you find a job, get married, buy a house, and raise a family without once ever having to leave the freeway.

1915. A taxi was creeping slowly through rush-hour traffic and the passenger was in a hurry. "Please," he said to the driver, "can't you go any faster?"

"Sure I can," the cabby replied, "but I ain't allowed to leave the taxi."

1916. I have a solution for all our traffic problems: Let no car on the road until it is paid for.   WILL ROGERS

1917. Things are rough. People are worried. I saw a man lying in the gutter. I walked up and said, "Are you sick? Can I help you?"

He said, "No, I found a parking space and I sent my wife out to buy a car."   HENNY YOUNGMAN

1918. Civilization is a family driving a $10,000 car pulling a $20,000 trailer looking for a free place to park.

1919. Few things in life are more satisfying than parking on what's left of the other fellow's dime.

1920. A headline reads: "Parking is a big problem in religion." So the pride in the family pew has been matched by that in an assured space in the parking lot at the church. Following the announcement that a church was being designed on stilts with parking space underneath for the worshippers' cars, a member predicted, "When the roll is called up yonder, I'll be in the basement, trying to find a place to park."

1921. The traffic signs in Berkely, California, have been changed from "Walk" and "Don't Walk" to "Right On, Brother" and "No Way, Baby."

1922. Sign on garage door: "Cars Illegally Parked In This Driveway Will Be Towed Away And We Won't Tell You Where."

1923. I solved my parking problem. I bought a parked car.

1924. Traffic Light: "A trick to get pedestrians halfway across the street."

Robert Henry and a few of his friends.

Vacations

1925. Summer Camp letter:

Dear Mom and Dad:

Please send me a map. I am planning to escape with Joey and Marty.

Love, Randolph.

1926. Two men who had traveled abroad were comparing their opinions about foreign cities. "London," said one, "is certainly the foggiest place in the world."

"Oh, no, it's not," said the other. "I've been in a place much foggier than London."

"Where was that?" asked his friend.

"I don't know where it was," replied the second man. "It was too foggy to tell."

1927. Why is planning a vacation always easy for a married man? . . . Because his boss will tell him when and his wife will tell him where.

1928. A vacationing hotel guest was completely fed up with the whole system of tipping . . . especially after one week of taking care of doormen, waiters, bellboys, hatcheck girls, and such. Then came a knock on the door. "Who's there?" called the guest.

"I'm your bellboy, sir. Telegram for you."

The tip tortured guest had a crafty gleam in his eye. "Just slip it under the door," he ordered.

"I can't sir," said the bellboy without a moment's hesitation.

"And why not?" growled the guest.

"Because, sir," explained the determined bellboy, "It's on a tray."

1929. Summer Camp letter:

Dear Folks:

It rained at camp on Monday, Tuesday, Wednesday, Thursday, and Friday. Please don't pay them for this week.

Your daughter, Stephanie.

1930. This summer one-third of the nation will be ill-housed, ill-nourished, and ill-clad. Only they call it a vacation.

1931. Two U.S. tourists, a husband and wife, were crossing Canada by car when they reached a major city in one of Canada's prairie provinces. Seeing no road signs, the husband asked a likely looking Canadian where they were.

"Saskatoon, Saskatchewan," he replied.
"What did he say?" the wife asked.
"Dunno. He doesn't speak English."

1932.   Nowadays, a voice crying in the wilderness isn't a prophet—it's a tourist who lets her husband read the map!

1933.   Trying to conserve funds, a vacationing hotel guest asked for the cheapest space available in the Los Angeles Hilton.
"It was comfortable and had terrific carpeting," he said, "but I woke up every time it stopped at a different floor."

1934.   He took one look at his passport photo and called off the trip. "If I look like that, I'm too sick to travel."

1935.   When you send your son to summer camp, you shouldn't think of it as losing a boy, you should think of it as gaining two turtles, a frog, and a garter snake.

1936.   Summer Camp letter:
Dear Mom:
I promiss to rite to you ever day from camp if you promiss not to send my letters back with the spelling corected.
Your son, Aaron.

1937.   Two women were chatting. "I was talking with Jean the other day about vacation plans and she tells me that you aren't going to Paris this summer."
"No," the other woman replied, "That was last year. This year we aren't going to Rome."

1938.   A tourist is a person on vacation who travels thousands of miles just to get a snapshot of himself standing beside his car.

1939.   The man who said "You can't take it with you" never saw a camper truck packed for a vacation.

1940.   Despite jets and missiles, they still haven't come up with anything that goes faster than a two-week vacation.

1941.   The easiest way to refold a road map is later.

1942.   One time, I stayed in a hotel room so small that you had to go out in the hall to change your expression.   CASEY STENGEL

1943.   Vacationing through the modern day South, a Northerner gazes into his empty billfold and recognizes the true meaning of "Gone With The Wind."

Voting

1944. Elections are things that are held to see if the polls were right.

1945. Sign outside a polling place: "Do not be taken in by silver-tongued orators, cheap rhetoric, phony promises, political claptrap, patriotic publicity, ballyhoo, slick commercials, spontaneous demonstrations, and campaign razzle dazzle. Just flip a coin."

1946. Nine state primaries and caucuses will be held March 13, which is being described as "Super Tuesday." This is just the beginning of 8 months of political razzle-dazzle by which we pick our national leader, a process that the Russians managed to boil down to one sentence: "Okay, Rudolph, you're it."

1947. The elections: "the time of year when the unemployed go to the polls to determine who will join them."

1948. A peasant in a small Russian village went to the polls on election day and was given a scaled envelope and told to drop it into the ballot box.

He began tearing open the envelope. The Soviet official shouted, "What do you think you are doing?"

The peasant said he wanted to see who he was voting for.

"Are you crazy?" yelled the official. "This is a secret ballot!"

1949. Next time, I'm going to vote a straight ticket—as soon as I can find out which party is going straight.

1950. After giving a typical stirring, double talking, promise making speech, the politician looked out at the audience and confidently asked if there were any questions.

"Just one," said one possible voter, "Who else is running?"

1951. Voter to candidate: "I wouldn't vote for you if you were St. Peter."

"If I were St. Peter," said the candidate, "you couldn't vote for me because you wouldn't be in my district."

1952. Man is the only animal that laughs. But then he is the only animal that votes. He's also the only one who blushes . . . or has need to.

1953. A key slogan in a recent election—"What You Vote For Today, You Live With Tomorrow"—produced 35,197 write-in votes for Bo Derek; 36,209 for Tom Selleck.

1954.   "What did you think of the two candidates?"
"I'm glad only one was elected!"

1955.   Fifty percent of all accidents happen around the home—the other half in voting booths.

1956.   A government official wound up in the hospital with a broken leg. He must have experienced mixed emotions when he opened an envelope and read the message on the get well card. "Your staff, by a vote of 14–10, wishes you a speedy recovery."

1957.   Heard it on the radio: "With six cemeteries still to be heard from—the election is still too close to call."

1958.   A Kentuckian had 17 children, all boys. When they came of age, they all voted the Democratic ticket—all except one boy. The father was asked to explain this evident fall from grace.
"Waal," he said, "I've always tried to bring them boys up right, in the fear of the Lord, and Democrats to the bone, but John, the ornery cuss, got to readin'."

1959.   After a local election in a town in Ireland, McManus was asked how he had managed to eke out a victory. "Twas like this," McManus explained. "I am aware that everybody who knew me voted for Sullivan, but on the other hand, everybody who knew Sullivan voted for me—and it turned out he knew more people than I did."

1960.   Several years ago, the hometown football coach at the local high school announced his candidacy for sheriff.
The coach had been at his job for about a dozen years. While he had had some success in the early part of his career, for the past three seasons his teams had been on the short end of the scoring in almost all of their games. As a matter of fact, in three years the team had a record of 4 wins, 3 ties, and 22 losses. A friend asked the coach: "With a record like that, how do you expect to get people to vote for you?"
"Well," replied the coach, "I'll just point out that if I don't get elected, I'll have to go back to coaching" . . . He won overwhelmingly.

Waiters/Waitresses

1961.   A typical waiter from a New York restaurant suddenly became very ill and was rushed to the emergency room of a hospital. He was lying on the operating table in great pain, when he saw

an intern walk by. "Doctor, you have to help me," the waiter pleaded.
"Sorry," the intern replied, "this isn't my table."

1962. A man, leaving a cafe said, "Waiter, I find that I have just enough money to pay for the dinner, but I have nothing in the way of a tip for you."
"Just let me add up that bill again, sir," replied the waiter.

1963. A father became exasperated when his teenage son failed to come to the table promptly when called.
"That kid's going to be a loser when he grows up!" stormed Pop. "Why doesn't he come when he's called?"
"Maybe he's made up his mind to be a waiter," said Mom.

1964. "May I help you with the soup, sir?" asked the waiter.
"What do you mean, 'help me?' I don't need any help!"
The waiter replied, "Sorry, sir. From the sound, I thought you might want to be dragged ashore."

1965. A waiter is a person who believes that money grows on trays.

1966. A customer told a slow waitress that the service was lousy.
"How do you know?" she yelled. "You ain't had any yet!"

1967. Show me a flying saucer and I'll show you a waitress who has been pinched.

1968. Why does the waiter always wait until your mouth is full to ask you if everything is all right?

1969. While ordering his lunch, an American tourist in Paris was using some of his high school French. "Garcon," he said, studying the menu, "je desire consoome royal, et un piece of pang et burr—nom hang it—une piece of burr. . . ."
"I'm sorry, sir," said the tactful waiter, "I don't speak French."
"Well, then," snapped the tourist, "for heaven's sake, send me someone who can."

1970. Unhappy diner: "This food is terrible! I want to see the manager of this establishment!"
Bored waiter: "Sorry, sir. He's out to lunch."

1971. "Waiter, this steak is so tough I can't eat it."
"Then, get out! This is no place for weaklings!"

1972. Man dining out told his waiter, "Put the rest of my steak in a bag for my dog, will you? . . . and put in a few slices of bread in case he wants to make a sandwich."

1973. The waitress at the local cafe isn't too sharp. A customer asked for coffee without cream and she told him: "We're out of cream. How about having it without milk?"

1974. Someday I hope to see a waiter with enough guts to lay the check face up on the table.

1975. Customer: "Waiter, what time is it?"
 Waiter: "This isn't my table."

Weather

1976. The suburbanite was nursing his car through a massive snowstorm that had caught the city by surprise in the early afternoon. He made some headway for while but eventually the drifts stopped him completely. He waited out the storm through the night until it was clear enough for him to leave the car. He made his way to a telegraph office and sent this message to his office: "Won't be in to work today. Not home yesterday, yet."

1977. The drought had continued for weeks and the population of the small Alberta farming community joined together in church. "Now I know all of you came here today to pray for rain," the minister told his flock. "So may I ask why not a single one of you brought a raincoat or an umbrella?"

1978. Do you realize that the size of your funeral is gonna depend on the weather. I know if it rains, I ain't comin'.

1979. Plan ahead. It wasn't raining when Noah built the ark.

1980. The dust got so thick one year that chicken hawks had to wear goggles and fly backwards.

1981. Lightning never strikes twice in the same place. Of course, it seldom needs to.

1982. I tell my children not to despair if all their dreams come out wrong. It might mean they have a future in weather forecasting.

1983. It only rained twice last week. Once for three days and once for four days.

1984. Local weather forecasters hesitate to call it rain. They prefer to call it dew. A friend stepped off his front porch this morning and they're dragging the dew for his body.

1985. Weatherman to radio announcer: "Better break it to 'em gently. Just say, 'Partly cloudy with scattered showers followed by a hurricane.'"

Weight Watchers

1986. I'm on a diet now. I have to stay away from mirrors.

1987. My husband is a big eater. When he wants a salad, I pour oil and vinegar on the lawn and tell him to graze.

1988. The latest fad is "The Chinese Diet." You eat American food . . . but you use chopsticks.

1989. He went on a diet because of fear tactics. His tailor told him he couldn't let out his pants anymore, but he could install landing lights.

1990. The reason she's dieting is because when she puts on her green stretch pants, she looks like Puerto Rico with a zipper.

1991. A chronic nibbler, the housewife simply couldn't stick to a diet. Finally she hit upon a reminder scheme that worked. She pasted a big picture of a shapely, briefly clad model on the refrigerator door. During the first month, she lost seven pounds. During the same time, her husband gained eight pounds because he couldn't stay away from the refrigerator!

1992. One of the best compliments a dieter can have . . . "Have you been sick?"

1993. It's not that my wife is overweight, but her pantyhose are called "Wide Load."

1994. I've got a new diet, guaranteed to work. If it tastes good . . . spit it out!

1995. The greatest thrill after a successful diet is being able to see your shoes without holding your breath.

1996. I had a friend on the low carbohydrate diet for two years. No sweets, no booze, no cake. Finally ate a piece of candy . . . had to cut her out of the living room ceiling.

1997. I've got to go on a diet. Last week I got a shoeshine and had to take the guy's word for it.

1998. If the Lord had meant for us to diet, He would have made everybody fat to start with.

1999. It's not that I was an overeater. I was a do-it-yourself famine.

2000. My Health Spa insisted I go on their most expensive diet. It worked. In two months, I lost $300.

2001. He's always been overweight. Who else ever complained that his Hula-Hoop was too tight?

2002.   To him, a "light salad" is the first row in the vegetable garden.

2003.   You're overweight if you step on your dog's tail . . . and he dies.

2004.   You know you're off your diet when it rains and nothing below your waist gets wet.

2005.   Sign outside reducing salon: "Return to slender."

2006.   My sister was so big when she was a kid, she could only play "Seek."   PHYLLIS DILLER

2007.   The doctor scared my fat uncle into dieting with six simple words—"Have you ever seen skin explode?"

2008.   Before starting on a much needed fitness program, a tremendously overweight person bravely stepped on the kind of scales that stamps your weight on a card. The card read, "Come back in 10 minutes . . . alone!"

Wives

2009.   A man approached another man and said, "I'll pay you one thousand dollars to run off with my wife."

"A thousand dollars," the other man replied. "Why should you want me to do that? Think of all the years you have spent with your wife. Think of what that woman has given you all those years."

"You're right," the man answered. "I'll make it two thousand dollars."

2010.   The psychiatrist came storming into the hospital director's office. "Jones has shoved me to the limits of my patience," he screamed. "Being nuts is no excuse. This time he has heaped the final straw on me."

"What happened?" asked the director.

"He asked me if he could have a date with my wife," yelled the psychiatrist.

"Was that your wife who picked you up in a station wagon after work yesterday?" inquired the director.

"Yes."

"Then put Jones under close observation," ordered the director. "He's crazier than I thought."

2011.   Wife to husband working on budget: "Perhaps we could borrow a little each month and set THAT aside."

2012.   Wife to husband: "All right, I admit I like to spend money . . . but name one other extravagance."

2013. Wife, at desk with checkbook, to husband: "Well, it balances. The checks total up to exactly the amount I'm overdrawn."

2014. Husband, looking up from newspaper, to wife: "What's happened between you and the retail merchants, dear? I see they say business is off 20%."

2015. Wife (on telephone): "I can't start the car, there's water in the carburetor."
Husband: "Where's the car?"
Wife: "In the lake."

2016. Woman: "Thursday is my husband's birthday. I want to give him a small lockbox to guard his papers."
Shopkeeper: "Anything else?"
Woman: "Yes, a second key for me."

2017. A woman went to the police to report her husband missing. "He's bald and skinny, has no teeth, and no personality," she said. "In fact, most of him was missing before he was."

2018. A soldier got a letter from his wife containing a sketch of their car's instrument panel. "This is exactly the way the dashboard looks," she wrote. "Do we need a quart of oil?"

2019. One woman was complaining to another about her husband coming home so late at night . . . often in the wee hours of the morning.
The other woman said, "My husband used to do the same thing. But I finally discovered a way to put a stop to it. When he sneaked up the stairs, I would call out to him, 'Is that you Hershel?'"
"But how did that help?" asked her friend.
"Easy, my husband's name is Virgil."

2020. Winning an argument from my wife is about as difficult as nailing jello to a tree.

2021. They now have a lie detector without wires . . . it's called a wife.

2022. Silent Majority: "That's my wife when she's pouting."

2023. My wife is never satisfied. I gave her a $50 gift certificate for her birthday. She took it back and exchanged it for two 25's.

2024. Only two things are necessary to keep one's wife happy. First is to let her think she's having her own way. Second is to let her have it. LADY BIRD JOHNSON

2025. At a factory the other day, a completely dependable employee had failed to show up for work, and the foreman was asked what had happened.

"Oh," said the foreman, "his wife left him yesterday and he took the day off to find a replacement."

2026.   By the way, his wife had to let the maid go . . . because he wouldn't.

2027.   It's a funny thing about men sitting at bars. They're there for one of two reasons. Either they have no wife to go home to . . . or they do.

2028.   Letter from wife to husband: "I'm so miserable without you, it's like you never left."

Women

2029.   No one hates to hear a woman admit her age like her older sister.

2030.   Confusion is one woman plus a left turn. Excitement is two women plus one secret. Bedlam is three women plus one bargain. Chaos is four women plus one luncheon check.

2031.   A woman went to a marriage counselor and complained of her husband's overwhelming self-interest. "It was evident from the minute we were married," she said. "He wanted to be in the wedding pictures."

2032.   When a man does something stupid, people say, "Isn't he silly!" But when a woman does, they say, "Aren't women silly!"

2033.   "Officer, this man is annoying me."
  "But he isn't even looking at you."
  "I know, that's what's so annoying."

2034.   "Woman's Intuition" is that special sixth sense that permits a woman to put two and two together and come up with any answer she feels like.

2035.   Practical advice to women for living the good life: "From birth to age 18, a girl needs good parents. From 18 to 35, she needs good looks. From 35 to 55, she needs a good personality. From 55 on, she needs cash."   SOPHIE TUCKER

2036.   The only way to win an argument with a woman is to be on her side.

2037.   A young lady said she met a guy and immediately knew he was no good because he started to insult her and used bad language. When asked how she met him, she said, "I ran over him in my car."

2038.   A sexy woman is one who wears her clothes so tight that a man can hardly breathe.

2039.   Statistics show that three-fourths of all women are secretive about their age. The other fourth lie about it.

2040.   Fifty-one percent of the nation's drivers are women and that's only counting the front seats.

2041.   There are two kinds of women—those who'll argue over nothing, and those who'll argue over anything.

2042.   The average woman should concentrate on beauty rather than on brains, because the average man can see much better than he can think.

2043.   It's not true that women change their minds frequently. Ask a woman her age and she'll give you the same answer for years.   EARL WILSON

2044.   It is said that a woman's mind is cleaner than a man's because she changes it more often.

2045.   Women are a problem, but they're the kind of problem men like to wrestle with.

2046.   Some women are regular magicians at Christmas time. They're able to get mink coats out of old goats.

2047.   The real reason women live longer is because they have whole closets full of dresses they wouldn't get caught dead in.

Women's Lib

2048.   The trouble with some women is that they get all excited about nothing—and then marry him.

2049.   When asked why she never married, an old lady used to say, "Hit takes a mighty fine husband to be better than none."

2050.   Isn't it funny that no one ever asks a man how he combines marriage and a career?

2051.   "Is your husband hard to please?"
   "I don't know. I've never tried."

2052. Bumper sticker on a Buick Riviera with a woman in a business suit at the wheel: "Women Who Seek Equality With Men Have No Ambition."

2053. One man to another, "Women are involved in everything today. I recently asked a woman executive what ever happened to dumb blondes? She said, 'I married one—he's home washing dishes.'" DON REBER, Times Cartoon Lines, Reading, PA

2054. The office of Vice President would be an ideal position for a woman. They're already used to situations where doing a great job won't get them a promotion.

2055. One woman said she wanted to leave her husband and go home to her mother—but she couldn't find out who her mother was living with!

2056. The modern woman's idea of remodeling the home? Brick up the kitchen.

2057. Bumper sticker: "When God made men, She was only fooling around."

2058. Some couples live together, have kids, then get married. That makes it a little hard on the kids. At the wedding, they don't know on which side to sit.

2059. Modern day girl: "I was so flabbergasted when he asked me to marry him, I almost fell out of the bed."

2060. Father: "You modern girls don't care how you look anymore. Your hair looks like a mop!"
   Daughter: "What's a mop?"

Index